MASTERING

BUSINESS MICROCOMPUTING

W0043826

MACMILLAN MASTER SERIES

Accounting	German
Arabic	German 2
Astronomy	Hairdressing
Australian History	Italian
Background to Business	Italian 2
Banking	Japanese
Basic Management	Keyboarding
Biology	Marketing
British Politics	Mathematics
Business Communication	Modern British History
Business Law	Modern European History
Business Microcomputing	Modern World History
Catering Science	Nutrition
Catering Theory	Office Practice
Chemistry	Pascal Programming
COBOL Programming	Philosophy
Commerce	Physics
Computer Programming	Practical Writing
Computers	Principles of Accounts
Economic and Social History	Restaurant Science
Economics	Social Welfare
Electrical Engineering	Sociology
Electronics	Spanish
English as a Foreign Language	Spanish 2
English Grammar	Spreadsheets
English Language	Statistics
English Literature	Statistics with your Microcomputer
Financial Accounting	Study Skills
French	Typewriting Skills
French 2	Word Processing

OTHER BOOKS BY THE SAME AUTHOR

Information Systems Development: A Data Base Approach
Information Systems Definition: The Multiview Approach
    (*with A. T. Wood-Harper and Lyn Antill*)
Microcomputers and their Commercial Applications
Management Information from Data Bases
    (*with T. Crowe*)
Information Systems Development: Methodologies, Techniques and Tools
    (*with G. Fitzgerald*)
Information Systems Development in the 1990s: Concepts and Methodologies
    (*with R. C. Reeve and T. J. Robbins-Jones*)
Information Systems Development in the 1990s: Techniques and Administration
    (*with R. C. Reeve and T. J. Robbins-Jones*)

MASTERING
BUSINESS
MICROCOMPUTING

SECOND EDITION

D. E. AVISON

MACMILLAN

First edition 1987
Reprinted 1989
Second edition 1990

Published by
MACMILLAN EDUCATION LTD
Houndmills, Basingstoke, Hampshire RG21 2XS
and London
Companies and representatives
throughout the world

British Library Cataloguing in Publication Data
Avison, D. E.
Mastering business microcomputing.
1. Business firms. Applications of microcomputer systems
I. Title
658'.05416
ISBN 978-0-333-52511-1   ISBN 978-1-349-11608-9 (eBook)
DOI 10.1007/978-1-349-11608-9

ISBN 978-0-333-52512-8 Pbk export

To my wife Marie-Anne, son Thomas, and nieces and nephews – Cathryn, David, Guillaume, Matthieu, Martin and Sophie

CONTENTS

CONTENTS

PREFACE TO THE
FIRST EDITION

This book looks at the business applications of microcomputers. It concentrates on those applications which are of especial interest to managers of small or medium-sized business or managers of departments in a larger company. It has also been designed to be useful to students of business computing on computer and business courses.

Up until the 1980s, the most prevalent way of using computers was achieved by sharing the facilities of very large mainframe computers and using the expertise of the in-house technologists. These computer programmers and systems analysts worked in the firm's data processing department. Now, many of the facilities provided on these large machines are available on microcomputers, available on tap, not at the mercy of the data processing department, but at the control of the user at the office desk.

This is a very exciting time in the development of computers. There are great opportunities for the manager . . . but there are dangers as well. The purchase of a microcomputer system requires much planning. The first stage is not to choose between microcomputers at an exhibition or at a firm of computer suppliers, but to decide on the applications that the company needs, and produce a full specification of these needs. Only then is it sensible to look at the market-place. This all takes time: there is a great deal of choice in both hardware and software. Although the microcomputer world is less complex than the mainframe environment, it is still complex and it takes time to learn about the systems available.

The book is designed to give the reader an overview of the commercial applications of microcomputers. It is intended for potential and present users of microcomputers, not professional technologists. 'Heavy' chapters on hardware and software are not included. My aim is to keep the book readable and to avoid unnecessary technical detail. The approach adopted here is to discuss hardware and software aspects in the context of a particular application where

PREFACE TO THE FIRST EDITION

they are relevant, so that potential buyers know what they are looking for when they are contemplating using microcomputers for a particular purpose. In general, brand names of hardware and software are avoided. The pace of change in this area is so rapid that the specific products mentioned would soon be 'old hat' and the book become out of date. This text discusses principles: how to make the best use of information technology. These principles will be relevant whatever the 'state of the art' happens to be.

The first chapter sets the scene. It looks at the possibilities that the 'new technology' gives the business professional. It is a very exciting field. But it is also full of dangers, and this chapter discusses some of the problems that salesmen are very unlikely to discuss voluntarily. Techniques are described which should help people avoid falling into any of the pitfalls that abound. Other chapters are devoted to the major business application areas of microcomputers: word processing and the electronic office, file and data base management, spreadsheets and financial modelling, graphics applications, accounting and related systems, project control and statistical systems, application generators, expert systems and integrated systems. A glossary of terms is provided at the end of the book.

D. E. AVISON

PREFACE TO THE SECOND EDITION

It is unfortunate for writers of computer books that the field changes rapidly, though it makes the subject exciting. For this reason I attempted to make sure that the first edition of the book was about principles and practices rather than particular machines or application packages.

However some applications which were stressed in the first edition are less important now, whilst other aspects were underplayed. Thus I have added or deleted paragraphs and figures as appropriate, reflecting the developments in each of the applications discussed in the book. In the three years since the publication of the first edition, other applications have become widespread. I have taken the opportunity to add new sections, such as that covering desk top publishing, which is a major extension to word-processing-type applications, or to add paragraphs on newer software, such as hyperdata. The number of types of supplier of computer equipment, software and advice has also increased, and a new section has been added to the first chapter in order to reflect this change. I have also taken the opportunity to change most of the photographs and to reflect the improvements in factors such as speeds of processing and memory sizes, which have continued unabated.

Many aspects, such as networks, security and control, are important for all application types, but in order to avoid repetition they are discussed once in the most appropriate place. This does mean, however, that the reader interested in only one or two applications may look at the whole book in order to gain a full appreciation of those and to get a 'flavour' of all applications.

I believe that human factors related to microcomputer applications are particularly important, indeed much more important in the success of the venture than choices relating to technology. I have toyed with the idea of writing a separate chapter on the human side of computing, but I have decided to keep to the original format and strenthen this aspect, so that discussions of human factors pervade the text, as indeed their importance pervades each application.

ACKNOWLEDGEMENTS

Although I have attempted to separate out principles from specific systems, I ought to acknowledge that my main experience has been gained by being involved in the purchasing decisions (as chairman of the relevant committee) and by using the many microcomputer systems available at the Department of Computer Science at Aston University. These include several Apricot, IBM, and Apple Macintosh microcomputers, many of which are networked, an NCR Tower, Orion, and several Apollo and Sun workstations.

I also list below the packages that have provided the basis of the various chapters. Some of these packages are relevant to more than one chapter and topic. My experience has been gained using these packages at Aston University and during various consultancy work.

WORD PROCESSING AND DESK TOP PUBLISHING

Byline
MacWrite
MicrosoftWord
PageMaker
Superwriter
Wordcraft
WordPerfect
Wordstar Professional

DATA BASE MANAGEMENT

dBase
Delta
Everyman
FoxBase
Ingres
Omnis
Oracle

ACKNOWLEDGEMENTS

SPREADSHEET

Excel
Lotus 1-2-3
MasterModeller
Multiplan
WingZ

GRAPHICS

Dreams
Gem
Graphics Gallery
MacDraw
MacPaint
Presentation Master

ACCOUNTING

Apricot Accountant
Pegasus
Tetraplan

INTEGRATED

Jazz
Open Access
Smart

STATISTICS

SPSS
StatGraphics

PROJECT CONTROL

Pertmaster
Project Manager Workbench

EXPERT SYSTEMS

XIPlus

By providing this list, I do not want to imply that these are necessarily the 'state of the art'. Packages on my list will be superseded by products from competitors or by updates from their own suppliers. The pace of change in microcomputer hardware and software is very fast. I have, however, omitted from the list systems that I have used which do not 'work' or have given me a number of 'unnecessary' problems. These could have been avoided by better design, testing and documentation.

A number of companies provided photographs and diagrams which have been used in the text. These are individually acknowledged with the company name. Copyright rests with these companies: Abtex Software Ltd; Apple Computer (UK) Limited; Apricot Computers; Brother Office Equipment Division; Compsoft plc; Digital Micro Systems; Digital Research Inc.; Hewlett-Packard Limited; IBM United Kingdom Limited; Kendata Peripherals Limited; Lotus Development (UK) Ltd; Mercia Software Limited; Penman Products Limited. I am grateful for this help.

I wish to thank my head of department, Dr Brian Gay, and other colleagues of the Department of Computer Science at Aston University, for the opportunity to look at the exciting field of microcomputers, and the many students at Aston, particularly M. Parrish, N. Sharratt and M. Vale, who have knowingly or unknowingly helped me. It is a cliché, but true nevertheless, to say that students teach their teachers at least as much as teachers teach their students.

I also wish to thank Blackwell Scientific Publications for being able to draw on my earlier book *Microcomputers and their Commercial Applications* (1983). Although this present text takes a different approach to the subject, I am grateful to Blackwell Scientific for this permission.

CHOOSING YOUR MICROCOMPUTER SYSTEM

This chapter starts by looking at the reasons for purchasing a microcomputer system. The second section looks at the application areas where such a system might be appropriate. The feasibility study is described in section 1.3. This looks at possible problems of the present way of doing things and at the requirements of the new system. It also looks at methods of evaluating alternative solutions. Sometimes it is difficult to obtain information about what *is* available, and methods of resolving this problem are described in section 1.4. The suppliers of systems are discussed in section 1.5. This is followed in section 1.6 by an introduction to the human factors associated with the installation of microcomputer systems.

Although this is not a book aimed at the technologist, it is still important to understand some of the concepts and jargon associated with microcomputers. A knowledge of these will help managers understand how the application might be carried out and enable them to ask the right questions of the salesmen and to understand their replies. Sections 1.7 and 1.8 introduce the basic terminology associated with computer systems, and this will be further developed in the context of different applications in later chapters.

1.1 THE MICROCOMPUTER MAZE

A quick look at any of the microcomputer magazines shows that the prospective purchaser of microcomputer equipment does not lack for choice. There are over a hundred computers to choose from. The purchaser is also confronted with choice of other hardware devices such as printers (to print out documents) and storage devices (to store data). There are also hundreds of software packages, some of which are designed for a particular purpose: for preparing text, managing data, calculating, analysing statistics or planning. They may run on a number of microcomputers, but many only run on one computer. Then there are the packages designed for particular market sectors such as hotels or shops.

Managers can be bewildered by the amount of choice and give up trying to gain a knowledge of the field of microcomputing. In truth, there are no experts of the whole field. It is impossible to keep up with the amount of hardware and software available and the pace of change. This bewilderment may lead to managers giving up attempting to be thorough and in consequence they are 'sold' a microcomputer system in the hope that it will be useful to the organisation, or they buy one because competitors or friends have one.

A computer system bought in this way is likely to prove inadequate for the needs of the company, and it may cause serious damage to the firm:

(a) **a loss of company data** – because adequate security measures were not taken;
(b) **a loss of customers** – because the service has deteriorated;
(c) **a loss of cash** – because buying hardware and software and attempting to use it is expensive; and
(d) **a loss of face**.

The computer becomes a rejected toy. Because of this experience, it may be difficult to implement a computer system in the future, even when it might be appropriate.

Although it might at first sight seem reasonable to place emphasis on the microcomputer and associated equipment (**hardware**) and to a lesser extent on the programs that make the hardware perform particular tasks or functions (**software**), it is much better to concentrate on the needs of the organisation. Once these have been determined, the manager can specify to the salesmen what the requirements are. This will help to reduce the choice by eliminating hardware and software that will not perform the required tasks or perform functions that are not required. By choosing the hardware first, it is very likely that equipment will be bought which proves inappropriate for the needs of the organisation.

A computer system might well be appropriate:

(a) where there is a large volume of data to be processed;
(b) where speed and accuracy are important; and
(c) where the processing is repetitive.

Typical application areas where microcomputer systems have proved effective are discussed in the next section.

1.2 TYPES OF MICROCOMPUTER APPLICATIONS

This text concentrates on the types of business applications for which microcomputers are suitable. About three-quarters of microcomputer applications are covered by word processing, data management, spreadsheet, graphics, accounting and integrated packages (which combine many of the facilities already mentioned). The programs to carry out these functions can be bought 'off the shelf' from a supplier and this **application package** should be chosen to suit the particular requirements of the purchaser as defined in the requirements definition. Most of the remaining applications tend to be industry specific or are of less general application.

Word processing and its extensions such as mailing, diary keeping, meeting arrangement, agenda and minute keeping and desk top publishing are discussed in Chapter 2. Most people handle text in their work, and the advantages of word processing over conventional typing come mainly because changes can be made to the text without wholesale retyping. But there are disadvantages too. Secretaries may not take to the technology enthusiastically, and an opportunity is taken in this chapter to discuss further the human and social problems associated with the new technology.

File management and **data base management** systems are discussed in Chapter 3. The computer can become an electronic filing cabinet which is capable of holding much more data in a much smaller space than clerical systems can achieve using paper, record cards and a filing cabinet. Computer systems are capable of holding all the facts relating to a business. They can retrieve the data as a printed report set out according to the user's wishes or displayed on a visual display unit, which is similar to a television monitor. Answers to specific queries can also be provided by the system. Information may be required about the customers, products, stocks or employees of the company. All this data can be held on separate or 'integrated' files, which are normally called data bases. This data can be used for mundane data processing activities and for decision-support systems which provide vital information for management decision-making.

Most sales managers will be particularly interested in **spreadsheet** programs. About one-quarter of their time may be spent preparing budgets. Traditionally, large spreads of paper were used for budget planning. These are slow to create and very difficult and inconvenient to amend. Most managers will need a few stabs at the figures before they are satisfied with the results, and these iterations are easy to make when using a spreadsheet package. They are particularly powerful at answering 'what if?' type questions. The repercussions throughout a plan of a particular move can be worked out by the computer system in a few seconds. If the repercussions are not palatable, the spreadsheet can revert to its previous form without the manager having to resort to erasers or correction fluid. The manager can then ask another 'what if?' question and see if the results of that strategy are better. Spreadsheet and financial modelling systems are discussed in Chapter 4.

All organisations need information in order to operate. Data is as much a resource of the business as stocks of products and machinery. The loss of data relating to customer debt will immediately show the worth of data. File management systems (discussed in Chapter 3) usually provide the information in the form of text or tables of data. Pictures may be a much better way of expressing the information in many circumstances. **Computer graphics** packages, which are discussed in Chapter 5, provide this facility. Data may be represented as a bar chart, graph, or pie chart, and by using colours or shading patterns a picture can indeed be worth 'more than a thousand words'.

In order to encourage managers to use computers, a graphics interface is provided on many computers. This is generally regarded as a much friendlier and easier way for users to get the best out of their computers, certainly in the short term. This graphics interface is also discussed in Chapter 5.

Ever since commercial entrepreneurs like Joe Lyons developed and used large (mainframe) computers in the 1950s for administrating the Lyons Tea Shops, the staple applications of computers have been **business accounting** routines such as sales ledger, purchase ledger, nominal ledger, costing and invoicing. These are also important microcomputer applications, along with related applications such as stock recording and payroll. These are discussed in Chapter 6. Some software suppliers have combined these programs to form an integrated package of accounting routines. These packages can be easier to use because the different parts of the company accounts are consistent and data need only be collected and checked once.

Chapter 7 looks at the various packages which integrate word processing, file management, spreadsheet and graphics facilities. These **integrated systems** may also have other facilities, such as diary management and communications modules. A communications facility will enable users on a number of computers to pass messages and data files. An opportunity is also provided in this chapter to look at other applications such as project management, and at statistics packages. This chapter also introduces the systems which enable users to build their own applications, not by using the professional programming languages such as Cobol, Pascal, or Fortran, which will take a great deal of time to learn and to use, but by using applications generators. These can be as powerful and are far easier to use. Expert systems, which attempt to simulate the role of the expert (accountant, solicitor or doctor) in making decisions, are also discussed in this chapter.

1.3 THE FEASIBILITY STUDY

When making a large computer investment in traditional data processing, a **feasibility study** is carried out, which:

(a) looks at the problems of the present system (what has to be put right?);
(b) sets up a requirements definition for the new system (what will the system do?);
(c) looks at alternative solutions (what are the ways to achieve these objectives?) and details their costs and benefits (what will each cost and what will it be worth?); and
(d) makes a recommended solution, which not only gives reasons for choosing this option but discusses its feasibility (how difficult will it be to carry out? and will it meet all the requirements?).

The purchase of a microcomputer system should be no different and no less thorough. It is always useful (and frequently disturbing) to compare this feasibility study with a report of the system – written about six months after it has been operational. The implemented system may give fewer benefits and cost more than the predictions.

This experience ought to be used to improve the accuracy of future feasibility studies. This process of **organisational learning**, where the business stores and uses experiences, is positive, as it can be used to teach new staff and retrain others, and it can also encourage adaptiveness to change.

In this section we will look at the four parts of the feasibility study in outline, and then look in more detail at the question of evaluating computer packages.

(a) Problems
A business could be having problems in an application area which may be solved by the use of microcomputer systems:

(i) The manual system may be falling apart as it was designed for the needs of the past which have since changed.

    (*ii*) Clerical staff may be difficult and expensive to recruit and to keep.

  (*iii*) The business may be going through an expansionary phase and more data processing is required.

  (*iv*) Customer service may be deteriorating.

   (*v*) Poor management decisions may be made because of:

      (*a*) a lack of information;

      (*b*) the wrong type of information;

      (*c*) inaccurate information; or

      (*d*) information provided at the wrong time.

Having identified a problem or problems, the next step is to write a **requirements definition** which lists all the requirements of the replacement system.

(b) Requirements definition

The requirements of the new system should be clearly defined. The requirements definition should be put together by all those people having a stake in the project: managers, users, and operators. It will include specific and attainable targets which have been quantified for the new system. Statements about desired service levels and the ability to deal with the new workload have to be particularised into the provision of:

    (*i*) reports;

   (*ii*) enquiry facilities;

  (*iii*) levels of security;

  (*iv*) volumes to be processed; and

   (*v*) timescales.

The requirements definition will also contain **constraints**, such as:

    (*i*) a budget maximum;

   (*ii*) personnel restriction; and

  (*iii*) a target date for implementing the new system.

(c) Alternative solutions

In considering a computer solution, a number of questions should be asked of each hardware and software option. For example, in evaluating a particular application package, the following questions should be asked:

(*i*) *Does it meet the functional requirements?*

This is of course the issue of fundamental importance. If the package does meet the functional requirements then:

(a) Is all the input required by the package readily available?
(b) Is its capacity large enough for present use or too restricting for the future?
(c) Does it process the data fast enough?

If only some of the requirements are fulfilled then some other questions should be asked:

(a) What percentage of the requirements are fulfilled without amending the application package?
(b) Are the limitations of the package acceptable?
(c) How easily can the extra requirements be fulfilled?

(ii) What resources are required to buy and run the package?

(a) What is the basic cost, maintenance cost and the cost of extra hardware and support required?
(b) What labour is required to set up and run the system?
(c) Can the package be run on other computers (which may be important later)?

(iii) How many people are presently using the package?

(a) Is it possible to get their reactions to it?
(b) Were there many setting-up and teething problems?
(c) Has it proved reliable?
(d) Are they presently happy with the system?
(e) Are they happy with the help provided by the supplier when it was requested?
(f) What would they have done differently now?

(iv) What is the quality of the documentation?
Is it geared to computer experts, or are the users of the system likely to understand it? Is it well written? The documentation should be judged on its appropriateness for the people who are going to use the package. Is it good for:

(*a*) *reading* (e.g. to give a general overview of the system)?
(*b*) *learning* (e.g. so that the user can use the package without too much trouble)?
(*c*) *teaching* (e.g. so that the trained user can teach others how to use the system)?
(*d*) *referring to* (e.g. so that the format of a particular command can be checked)?

(e) *reminding* (e.g. to allow the user to look at an overview of the system quickly)?

(f) *diagnosing problems* (e.g. so that the user can soon correct any mistake)?

(v) *Are the 'help' facilities provided by the package when using the system on the computer good?*
If the user does make an illegal command or response, are the messages sensible and does the system provide help to make the correction? This is a facility which is often overlooked when buying a package, but a good help facility is vitally important when learning about the system.

(vi) *Is there a disk tutorial system?*
Such a system should lead the user through the use of the package, with carefully chosen examples, in a structured way.

(vii) *Can the package be implemented without the need to employ computer professionals?*
This should avoid expensive setting up costs.

(viii) *Are other training facilities provided?*
These may be in-house or provided at the supplier's base.

We will look in more detail at the question of evaluating particular application packages later in this section.

(d) Recommending a solution
One way of presenting the various solutions is to create a matrix, listing the requirements (and therefore ignoring irrelevant features) on the left-hand side of a table, then listing the solutions that might be appropriate along the top.

Let us assume that the alternative solutions are three application packages. Where the package meets any criterion, put a tick at the intersection. For evaluating the package, the more ticks the better, and therefore the recommended solution will be the one with the most ticks. This is package A in Figure 1.1.

A package may only partly meet any requirement. The technique can therefore be improved by giving a mark out of ten for each package/criterion. The marks for each package can be added up and the package which scores the most is chosen. This is package B in Figure 1.2.

fig 1.1 *evaluating packages: a crude matrix method*

CRITERION	PACKAGE A	B	C	
1	✓	✓	✓	
2	✓		✓	
3	✓		✓	
4	✓	✓		
5		✓		
TOTAL TICKS	(4)	3	3	

fig 1.2 *evaluating packages: developing the matrix method*

CRITERION	PACKAGE A	B	C	
1	6	9	8	
2	6		9	
3	7		9	
4	7	10		
5		10		
TOTAL MARK	26	(29)	26	

The technique can be further improved by giving a weight to each criterion. Some requirements are more important than others. To emphasise the relative importance of criteria, a weight is allocated to each of them so that if a weight of four is assigned, then this criterion is considered to be four times as important as a criterion allocated a weight of one. Thus, if a package scores 7 out of 10 where the weight is 3, this counts as 21 on the total. Criteria which are considered essential can be given large weights, so that packages which do not meet these requirements will be excluded. In Figure 1.3, the allocation of different weights to criteria has led to package C being the recommended solution.

fig 1.3 *evaluating packages: including weights in the matrix*

CRITERION	WEIGHT	PACKAGE A	B	C	
1	(2)	6(12)	9(18)	8(16)	
2	(10)	6(60)	0(0)	9(90)	
3	(10)	7(70)	0(0)	9(90)	
4	(1)	7(7)	10(10)	0(0)	
5	(2)	0(0)	10(20)	0(0)	
TOTAL WEIGHTED MARK		149	48	(196)	

The example shows that different recommendations could be made depending on the way the technique is applied.

Having looked in outline at the feasibility study, we will look in more detail at some of the important considerations that need to be taken into account in evaluating and purchasing application packages and the hardware to run them. These include:

(a) **a requirements shortfall**, where not all the requirements defined in the feasibility study can be met by any one solution;

(b) **intangible costs and benefits**, which are difficult to evaluate in money terms but are nevertheless important in assessing alternatives;

(c) **extras**, which are frequently not included in an evaluation summary but when added up are an important consideration;

(d) **maintenance costs**, which include the costs of precautions which can be taken to avoid the system failing once it is running and those which ensure that the system is repaired should it fail;

(e) **hardware acquisition choices**, such as outright purchase, leasing, renting, hire purchase and second-hand purchase.

(a) A requirements shortfall

In some circumstances even the best hardware and software choice performs only some of the requirements defined. The business is then faced with a further choice in order to deal with this.

(*i*) Should it decide that microcomputer systems are inappropriate and continue with some sort of manual system, perhaps by reorganising the clerical procedures or employing more staff?

(*ii*) Should it purchase the computer system and application package and develop a manual system to perform those parts of the application not carried out by the computer system?

(*iii*) Should it call in the services of a consultant or software house to adapt the package so that it does conform to the needs of the business?

(*iv*) Should it pay a computer bureau to develop and run the system?

(*v*) Should it adapt the business to fit in with the requirements of the computer system?

All these are feasible in certain circumstances.

Whatever the choice, it is likely that some variation of the *80:20 rule* will apply: about 80% of the application requirements will be covered by the system, but about 20% will not be covered. Conversely, it is this 20% of the application requirements which will absorb something like 80% of the costs.

At least the prospective purchaser has had the foresight to detect the mismatch before purchasing the system. Too often the system has been purchased and the manager has discovered to his horror that some vital function is not performed. Further, as the problem was not analysed beforehand, the manager may have chosen an application package that is particularly difficult to adapt or a computer which will not run alternative packages.

It may seem surprising that the extra 20% of the requirements are so comparatively expensive. The reason is that the writers of an application package expect to sell many copies. This means that the initial expense of writing it is absorbed by the profit on the number of copies sold. Writing a package may cost thirty times its selling price. However, as soon as more than thirty copies are sold, the supplier begins to make a profit. The 'tuning' of the package for an individual user will be expensive. Although software houses design packages to be of use to as many prospective customers as possible, such a *generalised* package is unlikely to fulfil all the requirements of all of them. In estimating the costs and benefits of a computer solution in the feasibility study, it is essential that the cost of fulfilling *all* the requirements are included, otherwise the justification for the purchase will be distorted.

(b) Intangible costs and benefits
In evaluating systems, it is necessary to include these in the calculations. Intangible costs include:

  (*i*) the time and effort spent looking at potential packages; and
  (*ii*) the time and effort involved in training and educating people to use the computer system and overcoming their resistance to the new technology.

This second item is vital. The morale of staff may improve with the implementation of computer systems. But it might deteriorate if measures are not taken to maintain the confidence of employees. Staff may view computers as a threat because they may lead to a loss of work status, work satisfaction and employment. These intangible costs are difficult to evaluate.

Intangible benefits such as:

  (*iii*) greater speed of data processing;
  (*iv*) improved levels of security;
  (*v*) greater accuracy; and
  (*vi*) greater reliability

are equally difficult to evaluate in money terms, but should be included in the assessment.

(c) Extras
The most obvious costs will be those for the equipment and the application package. The equipment will include the computer, printer, visual display unit, storage device, and other peripherals. The costs of extras such as acoustic hoods for the printer to make it operate more quietly, paper stackers, and cabling should also be included in an evaluation. Again the cost of the application package may be included, but other software, such as printer drivers which will enable reports to be printed out on your printer, which might be necessary, omitted from the analysis.

In any case, hardware and software will probably account for only about one-half of the real outlay for the system. The wages of those people involved in setting up the system could be high. Less dramatic running costs include consumables such as the stationery, disks, and power supply. The rent of the space for the computer system should also be included. The equipment needs to be insured against fire and theft. Only a thorough analysis carried out in the feasibility study will ensure that all costs are included.

(d) Maintenance costs

Preventive maintenance is worthwhile: this includes regularly cleaning the equipment and checking the mechanical parts. Static can form and the voltage built up may lead to the loss of data on a disk because it is impossible for the computer to read that data. There are anti-static sprays available. A further danger of static is that it attracts dirt. Again, specks of dirt can do damage to disk drives and cause a loss of data.

Dust covers are available and ought to be put over the machines when they are not in use. Cigarette ash, food and drink might cause problems and 'good housekeeping' precautions to reduce or prevent their use in the vicinity of computing equipment may prevent very costly repair bills or a loss of data. A drinks spill, for example, can do great damage.

Even with preventive maintenance and good housekeeping measures, the system *will* fail at some time. By taking out a maintenance contract, very expensive repair bills will be avoided. Annual maintenance costs are usually about 15% of the purchase cost of the system. **Maintenance costs** therefore seem high and many managers may decide not to take out a maintenance contract. However, because the cost of repairing the system can be very expensive, computers may be left unrepaired if the system 'goes down'. This may mean that the business will suffer, especially if it has become reliant on the computer.

Maintenance contracts therefore are usually worthwhile, and it may be expedient to choose a maintenance contract which requires the servicing agency to replace the hardware with a loan machine when it is being repaired, because the system may take some time to repair. A temporary replacement machine could prove very useful in this situation.

(e) Hardware acquisition choices

In this section, we have assumed that once the decision to go ahead with a computer solution has been made, the hardware and software will be bought outright. However, outright purchase of the hardware and software represents only one of the **acquisition choices** open to the user. The system could be *leased*. In a leasing scheme, a finance house buys the equipment and leases it out over a fixed period at an agreed rental. Many smaller firms prefer to lease their microcomputer equipment. The arguments for and against a leasing scheme depend on the particular business and the company law and tax regulations operating at the time. It may be more advantageous to use *hire purchase* facilities. A *bank loan* might also be worth considering. Again, the arguments for and against will depend largely on tax and other legislation. *Renting* represents another option, although it is normally more appropriate for much larger computers. A final option is to buy *second-hand*. However, the pace of change in microcomputers is such that a machine over about two years old could already be out of date.

1.4 GETTING INFORMATION

Whereas with the larger mainframe computers there tends to be a wealth of help available from *in-house* data processing (or management services) departments, there may be far less expertise available to help develop microcomputer systems. This section looks at possible sources of information and advice. Some larger businesses *do* have information centres which have been set up for this purpose, but most people will have to go for outside help. Information sources include microcomputer magazines, suppliers, microcomputer advice centres, exhibitions and consultants. This section also discusses ways in which the supplier can be expected to support the system when it has been purchased.

In the past the in-house technologists – computer programmers and systems analysts – have tended to be disinterested in microcomputers and unable or unwilling to give advice on microcomputers. This attitude is changing, but it is by no means extinct. One sign of improvement is the **information centre** idea. Here, the data processing staff in a company make themselves available to give advice to the user departments. Following discussions with the user department, the data processing professionals may recommend a large computer solution. However they may recommend a microcomputer system with a particular application package.

Many firms opting for this approach have demanded that user departments standardise on one microcomputer model or at least on a small range of microcomputers. Similarly, with application packages, the user is expected to choose from a limited range of supported packages. The reason for this limitation is obvious: to enable the data processing professionals to gain a thorough knowledge of the systems that are supported and therefore be able to offer good advice in their applicability and use.

There is another reason for standardisation: there is a cost advantage of buying in quantity. The cost of ten copies of an application package, for example, is unlikely to be ten times the price of one. Thus a procurement policy defining a range of standard products is desirable unless the user can prove that the functionality of this range is demonstrably inferior to some item of non-standard equipment.

In time, these computer systems and application packages may not be 'state of the art'. This is not usually important (though such claims may sell computers). The most important criterion is whether they do the job defined in the requirements definition. In any case, the state of the art may not be 'on the shelves' or not tested properly. Unfortunately, many products are announced before they are available so as to stimulate interest. The temptation is then to put it on the market as quickly as possible. The first buyers thus become 'guinea pigs'.

With smaller firms this microcomputer venture may be the first for the business. The first source of advice may be one of the large number of **microcomputer magazines**. Most provide a very good and up to date introduction to the range of systems available. They will also give details about suppliers, from whom further information can be obtained.

Once the requirements have been defined and the range of solutions narrowed through studying the magazines and brochures from suppliers, the next step ought to be to have a closer look at the alternative solutions. Although there may not be an in-house information centre, there is a **microcomputer advice centre** in many towns where it is possible to look at a range of machines and packages, see how they run, and gain some 'first level' advice without charge.

A day spent at a **computer exhibition** can also be useful, but it is necessary to decide on what to look for first. Then it is possible to seek out the supplier, see a demonstration of the system, and ask questions relevant to *your* business and *your* application. Without this preparatory work, you will be very tired and none the wiser. Such a visit may also give an impression of the suppliers: whether they are likely to stay in business and whether the staff are interested and helpful.

This visit can be followed up by one to the suppliers or for them to set up a demonstration at your place of work. Ideally this will use the real application data, preferably enough of it to test the speed of the computer system in dealing with the data. It may be possible to borrow a demonstration version of the application package for a week or two in order to try out the system. This will provide an opportunity to assess aspects of the package, such as documentation, as well as the running of the system.

Another source of advice is the **consultant**. Consultancy fees can be very expensive, or at least seem so when compared with the prices of the hardware and software. Many consultants have a financial tie with a hardware or software supplier and their advice might be biased. It is best to take on a consultant who has been recommended by others. A general microcomputer person, with a knowledge of the application areas defined in the requirements definition, may help in choosing hardware and software at the beginning. If difficulties are experienced with an application package, then these will require a consultant with a knowledge of that particular package.

There are inevitably some unexpected problems in installing a hardware and software system and most people will need some advice unless they are happy to spend a lot of time (and accept some frustration) installing the system using technical manuals as instructions.

There are also pitfalls to avoid even if the package chosen is appropriate for the application and is installed to the satisfaction of the users. The average life expectancy of firms supplying hardware and software is probably less then the expected life of the system. Many suppliers are small, with a staff of around five people. If the firm is wound-up, maintenance of the hardware and software may prove to be a problem. In assessing a system, therefore, the likely level of support once it is operational must be taken into consideration.

The support may be provided by the dealer who sells and installs the computer system and application package. It may be provided by the manufacturer, wholesaler or distributor. It may be a mixture of a number of companies. Some manufacturers of hardware or distributors of software do not permit direct selling and require purchases to be made through a dealer. All this can be very confusing and may lead to difficulties about whom to contact should there be problems. It is obviously important to establish such arrangements before signing any contract.

The contract proposed by the supplier is important: it might be framed to put all the obligations on the purchaser (it will have been drawn up by the supplier's solicitor). Aspects such as:

(a) delivery dates, and what to do if they are not met;
(b) the level of free maintenance;

(c) the cost of further maintenance; and
(d) the provision for training

should all be agreed and written into the contract. The advice of your own **solicitor** could therefore be crucial.

Supplier support normally includes:

(a) training on how to use the system, preferably in the user's environment;
(b) a telephone 'help line' so that the user can obtain advice;
(c) maintenance of the system, should the hardware or software package go wrong or need to be altered; and
(d) the provision of new versions of the software incorporating improvements as they become available.

This level of support will not be free, but it should be provided by the supplier, and at an agreed cost. Dealers selling the equipment at a discount are unlikely to provide this level of service.

The training of staff is important, and when arranging courses it is important to check the qualifications of the teaching staff. If the course is conducted away from the user's place of work, there must be enough equipment for each person to get 'hands-on' experience.

It is also important to consider reliability when assessing hardware and software. Failure can be very expensive in terms of lost time, effort and reputation. Employees will not be happy to learn that the payroll system has failed and that they will have to wait a few days before getting paid. As we have seen, there may be times when even the most reliable systems fail. Arrangements could therefore be made with a **computer bureau** to run applications if the in-house hardware or software has 'gone down'.

It is necessary to take a backup of all data so that it is possible to recover in the event of failure. Archiving should also be carried out. This is the building up of a library of files which are no longer needed daily, but which might be needed for reference purposes in the future. These security measures should prevent an inconvenience becoming a 'disaster'.

1.5 SUPPLIERS

There is a wide range of computer products and services offered by a number of types of suppliers. In general, there is a trade-off between price and service. In other words, the lower the price, the less help and after-sales service is given. However, although this is generally the case, the 'rule' does not always hold true. If you are a first-time buyer, have little computing experience or have a specialist application, it may well be prudent to pay more for a specialist dealer who has a number of services available, such as advice, support and training, rather than go to a supplier who aims to 'push boxes' at the lowest possible price. The cut-price dealer is less likely to have the resources (and the enthusiasm) to give specialist advice. On the other hand, if the purchase is for equipment where there is already in-house experience, or a standard system, it may well be appropriate to go to the cheapest supplier. Noting that what follows is a generalisation and that there are exceptions, the categories of supplier are: high street stores, computer dealers of different kinds and original suppliers (manufacturers).

(a) High street stores

There are some high street stores, particularly the multiples, selling computer systems amongst other electronic equipment. They attract buyers on the basis of price, for few salesmen have much more than a superficial knowledge of the systems, apart from that required to sell them. Usually the choice is limited, and any non-standard item is difficult to come by. Indeed many offer a computer system consisting of the computer, disk drive and printer as part of the 'deal'. There is no choice.

Sometimes they will have limited stocks and there will be a few weeks' waiting. It is important that buyers are informed (or inform themselves) of any delay in supply. Another limitation of high street stores is the after-sales service, including maintenance. There may be a few weeks' delay while the equipment is returned to the manufacturer for repair. Unless the buyers can survive with their own expertise, expensive specialist help may be required. This may cost as much as the equipment did in the first place.

(b) Specialist computer dealers

A number of stores now exist which specialise in computer equipment. Some are multiples, with one or two stores in each major town, whereas others are one-offs and might have a local reputation of one kind or other. They are probably more expensive than high street stores, but advice may well be more available and the range of products greater.

Some dealers provide a fuller service, and sell a full range of business hardware and software packages. They may have staff that will customise the software for a buyer's particular needs. Many of these business dealers specialise in particular application areas, such as accountancy firms, solicitors, doctors' practices and so on.

There is a third level of specialist computer dealers, normally called systems houses. They usually sell to larger companies who are willing to pay for specialist services because they cannot afford the risk of failure. Again, they may specialise in a particular range of computer equipment and may be endorsed by the manufacturer. Most of their income comes from the specialist services, such as customising, training and advice, rather than the profit margins on the equipment. It is therefore important to find out that they will do a good job, and to demand references.

(c) Mail order companies

There are now a number of direct mail order companies. They may be similar to high street stores in terms of price, or be even cheaper. As with high street stores, the buyers need to have a clear idea of what they require. It is important to verify that stocks of the goods needed are available. Though many companies offer 'hot line' (telephone) support it is not possible for the buyer to see the products beforehand. Further, the goods arrive in boxes, and therefore the instructions need to be clear and the buyer adept and confident about setting up the system. If machines have to be returned, it may be expensive and it may take some time before they come back.

1.6 PLANNING AND USER INVOLVEMENT

All this discussion leads to the conclusion that it is necessary to plan the acquisition of the new technology very carefully. If a manager goes out to buy microcomputer equipment without first looking at the needs of the department, then the expedition is likely to be costly. It is essential that the needs of the organisation are analysed thoroughly and that the advantages and disadvantages of various solutions are weighed up before a choice is made. Even assuming that the hardware and software chosen will meet the objectives set, there are many further hurdles. As we have seen, the system has to be reliable and the supplier has to offer a good after-sales service. But the most important hurdle concerns the human dimension.

If people object to the technology encroaching into their working lives, even the best choices may fail. People may refuse to work with the technology, attempt to ensure that it does not work, or look for another job. A fundamental question is 'who *are* the users of the system?'. In this section we distinguish between professional users, regular users and casual users. Once they have been identified, it is essential to plan the coming of the new technology and to ensure that all users are involved in the decision and are trained in the use of the system. This will help to gain their support. Ergonomic factors are also important in ensuring the happiness of the workforce using the system, and these factors are also discussed in this section. If human factors are given the importance that they deserve, then the business stands a far greater chance of the computer system being a success.

(a) Professional users
The different kinds of user may include professional users, that is, data processing people who will use the computer system to develop programs and systems. However, professional users tend to use large computers and a department or small firm may not have these skills at hand. In this book we are more concerned with other types of user.

(b) Regular users
Clerical staff and secretarial staff may well be regular users and may access the computer system daily to input data or to process text. They are frequently referred to as the **operators** of the system. Assuming that steps have been taken to ensure their co-operation, they are likely to be willing to train in the use of the computer and application package so that they can use the system. These inducements may mean tangible things, like salary increases, and less tangible things, like improved status, job interest and security. When regular users are familiar with the system, they may be put off by the level of help given to the casual user. Regular users may find this unnecessary and irritating and it also slows down the running of the system.

(c) Casual users
Casual users are frequently middle managers or top managers. They may have had little previous experience of computing and their use of the new equipment may be very varied. They are unlikely to have the time or inclination to train to use each computer system and application package thoroughly, and their enquiries of each day could be related to different applications or different parts of the same application package. The **human-computer interface** for casual users must therefore be particularly helpful. Some computer systems and application packages have two or three types of interface which can be selected according to the experience of the user.

Managers as users have another function to perform. It is important that their involvement with the new technology should not end with their permission to purchase the hardware and software, nor should they exist solely as the readers of the reports that the computer system provides. Managers must *lead by example*. They should benefit most from computers and their commitment to computer systems will encourage others to participate positively in the change.

(d) Ergonomic factors

Ergonomic factors are also important. Ergonomics is about the working environment, and the prospective user or manager should consider these aspects. Although microcomputers do not require the air-conditioned environments needed by mainframe systems, it is a mistake to assume that the microcomputer can simply replace the typewriter on the same desk, using the same space.

Compared with much of the conventional office equipment, computer equipment is larger and often noisier. If there is a poor working environment, users may suffer bad backs, headaches, sore eyes, hand cramps, and other discomforts which may lead to an unco-operative, error-prone and possibly a frequently absent employee. Repetitive strain injury (RSI) can cause permanent damage to joints in the fingers and elsewhere. It is essential that operators take frequent breaks from repetitive tasks. Printers should be bought with acoustic hoods which reduce noise levels. Visual display units should have a sharp signal and should not flicker, and pregnant women should avoid prolonged exposure to VDU rays. Detachable keyboards and visual display units capable of being tilted can also help to reduce strain.

Furniture, layout, and lighting ought to be designed to avoid these problems. Chairs should be adjustable for people of different heights, and support the user in a relaxed working position. There ought to be room on the desk for the screen, keyboard and the user's papers, so that the design is not cramped. The lighting should be arranged with care. Many offices are too brightly lit and this is costly and can also obscure the image on the visual display unit. Finally, the colour of the office environment should also be carefully chosen to avoid stark contrasts.

We shall return to the human factors associated with implementing the new technology in section 2.10. To complete this introduction to microcomputer applications we will introduce some of the basic jargon associated with hardware in the next section and with software in section 1.8.

1.7 HARDWARE

(a) The microcomputer

The basic element of the computer is the **microprocessor**. This is an **integrated circuit** held on a piece of plastic forming the micpropro-cessor **chip**. This performs some of the basic logical functions of the computer. A microcomputer will have a number of chips, including those for the computer's memory, connected on one or more **printed circuit boards**.

fig 1.4   *the IBM PS/2 computer*
   Source: IBM United Kingdom Limited

All this is hidden from the user as it is contained in the microcom-puter box, but two aspects *are* of interest to the buyer: the particular microprocessor chip and the amount of memory. The particular microprocessor is important as it governs such aspects as the speed of the microcomputer in performing the tasks set by the user. Each generation of microcomputers (a generation being about three or four years) is usually based on a different microprocessor chip, with consequent improvements in the performance of the microcom-puters. However, unless the processing is very complex, the ability of the computer to process data is more limited by the slowness of getting data to and from the computer: in other words, disk speeds, printer speeds and the speed of the operator typing in data on the keyboard.

The amount of memory is also important. Computers operate on groups of **BI**nary dig**ITS (bits)**. Each bit can be on or off (0 or 1) and a group of them can therefore represent a number or character. The most common grouping is a **byte** consisting of eight bits. Thus 00000000 may represent the number 0, 00000001 the number 1, 00000010 the number 2, 00000011 the number 3 . . . and 00001001 the number 9. The decimal number 416 will be held as three bytes as follows: 00000100 00000001 00000110. Following the decimal number 9 (00001001), the other possible combinations of a byte can be used for the characters of the alphabet and special characters such as %, *, $ and +. The combination 00001010 could represent the letter A, 00001011 the letter B, and so on.

The user is interested in the memory of the computer expressed in bytes. The larger the memory, the more data can be stored in the computer, and the larger the programs that can be run efficiently. Memory is usually quoted as a multiple of one 'k' bytes where one 'k' is 2^{10} or 1024 bytes. The minimum business computer memory requirement is 512k, but many microcomputers have much larger memories, frequently one megabyte (1024k) or more, and microcomputers with memories of four megabytes are now available. Some computers can be expanded by adding a memory expansion board which provides extra memory on a printed circuit board with extra memory chips. Commonly this gives the computer a memory size of 4, 8 or 16 megabytes. This will be placed in one of the computer's **expansion slots**. These expansion slots could also hold a **network board** so that your computer can be connected to others on the **network**. This is a communications system which allows computer users working on different computers to 'talk' to each other and use each other's resources.

As well as internal slots, the microcomputer will have a number of external slots or **ports**. These are available for any external devices, such as printers, that need to be connected to the microcomputer. If networking is contemplated, that is joining together computers so that data can be passed between them, the prospective purchaser should be aware of compatibility problems. It may be difficult to connect disparate computer systems. It might, for example, be wise to adopt a policy of purchasing computers which are made by the same manufacturer or have the same operating system (see section 1.8)

The total memory available may be described in terms of RAM and ROM. **Random access memory** (RAM) is memory available to the user for programs and data. **Read only memory** (ROM) is used for the operating software of the computer and, unlike RAM, its contents will not be lost if the machine is turned off. RAM is therefore for the temporary storage of data and programs, and on finishing the session the user must transfer the data on to backing storage if it is worth keeping.

Another aspect of some modern microcomputers is their ability to enable more than one person to use the computer at the same time. The alternatives – a queue of people waiting to use the computer or purchasing a number of computers – may be comparatively inefficient or costly. **Multi-user** microcomputers may cope with about 3 to 10 users accessing the machine 'at the same time'. Multi-user microcomputers are frequently referred to as 'super-micros', for they can perform as well as many minicomputers, although with ten users their performance is likely to be decidedly sluggish.

Perhaps at the other extreme are the range of **portable computers** now available. They can be transported to and from work so that they can be used at work and at home without having problems of setting up, though it is stretching a case to say that they are likely to get much use on the train (as many advertisers have claimed). Most can work both by battery (although users complain of a short battery life) and by mains power supply. Those which do not have a battery are often referred to as 'luggables'. Despite the apparent problems, portable computers, such as that shown in Figure 1.5, are becoming popular and more powerful and many are of comparable power and performance to desktop microcomputers.

Portable computers are designed to be light and should not take much room. Most have a computing capability, a keyboard, and screen all in one box. The screen is likely to be liquid crystal display (LCD) or gas plasma because these require less space than a conventional visual display unit, although some are more difficult to read. Many portable machines have a floppy disk drive and there are also hard disk versions. If portables are used as stand-alone computers, their main use is likely to be as word processors and diary managers, and to hold files of names and addresses.

Some portable computers have communications facilities and this would seem very useful, if not essential. This facility enables the user to dial an in-house computer using the telephone system, and the portable computer acts like a terminal to that computer. The entry of data relating to sales by sales people away from base, illustrates this type of use. Some microcomputers which are not designed to be portable also have communications facilities.

fig 1.5 *the Compag SLT/286 with large detachable keyboard*
Source: Compag Computer Limited

Computers are usually described as falling within one of three categories: **microcomputers, minicomputers** and **mainframe computers**. In general, these can be distinguished by their cost and power: in other words, the larger the computer (from micro to mini to mainframe) the more they cost and the greater their power. This power can be measured in terms of:

(*i*) larger volumes of work processed;
(*ii*) a wider range and number of hardware devices that can be attached;
(*iii*) a wider range of programs that can run;
(*iv*) a greater number of users using the computer at the same time; and
(*v*) the speed of processing work.

Over the last few years the power range of each category has increased greatly so that many micros today are as powerful as the average mini of, say, five years ago, and the average mainframe of, say, ten years ago.

The term **workstation** further blurs the distinction because a workstation is usually defined as a very powerful microcomputer system which has one user but is often connected to other computers in a network. Workstations may have, for example, a minimum of 8mb internal memory, a very fast processing speed, and external disk storage of, say, 256 megabytes. Comparable figures for a standard microcomputer may be, say, 2mb memory and 40mb disk capacity.

As we saw in section 1.3, the prospective buyer needs to form a requirements definition and decide which category of computer (as well as which computer system within a category) adequately fulfils this requirement, allowing for likely needs of the next few years. Not all users require the facilities of the largest computers. The number of applications and the amount of data to be processed may be limited, and the capacities of microcomputers sufficient. Microcomputers can offer distinct advantages:

(*i*) they are cheaper than minis and mainframes;

(*ii*) they are comparatively small and may fit conveniently on an office desk;

(*iii*) they may be portable;

(*iv*) they do not need special air-conditioned environments to operate;

(*v*) they do not need professional operators; and

(*vi*) the applications are frequently designed for use by casual users.

The term 'user friendly' has been over-used, but people untrained in computers are much more likely to want to use (and be successful in using) micros than minis and mainframes.

A microcomputer (or two or three microcomputers) may well be adequate for the small firm. The decision to buy microcomputers may also be taken in larger firms. In this case, it is likely that the departmental micros will be used for applications which are internal to the departments. Departments may also use the company main-frame for some tasks. In this case the micro may be connected to the mainframe so that, for example, data can be collected in the department, validated on the departmental micro and then sent to the mainframe for processing.

(b) Backing storage
Connected to the computer will be a disk storage system which will be
used to hold computer programs and data. There are two sorts:
floppy disks and hard disks. The text of this book is held on a 3½"
floppy disk. Each disk can hold 720 000 bytes of data (about 100 000
words of text). There is enough main memory on my microcomputer
to hold a chapter at a time, which is enough for me to work on. As
each chapter has been edited, it can be written on to floppy disk and
another chapter loaded into memory for editing.

Floppy disks can also be used to transfer data. It would be possible
to send this text, held on a disk, through the post and for it to be
typeset by the publisher directly from the disk.

A computer program may also be held on a floppy disk. An
application package may be held on one disk or be so large that it
needs a series of three or four disks. There are other floppy disk sizes,
notably 5¼" and 8". The 3½" **microdisk** is protected by a harder
casing and is more sturdy.

Data and programs are important, so **backup** copies ought to be
kept in case a floppy disk drive malfunctions and the data on a disk is
lost. Floppy disks have a write-protect notch which can be activated
to prevent data on it being overwritten.

Hard disks will hold much more data. The smallest can hold
around 20 megabytes, but 40, 60, 80 and 100 megabyte capacities are
common, with some larger capacity hard disks available (more
common, perhaps, in workstations). The disk is sealed in a disk unit
and is therefore protected from dust, fingerprints, and so on. Data
and programs can be retrieved about fifteen times faster from hard
disks and they are generally more convenient than floppy devices
(and considerably more expensive).

Recently a new kind of backing store has become available,
so-called 'floptical' disks. There are two basic types: WORM (Write
Once, Read Many) and WARM (Write and Read Many times).
These devices allow large amounts of data (typically 256 megabytes)
to be stored on special 5¼" disks. Since these disks are interchange-
able, large volumes of data can be stored in a very compact form.
These devices are comparable in speed to a medium to fast conventional hard disk.

It is important to copy the contents of a hard disk onto floppy
disks, or better still **streamer tape**, so that it is possible to recover
from a hard disk malfunction or a human or program error. By using
streamer tape (magnetic tape housed in a cartridge) it takes about
five minutes to back up a 20 megabyte disk. This process would take

more than an hour using floppy disk and would require a lot of disk handling procedures.

(c) Visual display unit (VDU)

A VDU, which is frequently referred to as a monitor, is like a television screen. Televisions can be used as VDUs, although the image on a purpose built monitor will be sharper and less liable to give the user 'real' headaches (a TV set will tend to flicker). The computer can send messages to the user on the monitor. The user can return messages by typing on a keyboard attached to it. There are colour as well as monochrome VDUs and they vary in size (normally 12″ or, more commonly, 14″). By using an anti-reflective panel over the screen, the nuisance of other light sources can be avoided. This can be particularly troublesome where strip lighting is used. The more expensive VDUs may be necessary for some graphics applications. VDUs are discussed further in Chapter 5 (on graphics).

A **cursor** is a marker on the VDU which appears at the position where an operation will take place. On switching on, the cursor appears at the 'home' position on the VDU screen which is at the top left-hand corner.

Some VDU screens (such as that in Figure 1.6) are touch sensitive, so that the user chooses an option from a list on the screen by touching the name of the required option on the screen. The UK Stock Market has adopted touchscreens for fast selection of options. Alternatively a hand-held **mouse** connected to the computer by a wire can be used to move the cursor to point to the required option, which is then activated by using a button on the mouse. There is a ball at the bottom of the mouse and it is the movements of this ball which move the cursor. The computer seen in Figure 5.23 has a mouse attached to it. The conventional way of giving instructions to a computer is to type them in on the keyboard.

(d) Keyboard

This is based on the conventional typewriter keyboard, although there are additional keys. The 'break' key, for example, is used to abandon a particular job (present work on it will be lost). Most keyboards also have function keys which are used to perform special functions. The function key 'help' is pressed to give the user information on how to use the system. Arrow keys, again present on most but not all keyboards, are used to move the cursor up and down and left and right on the screen. Most computer keyboards also have a **numeric pad**, which is used to input numeric data efficiently. In order to use the keyboard efficiently, some typing skills help, and it may be a good investment of your time to learn how to type by joining a class or following a 'teach yourself' course.

The main part of the keyboard in Figure 1.6 (similar to that on a standard typewriter) is shown in the centre. The keys at the top of the keyboard are function keys. The set of keys to the right are the numeric keys and the lighter keys to the left of them include the arrow keys.

fig 1.6 *HP Vectra computer*
   Source: Hewlett-Packard Limited

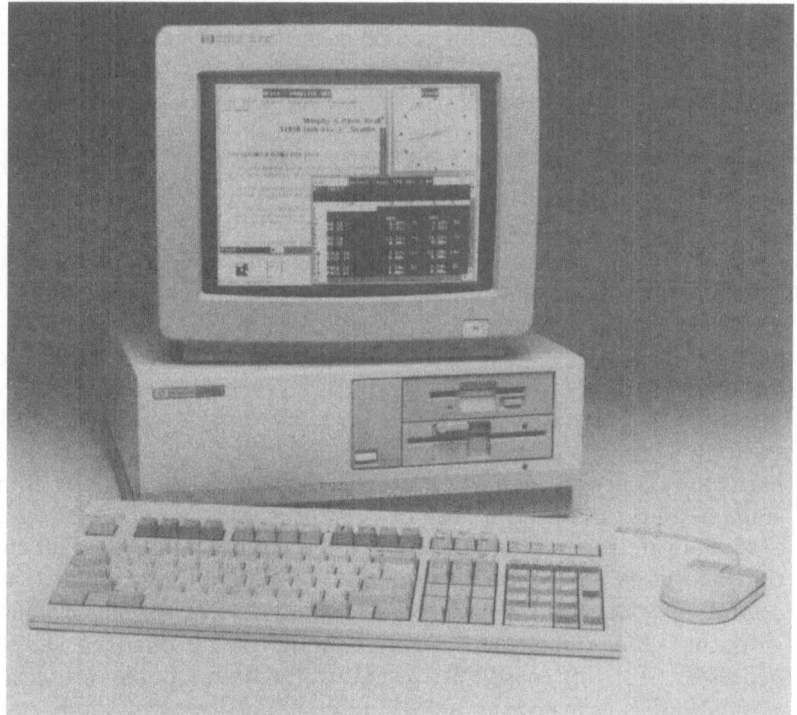

(e) Printer

Whereas messages on the VDU ('soft copy') are not permanent, a 'hard copy' can be obtained by attaching a printer to the microcomputer. Reports, payslips and letters can all be printed. There are different kinds of printer available and the quality of the print and the speed of printing vary a great deal amongst them. A more detailed description of the range of printers available is given in Chapter 2.

1.8 SOFTWARE

Software drives the computer system in such a way that a particular function or set of functions is carried out. It is therefore a set of logical instructions. There are two broad types of software: the **operating system** and the **user programes** which can themselves be of two types: user-written **bespoke** programs and **application packages**.

(a) Operating system

The operating system organises the running of user programs and the transfer of data between the various devices. It monitors and controls the use of the hardware. This can be described as the software which carries out the computer's housekeeping (to be contrasted with the applications software which carries out the users' requirements).

The most popular operating systems at the time of writing are MS-DOS (known as PC-DOS on IBM computers), OS/2, a more powerful operating system running on more recent IBM computers, and versions of Unix (for example, Xenix). MS-DOS has disadvantages, in that only one user can be using the machine at any time and software running on the system is limited in features. However, it is well used and there is a vast amount of software available for it. Unix, and its derivatives such as Xenix, is multi-user (a number of terminals, and therefore users, can be using the same computer at the same time). Unix is also the standard operating system for workstations. Unix can also run on a number of different manufacturers' hardware. Software can therefore be 'portable', that is, the same software can run on a number of computer systems. OS/2 is single-user, but can be performing a number of different tasks in parallel for that one user. A number of different computers have one of these operating systems, and packages are likely to run on any machine with the same operating system, although some changes will be necessary. For this reason it is usual to purchase a computer with a standard operating system, unless there are particularly good reasons for deviating from this rule. Operating systems can be particularly difficult for non-computer people to understand. Yet they need to load in programs, copy data on disk and print out documents.

For this reason, there has been a movement towards designing a user interface to an operating system which is easier to use than the standard operating system command languages. The 'WIMPS' interface, which is discussed in section 5.3 offers a pictorial presentation to the user, and has been adopted as standard on some computers and as an option on others. For example, there is a WIMP interface available for OS/2 users.

(b) Bespoke programs
The computer actually manipulates sets of binary digits ('0's and '1's). Any program is translated into this **binary code** from the source language. This translation process is known as **compiling** or **interpreting**, depending on the exact process involved. The user-written programs are written in a source language such as Basic, Cobol, APL, Pascal or Fortran. The choice of language will depend on the task in hand, as each has been designed for a particular range of tasks. None of these languages is easy to use.

Even if users are familiar with a particular programming language, the programs need to be designed, written and tested before they can become operational. This all takes time and is very costly. Should an application package be available which covers the required function, it is very unlikely that bespoke systems will provide a cost-effective alternative. Even so, where a package does not meet the user requirements exactly, it may be necessary for the user or consultant to write routines in a programming language and amend the package so that it more closely meets the requirements definition.

(c) Application packages
As we have seen, the purchase of an application package is likely to be the best way of implementing an application. Packages can be low cost and they are usually implemented much quicker than bespoke programs. The assumption of this book is that such a package will be available for most of the applications required by the business. This is, on the whole, true, especially in the personal computer (PC) market, but of course there are still problems. These include training the users, collecting the data, and testing the system to ensure that it works as expected. As we have already mentioned, if the system needs modification, the costs involved are likely to be relatively high.

In this text we discuss the main types of packages on microcomputers, judged by the numbers of users of these packages and by the number of them offered in the market place. These are:

(*i*) word processing and related applications (electronic mail and diary systems);
(*ii*) file management and data base management;
(*iii*) spreadsheet and financial modelling;
(*iv*) graphics and computer aided design;
(*v*) accounting and related applications (sales ledger, purchase ledger, nominal ledger, sales order processing, stock recording, invoicing, payroll and integrated accounts); and
(*vi*) integrated packages, project management, statistics, application generators and expert systems.

However, there are hundreds of packages available. Some are general purpose, like the above packages. Others are designed specifically for certain types of businesses, such as:

Architects
Agriculture
Builders and construction
Caterers
Dentists
Education
Employment agencies
Estate agents
Fleet management
Hotels
Insurance brokers
Market research
Newsagents
Pharmacies
Plant hire
Share management
Quantity surveyors
Video dealers

Most of these packages will cover one or two applications for that particular business. The package for the architect could be a drawings register, that is, a system to enable architects to keep track of drawings and documents. The package for dentists may be a patients register which makes appointments and handles cancellations. The system for estate agents could attempt to match properties on a register with prospective purchasers, and print off standard letters (such as valuation reports) and control advertising. A hoteliers' package may handle reservations, check-ins, and payment routines. A system for newsagents could deal with deliveries: hold customers' names and addresses, produce delivery boy/girl schedules, handle cancellations and control holiday stops. A video package will handle hirings, produce lists of films and customers, and work out and print a 'top 100' chart.

These applications could be devised by using a word processing, data base, spreadsheet or integrated package, but if there is a package available for your particular needs, it may well be a good option to purchase a business-specific package, as implementing the system can be considerably quicker.

Software packages normally come in a cardboard or plastic box or some form of folder in cardboard or plastic casing. This includes a set of disks, documentation, and licensing agreement. The package may have security devices of some sort. A **dongle** is a piece of hardware connected to the machine which has to be plugged in for the program to work. It is also possible to make disks very difficult to copy, or design the system in such a way that only one or two backup copies can be made. A further method of security is to design the program so that the system asks for a master disk to be inserted every now and again. All these methods are a nuisance to the purchaser but are aimed to prevent software piracy. Programs would otherwise be easy to copy and therefore cause a loss of income to their suppliers. Nevertheless there has been a movement away from making software difficult to copy.

One hardware/software combination which has been designed for easy and immediate use is a **turnkey system**. Once it is delivered and set up, it should be utilisable 'at the turn of a key'. Such systems are provided by a single supplier and normally address a single task such as work processing. Some turnkey systems are bespoke systems and therefore designed and implemented specifically for one customer. Purchasing a dedicated system usually limits the potential of the computer investment because the system has not been designed for flexibility, but this choice can be effective where this one application is of great importance and the requirements specification for it is unlikely to change.

WORD PROCESSING

AND THE

ELECTRONIC OFFICE

This chapter looks at the whole range of applications associated with the processing of text. The first section describes word processing, its uses and the advantages that it possesses over typing. The next three sections look at the main steps in processing a text document on a computer: creating and correcting the text (editing), storing the text on computer files, and printing the final document. Section 2.5 describes an additional feature of many word processing systems, that of a spelling checker using a dictionary stored on disk.

Computers can be used to set up and store text and print it out. They can also be used to send documents to other people. This application is known as electronic mail, and it is described in section 2.6. Section 2.7 looks at other features which may be present in an electronic mail environment, such as dictation, phototypesetting, facsimile, telex and viewdata. In order that mail can be sent electronically, the computers have to be connected in some way. Local area networks are a common way of doing this, linking computers in different offices in a building, and strategies for their implementation are described in section 2.8. The sophisticated applications of desk top publishing are examined in section 2.9. Some of the human factors related to microcomputer applications were looked at earlier, in Chapter 1, and this topic is developed further in the final section of this chapter. Many of the points made in this section have relevance to all computer applications.

2.1 WORD PROCESSING

Word processing is the preparation of text using computer techno-logy. It can be used as an alternative to pen and ink or typewriter for the preparation of papers, reports, and letters, in fact any text.

Documents, such as memoranda, can be transferred between people, perhaps in different offices. There is no need for any printing stage. A message, such as that shown in Figure 2.1, can be sent and replied to quickly. This possibility gives rise to the concept of the *paperless office*. As we shall see, this remains a concept: word processing has probably increased, rather than decreased, the use of paper. The **electronic office** is a development of the new technology to automate more and more aspects of office work. In this chapter we will look at these aspects as well as at how managers can best go about implementing the new technology in offices. But we start by looking at the basics of word processing.

Old-fashioned typing work requires the manager to dictate the text to the secretary or write it in longhand. Dictation is more usual because it is quicker and most secretaries will take down the text in shorthand notation. The next task is to type the text on a typewriter from these notes. Alternatively, the secretary can type from dictated instructions held on a cassette tape. The manager then checks and amends the text. Evidence of widespread use of error correction fluid looks unprofessional, so that unless the corrections and amendments are very minor, the secretary will need to retype *all* the text. This may lead to a further problem. The typist makes errors that were not present in the first version. The manager therefore has to recheck all the text...and so the process continues.

The steps of word processing need not be markedly different, the secretary simply uses a computer rather than a typewriter. But the last stages are different in one fundamental aspect. The secretary keys in the corrections and amendments *only*, and the manager need only check these changes. The rest has been untouched – it remains on disk storage – and therefore no new errors have been introduced. This makes word processing far more efficient than conventional typing.

This increased efficiency can come about for another reason. If we look at Figure 2.2, we see that the replies and acknowledgements of much commercial correspondence are standard. The texts of these can be held on disk and used over and over again. In dealing with general enquiries from customers, the only *genuinely individual* aspect of the reply and acknowledgement may well be the customer's name and address and the salutation, 'Dear *Mr Avison*'. All this information can be stored and picked out from a name and address file. Alternatively, if it is a new customer and not on file, the operator can key in the name and address when instructed by the system. Even the date can be put in automatically, as it will be stored by the computer.

fig 2.1 *word processing and the paperless office*

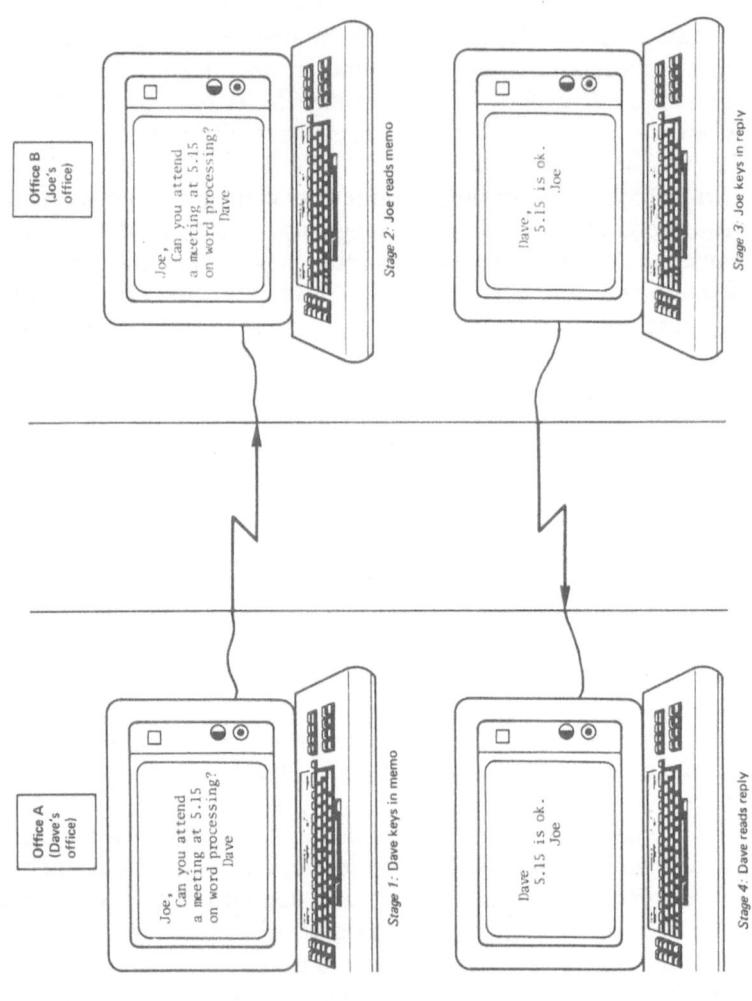

Office A (Dave's office)

Stage 1: Dave keys in memo

Joe,
Can you attend
a meeting at 5.15
on word processing?
Dave

Office B (Joe's office)

Stage 2: Joe reads memo

Joe,
Can you attend
a meeting at 5.15
on word processing?
Dave

Stage 4: Dave reads reply

Dave
5.15 is ok.
Joe

Stage 3: Joe keys in reply

Dave,
5.15 is ok.
Joe

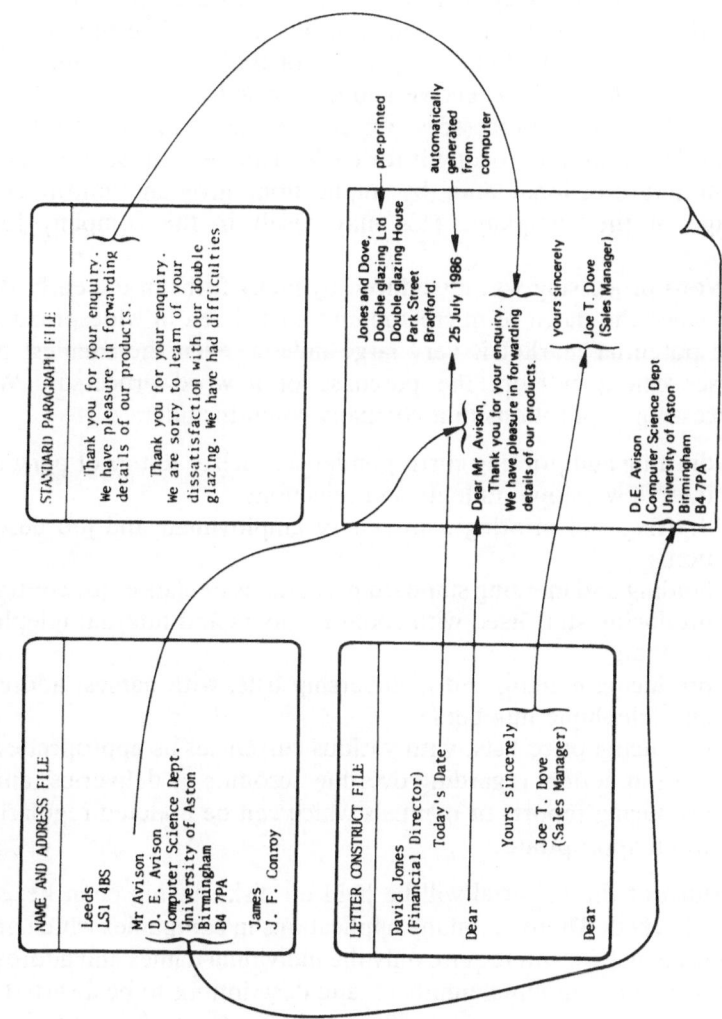

fig 2.2 *constructing a letter from files*

37

The **communication cycle**, that is the time and effort to process one communication, will be reduced. One example was shown in Figure 2.1. Using the company's internal mail system, memos can take 24 hours before a reply is received. With word processors in all offices, the communication cycle can be reduced to a matter of minutes. Another example of this is shown in Figure 2.2. The time taken to receive an enquiry about the product of the company, reply to the enquiry by letter, and receive and acknowledge the order is greatly reduced by word processors. Of course the company could use a typed letter and photocopy it for each customer, but such letters do seem unprofessional and, by implication, give an unprofessional image of the company. This may result in the company losing business.

Word processing was introduced by many firms in the early 1970s and since the dawn of microcomputers has been in widespread use. The potential market is very large indeed, even the smallest businesses can gain from the purchase of a word processor. Word processing applications in a company could include:

(a) drafting and printing correspondence, such as letters of personnel interviews, appointments and rejections;
(b) drafting and printing contracts of employment and job descriptions;
(c) holding and merging standard paragraphs or clauses for contracts;
(d) producing staff lists, with room numbers and internal telephone numbers;
(e) producing mailing and membership lists, with names, addresses and telephone numbers;
(f) producing price lists, with various currencies as appropriate;
(g) printing letters regarding overdue accounts or deliveries; and
(h) producing reports or manuals which can be updated regularly or when appropriate.

Much of the material will be held on disk, having been keyed in and checked. There are many applications in companies which are of a routine nature and require only the individual names and addresses, dates, money amounts, numbers, and descriptions to be inserted into the text where appropriate. This is obviously quicker and cheaper than producing an individual letter each time, but its appearance is the same as a freshly typed letter. Word processing systems can also print off several 'top' copies of a document. These will have a far better appearance than photocopies and take little or no more time and effort to produce.

The accuracy of mailing lists, membership lists, and staff lists may also be relied upon as they can be updated and distributed regularly. This increases the use of paper in the office. However, if all members of staff have access to microcomputers in an office network, the distribution of paper lists is not necessary. Following a 'one per desk' philosophy, an internal telephone number or a name and address can be obtained conveniently by accessing the relevant files from *your* computer. We will return to office networks later in this chapter.

Another gain of word processing is the reduction of the tedium associated with many of the tasks carried out in offices. Many firms hold standard paragraphs in file which give details of the company and good references about the products of the company. They may wish to use these frequently in correspondence. Instead of retyping these each time, they can be merged into a letter or document and printed off when the complete letter has been assembled. This reduces much of the boredom normally associated with the typist's job. As we showed in Figure 2.2, the letter can be constructed from computer files: a letter construct file, a standard paragraphs file, and a name and address file. All these can be held on disk. The only job that the sales manager has to do is to sign the letter.

A particularly difficult task in offices is the design of forms. Good form design is usually the result of many iterations of the drafting, getting comments, and redrafting cycle. Again, in a non-computer system the redrafting means a complete redrawing of the form, whereas in a computer solution the **soft copy** (VDU) form is filed and retrieved and amended as required.

There are obvious advantages to word processing systems, but they are not appropriate for all applications and the typewriter should not be thrown away. The process of filling in external forms (that is, forms not designed in your computer) is one of the few applications where conventional typewriters are superior to word processing systems. It is very difficult to judge the correct spacing. Many printers have keyboard attachments which effectively convert the printer into a typewriter for this purpose. An important second reason to retain a typewriter is to insure against the possible breakdown of the computer system. There is also a problem with temporary staff as they cannot be expected to know how to use *your* word processor, although they are sure to know how to use a typewriter. Firms cannot afford to train temporary staff.

Word processing does require different skills to be learnt by both the typist and the manager. Whereas the typist sees the printed text on paper immediately, word processed material is displayed on the

VDU screen as the text is keyed in and stored on disk. The text is printed only when the operator has keyed in all the text and checked it on the VDU screen. Unfortunately, the text displayed on the screen may be different in appearance to that which is eventually printed off. The line lengths may be different and the displayed text may have special commands mixed in with the text which instruct the printer to start a new paragraph, underline, italicise or embolden characters in the document. This lack of correspondence between the displayed text and the printed text can be very disconcerting and unhelpful. For this reason there are now many packages which are designed in such a way that *what you see is what you get* (frequently abbreviated to *wysiwyg*).

Even when there is not an exact correspondence between the text displayed on the VDU screen and the printed copy, there should at least be a similarity between what you see and what you get, otherwise the production of letter quality work is difficult and leads to unnecessary printing. An A4-sized VDU screen is of obvious benefit here, so that one VDU screenful represents one A4 page. However A4-sized screens are usually associated with turnkey systems dedicated to word processing, because they can be awkward when used for other applications such as spreadsheet and file management.

A colour screen can also be useful in a word processing system. By using different colours, it will be possible to separate the text from commands to the printer and from information provided by the word processing package, such as error messages and a status line. However, not all word processing packages take advantage of colour facilities.

Figure 2.3 shows the contents of a VDU display. The most obvious part is the text itself set up in the **display area**. The top part of the screen shows the **option area**, which lists the various options that the user can choose from. This list is often referred to as a **menu**, and the option is selected by pressing the function key associated with that option. These might include **HELP** (to obtain details on how to use this part of the package), **READ** (to put a text file into memory), **WRITE** (to put the text being worked onto disk), **PRINT** (to print the text on paper) and **RETURN** (to abandon work on the text).

The bottom part of the diagram shows typical contents of the **status line**: the file name, the line number and column number, and whether the user is operating in insert mode or replace mode. The column and line number refer to the position of the cursor. Insert mode puts the next character typed at the cursor position, the rest of the text will be moved to the right; replace (or type-over) mode will replace the

fig 2.3 *word processing – status line, display area and option area*

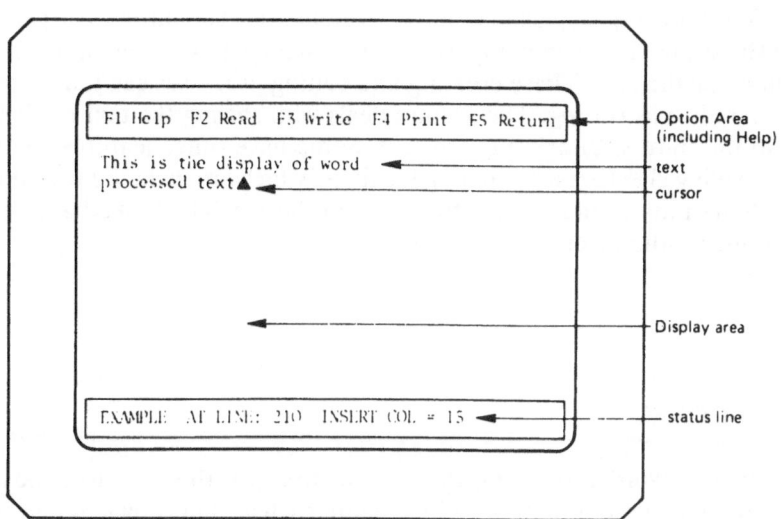

character at the cursor position with the new character. There may be other information provided on the status line such as margin and tabulation settings. In many packages, the status line appears in *inverse video*, where the characters appear in the normal background colour and vice versa.

Option areas and status lines are used in most but not all application packages. Those packages which do not use this form of user interface should give the same information to the user by other means. For example, options may be displayed after pressing a particular function key. Alternatively, options can be presented to the user in pictorial form. This graphical form of displaying the alternatives open to the user will be discussed in section 5.3.

With word processors, the text can be altered until the best wording and layout have been achieved. With typing, the manager may put up with second-best. Alternatively the typist may be asked to type the same material a number of times. It has been estimated that conventional typists spend less than 25% of their time typing 'new words'.

But word processors have disadvantages too. They can encourage rushed first drafts and poor editing. Their use can also lead to managers becoming too perfectionist, as they feel it necessary to perfect 'acceptable' text. This results in overfull waste paper baskets and offices which are far from paperless.

Word processing packages have several parts. The three basic parts of the system are seen in Figure 2.4. The first deals with keying-in and changing the text. These creating and editing processes can jointly be referred to as **editing**. The second deals with **storing** the text on disk and the third with **printing** the text. Some have other features, such as spelling checkers and mailing facilities, which are included with the system or are available at extra cost, but these will be looked at after discussing the three basic processes.

2.2 **EDITING**

A typical word processing system will first ask the user to choose between a number of options in a menu, such as that shown in Figure 2.5. This may be shown on the screen immediately following the request to use the package. When choosing option '1', the user will *name* the text so that it can be distinguished from all other texts and give some other information about it, such as the name of the author. The word processing system will keep this reference material along with the text and will add information of its own, such as when it was created, and subsequently changed. The user will also give information about the printed format of the text and then type in the draft. Many keyboard operators ignore errors at this stage and wait until all the text has been typed in before editing the draft (by choosing option '2' of the menu).

Most word processing systems are *menu-driven*, although many are *command-driven*, once an initial menu has been presented. This means that each instruction to the computer system is entered in the form of a command. Each command could be an English word such as **PRINT**, **STORE**, or **NEXTPAGE**. Alternatively, the commands may be keyed in using the **CONTROL** key on the keyboard and P (for Print), control and S for (Store), and control and N (for Newpage). These commands have to be remembered by the users, or they may need to make frequent reference to a 'facts card' which gives brief details of all commands.

The information about the printed format of the text will include many of the options listed below, some of which are shown in Figure 2.6.

fig 2.4 *the three parts of word processing*

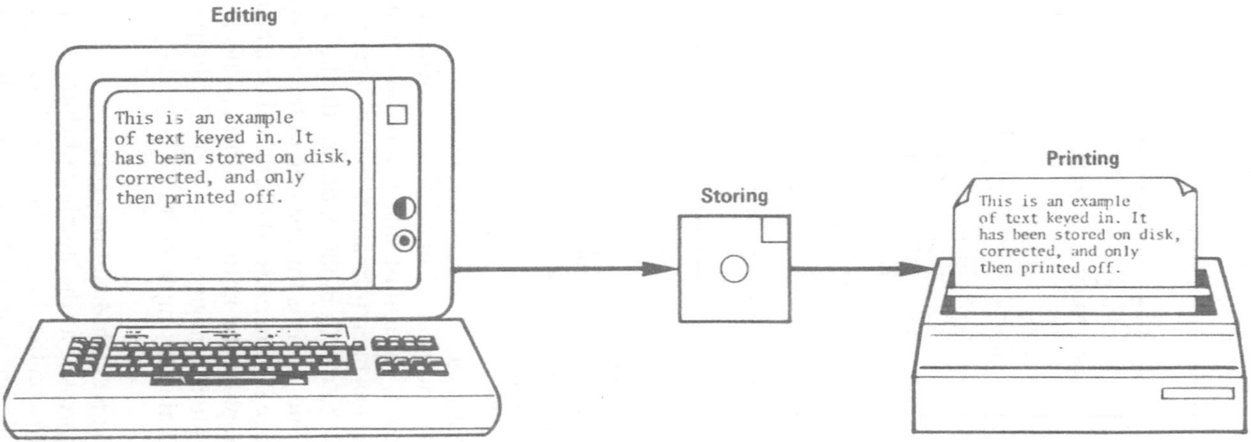

Editing

This is an example
of text keyed in. It
has been stored on disk,
corrected, and only
then printed off.

Storing

Printing

This is an example
of text keyed in. It
has been stored on disk,
corrected, and only
then printed off.

fig 2.5 *main menu options*

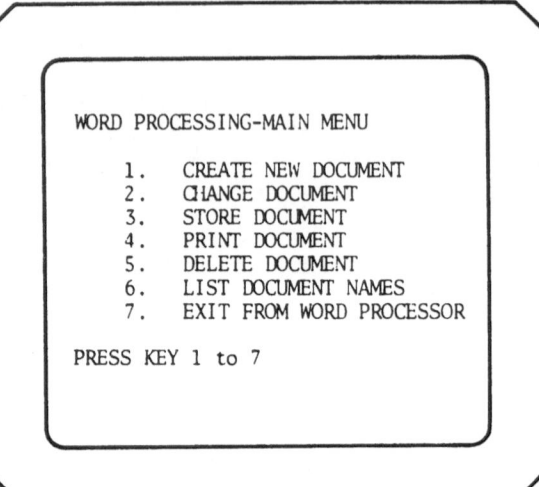

```
WORD PROCESSING-MAIN MENU

      1.    CREATE NEW DOCUMENT
      2.    CHANGE DOCUMENT
      3.    STORE DOCUMENT
      4.    PRINT DOCUMENT
      5.    DELETE DOCUMENT
      6.    LIST DOCUMENT NAMES
      7.    EXIT FROM WORD PROCESSOR

PRESS KEY 1 to 7
```

(a) Length of the line

This is expressed as the number of characters in the line, For A4 paper, this will be around 66 characters if they are to be printed off at 10 characters to an inch or about 80 characters at 12 to an inch.

(b) Length of a page

Expressed as a number of lines, this is obviously required for text printed in pages, as against that printed on continuous stationery. When the text has been formatted on one page, the rest will go to the next page and so on. Computers do not think, but some systems will use an extra line if this is the last one of the paragraph, and will skip to the next page if, otherwise, there would be a heading or first line of a new paragraph at the bottom of a page. This is the sort of feature which is frequently neglected in a computer package, but a good secretary will always 'implement'.

(c) Left-hand and right-hand margins

These are expressed as the number of character positions which will be left as spaces on the sides of the text. Typically, ten or more spaces are kept on the left margin, thus making allowance for binding, and five on the right.

fig 2.6 *word processing examples (created using Microsoft Word)*

Page 1   EXAMPLE OF WORD PROCESSING

Created on 27/6/89 at 15:03

This text shows some of the facilities available in a word processing system. The text can be **boldfaced**, underlined, double underlined, strikethrough, *italicised*, in outline or shadow, and can be superscripted ^{1} or subscripted $_2$. Another possibility is to:

centre some text

which requires some mathematical skill when typed, but is very easy to achieve using word processors.

It is very often convenient to use lists which are numbered and the following example also lists three of the fonts available:

1   **Chicago**
2   Times
3   `Courier`

or to use bullets, as in the following example

Headers or footers can have:
- titles
- today's date
- present time
- page number.

Many word processors have style sheets so that different styles can be incorporated in documents. There may be one style for text, another for lists, and a third for tables as in the following example:

123.5	136.4	94
4.9	7	123.5
129.5	836.78	94

Note that the three lists of numbers have been aligned on the decimal point. Note also that the last two paragraphs have been aligned on both the left and right margins (left and right justification).

(d) Character spacing

This can be 10, 12 or 15 characters per inch or proportional spacing. In the latter case, there are wider spaces left for wide letters than for narrower ones. Some printers do not offer all these options. When choosing a printer, compatibility with the word processor is an important consideration.

(e) Top and bottom margins

These represent the distance between the top of the page and the first line of text, and the last line of text from the bottom of the page.

(f) Page headings and page footings

These give the user the opportunity to put the name of the report or the title of the chapter either at the bottom or top of every page, possibly along with the time and date produced automatically by the system. This eliminates time-consuming data entry that would be necessary using a typewriter or a word processing system without this facility.

(g) Page numbering

This numbers all the pages of the document consecutively for printing out. Some systems will merge documents for printing out together and maintain the consistency of page numbering and other printing commands.

(h) Linespacing

This will usually be set to single or double spacing. It ought to be possible to change this specification within a text so that, for example, standard double-spaced text can be changed to single spacing for quotations. Some systems and printers also facilitate one-and-a-half spacing.

(i) Right and left justification

Right and left justification fill up the lines of text in such a way that the margins are aligned, giving a typeset appearance. The option to centre text on a page is also available. Typescript is left justified but not right justified, and many users 'switch off' right justification when using word processors for printing correspondence, as this will give the appearance of typewritten copy. Many people prefer receiving a letter of typed appearance as they think that typed copy is more personal than that produced by computers, just as people used to prefer handwritten copy.

(j) Semi-right justification
This keeps a ragged right margin but tidies up spacing and is also sometimes available. There may also be a **multiple column facility** which prints two or more columns of script for each page. Newspapers and some books and manuals are typeset in this way.

(k) Tables and overhangs
These facilitate the creation of columns of data or words in the text and indentations of some of the text. The system may number the lists or columns automatically. Some systems left and right justify columns, centre them, and align numeric data on a decimal point.

(l) Chapter and section numbering and indentation
These can be very useful for long texts and reports which can be awkward to set up using the word processor commands. The table of contents including the relevant page numbers can also be produced automatically by some packages, as can a list of figures and tables. Some packages can keep a list of cross-references, particularly useful when writing a book or long report.

(m) Word count
A word count provided on screen can be a useful addition for authors of texts and articles who have to work to a maximum number of words or keep within a range in the number of words.

(n) Indexing
Indexing is provided by some systems to help authors compile an index for a text. The user marks all words required to be indexed, and the system will compile the page numbers where they occur in numeric order and sort the words into alphabetical order.

(o) Special type
This is available on most systems to specify underlining, double underlining, boldface characters, italic characters, strikethrough, subscripts and superscripts. It is important that the printer also supports these features.

(p) Other facilities
Calculation facilities are provided by some word processors because some arithmetic may be required in the construction of a letter or report. In the same way, limited graphics facilities may be provided to enable a drawing or graph to be included within a text. Some packages enable the user to outline the document first and the system

helps the writer to follow this structure. 'Style sheets' are also available in some word processors. Regularly used formatting styles can be stored, and referred to as standard. A stylesheet could be set up for standard paragraphs, when using bullets and indents, and so on. Word processing systems may also perform such functions as locating the names and addresses or telephone numbers in a document and using the information to compile lists of addresses and telephone numbers.

Where a particular requirement is not specified by the author, the word processing system will normally 'assume' a value, known as the **default**. This is originally set by the producers of the package to be the most likely value. For example, the page-size options are likely to be set to A4 paper specifications. These default options can normally be reset by the company using the package, and can be set to conform to the *house rules* regarding margins, spacing, and so on. For most purposes, therefore, the user need not specify many of the options, as the default will be appropriate.

As with all packages, the prospective purchaser should not only see a demonstration of the package but also use it for the particular purpose required. The demonstration will look smooth if used by an experienced supplier. If *you* use the system then it will be possible to judge how easy it is to use. The package may be very advanced and have lots of facilities, but you may have specific requirements that the system lacks. It may not be able to handle footnotes, a foreign language, or columns of justified text. If these facilities are required and the package chosen does not have them, then the mistake can be very costly.

Having keyed in the draft of the text and set up the characteristics of the text for printing, the operator may either print it off 'to see what it looks like' or look through the text for errors before printing. This latter choice is preferable because it avoids waste in printed matter.

In this editing process, the user ought to be able to move about the text on the VDU screen freely and conveniently, using the features of the system. This freedom is provided by **full screen editors**. (Some packages used only to allow the user to move horizontally around the bottom line of text). A full screen editor allows the user to move the cursor up and down the text, and forwards and backwards in a line. Simple movements are usually achieved by using one of the four arrow keys on most keyboards. Most systems will give further freedom of movement, so that the user can move the cursor forwards and backwards by a character, a word, a sentence, a paragraph, a screen, or to the beginning or end of the text. Alternatively, the cursor movements can be made by using a hand-held mouse.

Once the cursor is situated at the correct position, the user may wish to delete, move or add text. Again, many word processors make this easy by having commands which will delete a character, word, line, sentence, paragraph or a block of text. Exchanging characters or words is also facilitated conveniently in many systems by a single command.

For deleting or moving a block of text, the user is required to *mark the block* by placing a marker at the beginning and at the end of the text and then deleting or moving the block as required. Marking the block enables the system to identify the part of the text to be processed. If the block of text is to be moved, it will move from its previous place in the text to the present position of the cursor. This operation is referred to as *cut and paste*. The term comes from journalism where a section of text is cut out and put in the correct place ready for printing.

Most systems also allow the user to copy text. This is similar to the move, except that the marked text remains in its present position as well as in its new position.

Sometimes the user wishes to change a word throughout the text. This requirement could come about where the operator has realised that a word has been misspelled consistently in the report. Most word processing systems allow the user to *search* the text for a particular word and leave the cursor in that position, or *search and replace* where the word is located and corrected. The search and replace option can be used throughout the text or used for a specified number of times.

Most systems allow a search where not all the characters are known. This is called search with *wildcard*. If, for example, correspondence had been spelt correspond*a*nce, by searching for

'corresponda*'

it is possible to locate occurrences of 'correspondant' and 'correspondance' and spell them correctly. Other enhancements include the change of *case* from small letters to capital letters, and vice versa.

Each of these instructions is carried out by a command to the system. For some systems a list of commands is displayed in a menu at the top or bottom of the screen. To activate a particular command, the user points the cursor at the relevant command or types in the first character(s) of that command.

Alternatively the command can be specified by using the *control* key followed by a character, the *escape* key followed by a character, or by using one of the *function* keys on the keyboard. Thus control and 'd' may signify 'delete the last character' and escape and 'd' signify 'delete the last word'. On the other hand the choice of one function key may lead to another set of options from which the user chooses. Thus one function key may be 'delete'. On pressing this, the system gives the options relating to the delete function. Obviously systems with a larger number of options can be difficult to use and it may take time to master, though in the end it is these packages which might prove the best choice because of their powerful facilities. It is usually easiest for the user to learn a subset of the system first. This subset will include all the basic options. The 'advanced' options can be learnt later.

Where the system uses function keys for commands, stickers with command names can be attached to the keys, although this may confuse when the computer is used for another purpose. It may also be possible for users to program some of the keys for their own use if any are 'spare'. For example, a function key could be used to hold a name or phrase which needs to be recalled frequently in a text. Pressing this key will place the phrase at the position of the cursor.

Although these commands are likely to be mnemonics with most packages, the newer user (and sometimes even the experienced user) is likely to need help in finding out or being reminded of all but the most common commands. Probably the most cumbersome way of doing this is by searching through the written documentation. The standard of documentation varies between packages. Indexes are frequently incomplete and, worse still, there is often a lack of correspondence between the manual and the system itself. At best this is disconcerting. Usually, however, there is a *facts card* provided with the documentation, which lists the commands along with a brief explanation of each of the options. Information about the range of function keys can be provided on a template which is placed over the keyboard, and this is particularly helpful.

Many systems provide *on-line help* which is usually invoked by pressing a function key. The better systems provide *help in context* whereby the user is provided with information about the range of options open at that particular stage. Many packages also provide a *tutorial disk* with the system and this can be particularly valuable to the new user. Such a tutorial will usually explain each aspect of the system along with an example that the user has to carry out.

Adding text is achieved by positioning the cursor at the place where the text is to be added, and keying-in the new text. Most systems give the user the opportunity to opt for *insert mode* where the text is placed in the cursor position and the rest of the text is moved to accommodate it, or *typeover mode* where the inserted text replaces the old text on a character for character basis. On inserting data most systems will format automatically and dynamically. Some systems require the user to reformat before justification is complied with. Formatting may be effected in this case by pressing the relevant function key.

When a line is filled, the next word will usually be placed on the next line automatically by the word processing system. There is no need to press the carriage return key (or next line key) to go to another line. This feature is known as *word wrap*. A conventional typist usually finds this difficult to get used to. Pressing the carriage return key may have other significance, such as specifying a new paragraph. On some systems it simply causes a very messy printed page.

Right justification frequently leads to a waste of space or an inelegant printout when the line has many blanks between words. This occurs where the last word in a line would otherwise be too long and is therefore word wrapped to the next line. Some systems allow the user to place a hyphen in long words where the word can be split between lines. These systems may 'ask' the user if and where hyphens should be placed where space on the paper would otherwise be wasted. This is usually more successful than computer attempts at word division because the rules governing it, 'natural' to a good typist, are complex. Some systems compile a dictionary of previous experience so that if a word is to be divided again, it does not refer to the user. This is sometimes referred to as a *soft hyphen*, it will only become 'hard' if the word needs to be divided.

Of course, there are many different word processing systems available, and all are different in points of detail and in their range of facilities, but they are likely to be based on the principles described. Frequently their differences are caused by the particular hardware and operating system that they are designed to be run with.

In discussing the input of text, we have assumed that the data will be keyed-in on a keyboard and displayed on a VDU for checking. These basic components of the microcomputer system were described in the first chapter. But there are alternative ways of inputting data. Two possible ways are optical character recognition and voice recognition.

(a) Optical character recognition (OCR)
An OCR device can read text directly from a book or a report. Until recently, OCR devices for micros required a standard typeface such as Elite and Courier or the OCR standard fonts OCR-A and OCR-B.

They were restricted in other ways, such as requiring double-spaced typing, wide margins and special quality paper. As the technology has improved, such restrictions have proved to be temporary phenomena, as it is possible for some OCR readers to be 'trained' so that they could read non-standard fonts. Some systems have already been developed that can read a newspaper page with headline, captions and the body of the text, even though they are in different fonts. Even poor quality photocopies can be read with good results. Other OCR readers can read neat and regular handwriting.

(b) Voice recognition
This is a likely development, although it is very complex as there are so many sounds in a natural language. Further, the same word spoken by different people may not be recognised by the computer. The error rate can be very high (30% being common). More realistic in the short term are systems which can recognise some sounds, say up to 200 commands such as *paragraph, new line,* or *underline* when setting up text, or *up* or *down* when editing text. This is achieved by digitising the words spoken through a microphone in a 'setup' session. Most systems require the commands to be repeated a number of times by the user at the initial input stage, and once they are known by the system it will maintain good levels of accuracy. As these commands are used frequently, such systems save on keystroke time. Further, each command could link up several keystrokes, effectively creating a library of voice-driven keystroke macros.

Voice recognition systems will be of great help to many disabled users and there are many uses for the able-bodied as well. At present, however, they are rather slow and frustrating to use and as yet the technology has not fulfilled the promise of science fiction writers. Nevertheless voice recognition will surely play an important part in the future of computing.

2.3 STORING TEXT

Once the user has finished creating and editing the text for the present, the document can be saved on disk for re-editing or printing out later. The new version of the document can replace the old version, thus *overwriting* the original, or the system may retain the old version for backup purposes. It is advisable to keep at least two backup versions on different disks. This ensures that if a floppy disk develops a fault or the file is deleted inadvertently, there will be a version of the document from which to recover without too much repetitive work. Each copy should be labelled with the name of the document and the date when it was created. Obsolete copies should be deleted so as to avoid confusion. Even when creating a document, it is necessary to take frequent backups. The loss of text is very disheartening and frustrating. There are extra precautions necessary for long jobs, for without intermediary backups a fault will require reprocessing the whole job.

As well as having a file name, each document is likely to have other information stored relating to it. This information can include the version number, and this will be incremented by one after each amended version. It may also store the author's name, date of creation and its size in characters.

Some systems (but fortunately fewer nowadays) limit the size of documents and this limit can be as low as 32 000 characters (about 5000 words or 12 pages of A4 text, single spaced). Such a design is shown as Figure 2.7. However, texts can usually be joined together later for printing out. The reason for this limitation is usually to allow all the text to be in main memory for editing. Alternatively, the system may allow files to be of 'any' length, giving the user a large **virtual memory**, limited only by the capacity of the disk. This arrangement is shown in Figure 2.8. In the case of floppy disks, the total document size could be ten or twenty times the 32k allocated for the document in main memory and at least a further factor of ten in the case of hard disks. The problem with this option is that the user

fig 2.7 *allocation of the memory of the computer-fixed document size*

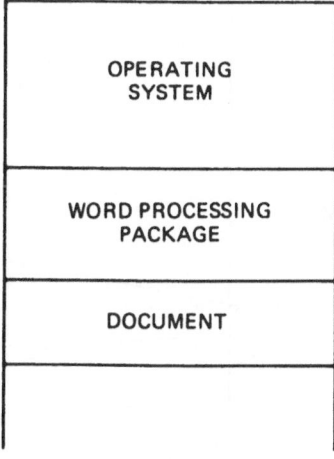

will find that editing can be a considerably slower process, particularly with floppy disks, as parts of the document are continually being swapped in and out of the computer's memory from disk.

Where the whole document is in main memory, the user can traverse through the document without any such delays. With microcomputers now having main memories of one megabyte or more, it is possible for much larger documents to be held in memory. As Figure 2.8 shows, the memory of the computer will be used to hold the operating system, the word processing system, and a fixed and limited space for the text. However, many systems were designed in the days of computers with memories of 64k or 96k bytes or have limited features so that they *can* run on smaller computers. Packages are *generalised* to maximise their sales potential, and this frequently means that they are reduced to the lowest common denominator.

A text is stored by the computer system as a file. Programs and data are also stored as files. A feature of file-handling in computer systems is the ability to merge complete files or parts of files. A possible application is the merging of a standard paragraph into an otherwise original text. Most systems facilitate this by allowing the user to read a second file into the text. This could be a complete file or a part of a file that has been *marked*. Some systems allow the user to read the file one screenful or page at a time. The user then specifies whether that page should be incorporated into the text or not. This process was seen in Figure 2.2.

fig 2.8 *allocation of memory of the computer-variable document size using virtual memory*

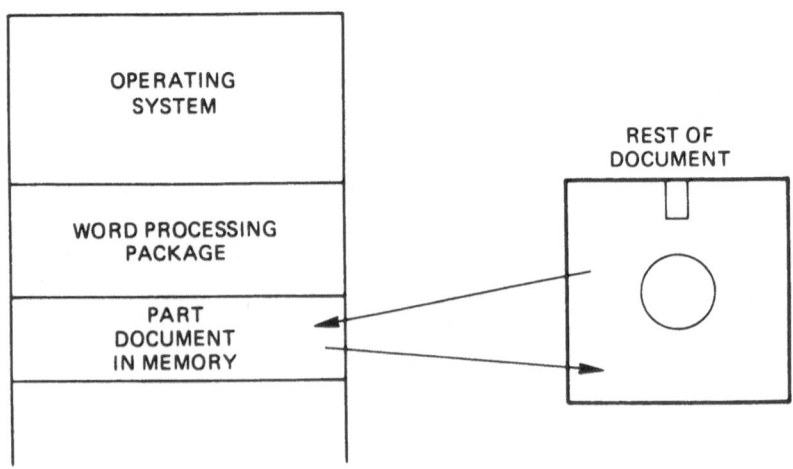

Some word processing systems allow the user to see more than one file on the screen at the same time. The screen is split up into **windows**. In the previous example there could be three windows: one for the standard paragraph file, one for the original text, and one for the new file, which will contain the result of editing the other files. This is called **split screen editing**. Figure 2.9 illustrates an application of split screen editing where a text on one window is merged with figures from another window, along with new text, to compile a third text. With two or three windows it is not usually difficult to move around each of the files, and the system has the facility to copy and move words, sentences, and paragraphs between windows, in the same way as it can within a file.

2.4 **PRINTING**

Good quality printed output is a result of good quality printers as well as a good word processing package. Some of the features of a word processing package will not be seen in the final printed copy if the printer cannot support such features; conversely, some of the features of an advanced printer cannot be reflected on the hard copy if a basic word processing package is being used.

(a) Types of printer
There is a great deal of choice between printers, some produce hard copy as good as the best typist's top copy, others produce copy only good enough for internal memo work or to produce draft copies.

(i) Daisy wheel printers
Daisy wheel printers (see Figure 2.10) produce 'letter quality' output but are rather slow. Their printing speed ranges from about 15 characters a second (about 150 words a minute) to about five times this figure. A printer printing off a text at less than one page of A4 in a minute will appear very slow, and too slow for most businesses. A page of A4 has about 400 words.

A daisy wheel is a plastic or metal disk in the shape of a flower head. It has 96 'petals', each containing one character. The daisy wheel can be interchanged so that mathematical symbols, foreign languages, or alternative character fonts such as Courier, Prestige, or Italic can be printed. If the printing facility will be used for graphics (pictures and designs), then the daisy wheel printer will not be suitable.

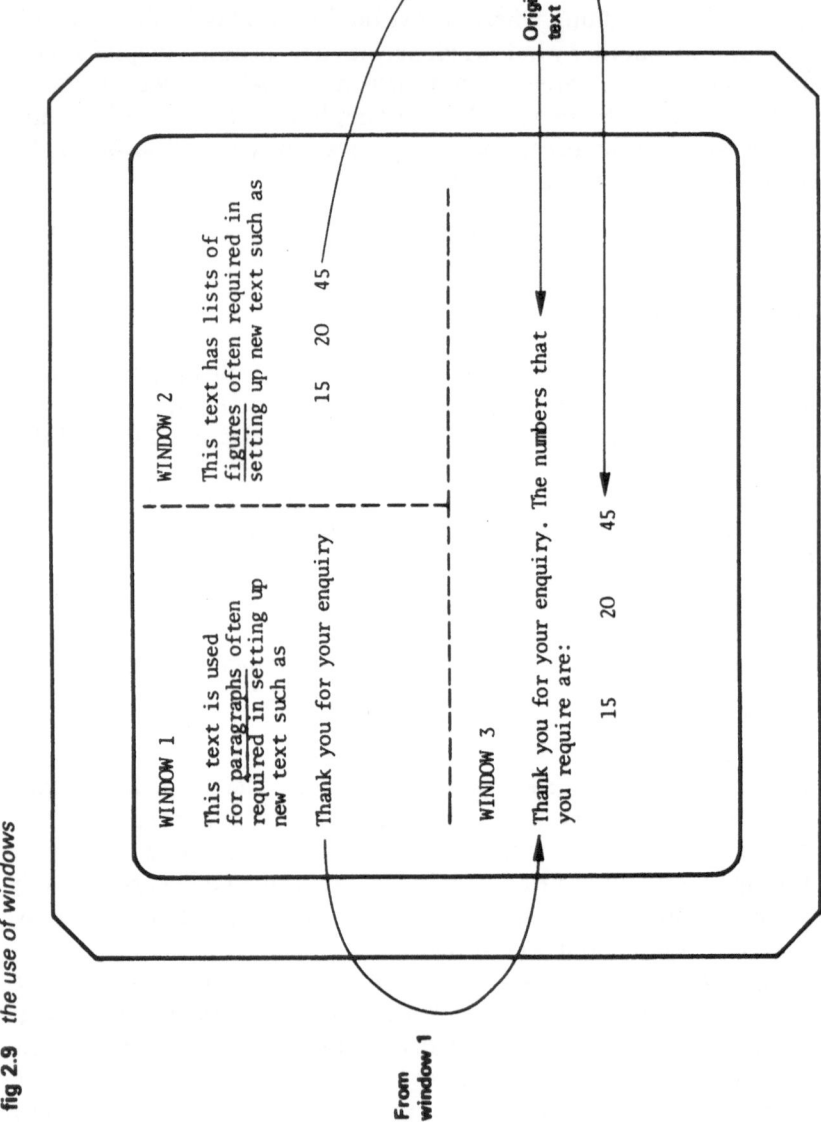

fig 2.9 *the use of windows*

fig 2.10 *daisy wheel printer (Brother HR–25)*
Source: Brother Office Equipment Division

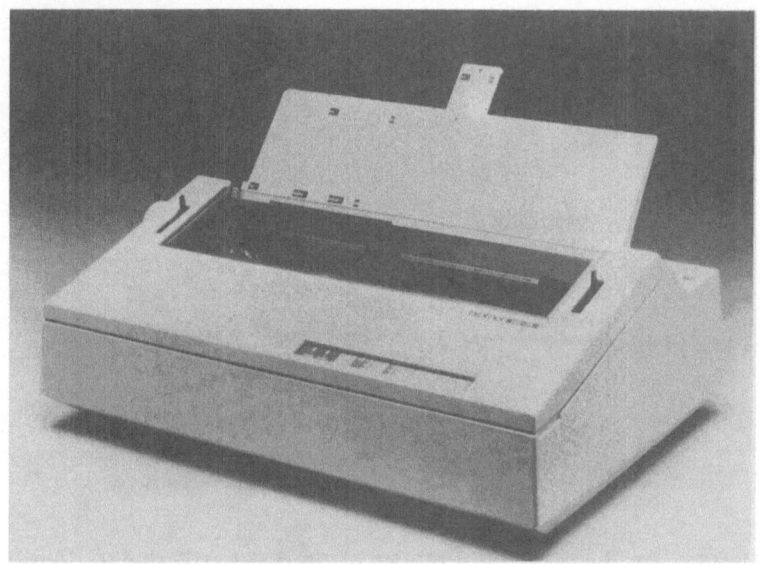

As dot matrix printers have improved the quality of their output and laser printers have become available at the 'top end', the market share of daisy wheel printers has declined.

(*ii*) *Dot matrix printers*
Dot matrix printers (see Figure 2.11) provide 'draft quality' printing and are generally the cheapest option. The characters are formed from a matrix of needles. So as to form a character, some of the needles are made to hit the typewriter ribbon and therefore mark the paper. Speeds of over 200 characters a second are commonplace, and speeds of five times this figure can be achieved by some printers. Near Letter Quality (NLQ) printers usually achieve their results by printing over the character more than once, slightly offset. Better definition can also be achieved by using a larger matrix of needles (this amount ranges from 7 to 48 needles per column in a matrix) and this also can give rise to good quality graphics work. Dot matrix printers are therefore multi-purpose, being suitable for good drafts of text, rough text, and graphics (many enable colour printing), and they are fairly fast, particularly when compared to daisy wheel

fig 2.11 *Brother 1818 18 pin dot matrix printer*
  Source: Jones and Brother Office Equipment

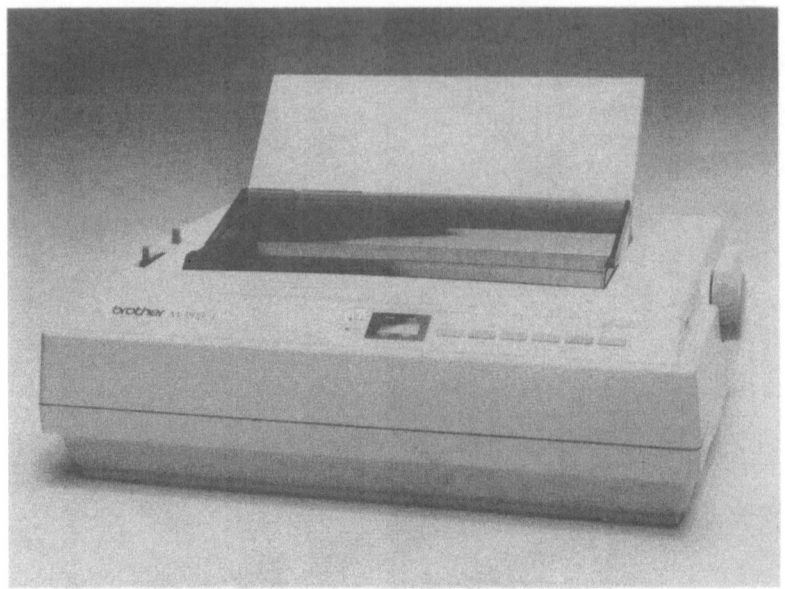

printers. The success of dot matrix printers is partly due to their unit price and low running costs. However, they are noisy and output does not match some other types of printer.

Daisy wheel printers and the dot matrix printers so far described are *impact* printers, that is they hammer through an inked ribbon to produce the characters. There are alternatives, such as *ink-jet* printers, which work by squirting jets of ink through a series of nozzles to form the characters on the paper. These can be more expensive but are quieter, less subject to wear and potentially faster than dot matrix printers, at whose expense their market share has increased. One disadvantage is that, because there is no impact, the technique does not enable carbon copies to be produced. There are other types of non-impact printer available, but laser printers, also non-impact, have become the standard quality printer, particularly as their price has fallen.

(iii) Laser printers
Laser printers (see Figure 2.12) represent a more expensive alternative, but where printers are shared the added cost of a high quality and fast printer is soon justified. They can be fast, relatively quiet (because they are non-impact) and the quality of output is excellent.

fig 2.12 *laser printers (HP series II and IId)*
Source: Hewlett-Packard Limited

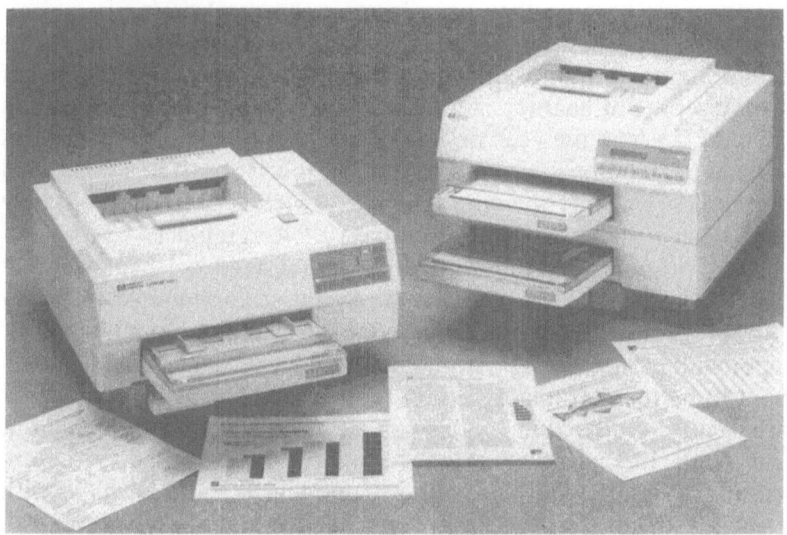

Laser printers can print a page at a time, from 8 to 15 pages a minute, and can offer options such as a number of type fonts, even on one page, and facilitate graphics. They work by using a small laser to draw characters onto a drum (similar to a photocopier, except that photocopiers use ordinary light). The drum picks up toner powder which is like dry ink and thereby transfers the image onto paper. Many laser printers can only print one copy of single sheet paper – not multiple copies – and none use continuous paper. Paper is fed from a tray holding up to 200 sheets of A4.

Running costs are about three times as much for a laser printer as for a dot matrix or daisy wheel printer. The most expensive item is toner, as a cartridge can cost up to £100. It can last for up to 4000 pages.

Even within a printer type there is a great deal of choice. Quality of print is frequently measured in 'dots per inch' (DPI). Matrix printers give a range from 60 to 360 DPI (the latter for 24-pin printers). Laser printers work at 300 DPI and upwards. A photo-typesetting machine works at between 1000 and 3000 DPI. Even so, some printer manufacturers are advertising their products as 'near-photographic quality'. Laser print looks better than even the best matrix printer because the dots are finer on the laser. As well as speed, sound level, cost and quality of print, there are other considerations. Printers have a number of mechanical parts and they tend to go wrong more frequently than computers. Reliability is therefore an important consideration in any purchase. In general, non-impact printers are more reliable because they have fewer mechanical parts.

Another consideration is their **buffer** size. This is the amount of memory in the printer itself. This is frequently around 32k (the size of a small report or chapter of a book). One chapter can therefore be printed off whilst the user works on the text. A printer may have as much as 512k of memory built in and can therefore store a great deal of graphics (which is 'memory hungry') as well as text output. It may need 1.5 megabytes to print a full page of A4 graphics.

Many printers are sold without a tractor feed or a single sheet feeder. These are 'extras'. A **tractor feed** uses continuous stationery with sprockets on each side (and hence sprocket holes on the paper). Paper with perforations surrounding the A4 size, which enable an A4 sheet to be torn off neatly, can be purchased. This gives reasonably satisfactory results, although a **single sheet feeder** is a better solution. This feeds one page at a time. **Hoppers** hold the paper before printing. Printers with two hoppers, one which could be filled with blank A4 sheets and the other with headed stationery, present an added sophistication, although not all word processing packages can cater for this.

(b) Print facilities

Printing off text is noticeably slower than display on a VDU. For this reason some word processors offer the option of a view of the text that will be printed off, on screen before printing. This is especially useful where the word processing editor is not of the *what you see is what you get* sort. Many word processing packages also allow the user to specify a quick print option where the formatting necessary to convert the text on computer into a printable text is limited. It will be used in circumstances where speed gains offset the reduced quality of the printed copy. It could be used to check the draft or obtain a copy good enough for internal work. Many printers are capable of printing:

  (*i*) multiple typefaces;
 (*ii*) bold;
(*iii*) italic;
(*iv*) underline;
 (*v*) double underline;
(*vi*) subscript; and
(*vii*) superscript characters.

Some of these facilities were shown in Figure 2.6. Some printers will also facilitate a ribbon colour change during printing. The use of these features will slow down printing and it may be reasonable to request the quick print option, which will ignore these sophistications, on all but the final printed copy.

The printer has to be configured to the word processing system. Frequently this is very simple, as your printer will be listed amongst those already pre-configured. Configuring defines the capabilities of the printer to the word processing system. These include all the options, such as typeface, which were listed in the previous paragraph. Additionally it will be used to define whether the printer will print bidirectionally (which will increase printing speed), whether it will print 6 and/or 8 lines per inch, and whether it handles proportional spacing, as well as 10, 12 or 15 pitch (characters per inch across the page). It also establishes the codes by which the word processing system communicates these requests to the printer.

(c) Spooling

One of the frustrating elements of printing in many systems is that the user cannot gain access to the computer whilst the printer is printing off text. One way of reducing this problem is to purchase a printer with a large memory buffer. This means that the printer itself has a memory and can hold text ready for printing. Alternatively, it is possible to buy one of the add-on memory buffers available.

A far more satisfactory solution is to use the spooling facility (sometimes called concurrent printing) which is available on many word processing systems. Spooling refers to the simultaneous printing of a text whilst the user is engaged in some other activity, such as editing another text. To achieve this, it is first necessary to format the printed text on disk. This is a much faster process than printing directly. Once the text has been filed on disk, it can be printed out in 'background' whilst the user edits a new text. Editing will gain the priority of the computer's resources and therefore printing will often stop and start whilst the computer is being used for editing. A few word processors queue the formatted texts in an order determined by their priority, and print them out in background following this schedule.

2.5 SPELLING AND DICTIONARY

Most word processing systems have spelling routines and a dictionary as an integral part of the package. In some instances the spelling checker is purchased as an extra. A spelling system will check all the words of a text against a dictionary of 100 000 words or more, depending on the system, and mark all words in a text that are not found in the dictionary. Some systems can recognise plurals and suffixes and prefixes such as '-ing', '-ed' and 're-', and reduce words containing them to their stem, which will be held in the dictionary.

Many proper names also need to be checked and these should be added to the dictionary. It would, for example, be particularly embarrassing to misspell a client's name. Some obscure words or proper names, peculiar to one communication, may be marked 'not to be checked' so as not to slow down processing unnecessarily. However the checking of text can be fast. A typical rate is 300-500 words a second. Even so, it is useful if it is possible to select sections or pages for proof-reading. Once the unmatched words have been identified, it is usual for the system to give the user an opportunity to:

(*i*) change the words in the text (or mark them for changing);
(*ii*) ignore the mismatch; or
(*iii*) add the word to the dictionary.

Many systems go further than this and suggest possible corrections which are a 'near-fit'. The user can accept one of these, and the word chosen will replace the misspelled word in the text.

Whereas most spelling checkers are used once the text has been created, some systems provide a facility known as 'check as you type'. This has come about as spelling checkers have become faster, so that, as a word is typed, it is checked and a warning given if the word is not recognised. However, some users do not like to be interrupted in this way.

Most dictionaries are expandable by the users, who will want to add words commonly used in their area. Many packages require conversion from American English to UK English. Many packages have foreign language and specialist dictionaries to use in medical, legal and insurance environments.

At present there is no word processor which is **context specific**. For example, if you wrote 'the sands of thyme', it would be acceptable, even though you meant 'the sands of time', because both words are in the dictionary. These difficulties, which also represent one of the many difficult aspects of natural language translation, will surely be at least partly solved in the next few years.

A further sophistication is the inclusion of a dictionary of phrases (sometimes called a glossary) and a thesaurus. Phrase recall is the ability to hold a number of useful phrases which can be allocated a code and recalled when required into the text. In this chapter the phrase 'word processing' would be a useful one for phrase recall. For mailing purposes the phrase 'Yours sincerely' will be an obvious one to include in the dictionary. The thesaurus can be used to avoid the over-use of certain words, detect clichés, or clumsy and incorrect expressions. Synonyms for words can be displayed on request, and dictionaries can provide full definitions of words.

Large items such as a thesaurus, standard dictionary, dictionary of quotations, translator's dictionary, lists of references, or even the complete works of Shakespeare can be held on **CD-ROM** (compact disk, read-only memory). We looked at other backing storage devices in section 1.7(b). CD devices can be connected to the computer in the same way as floppy disk drives, but have the advantage of huge memories and fast access.

2.6 ELECTRONIC MAIL

Word processing is the most well known and possibly the most important single application of the 'new technology' in many offices. But there are many other applications in the office. When a number of these have been implemented it is often referred to as an *electronic office*. These other applications include:

(a) electronic mail, where users convey messages to each other using computers and terminals;
(b) dictation, for word processing later;
(c) photocopying and phototypesetting, which is electronically controlled;
(d) facsimile, the transfer of pictures and text;
(e) teletex, a 'super telex' service which is publicly available;
(f) viewdata, a publicly available service, using adapted television sets but data is transferred in the telephone system; and
(g) teletext, which also uses television sets, and data is transferred using the televised signals.

Electronic mail applications will be discussed in this section, and the other facilities in section 2.7.

The term 'electronic office' has been interpreted here to include the whole range of text applications in the office. Some writers use the term to include applications such as accounting, spreadsheet and file management, which are regarded as separate applications in this text. The essential feature of the electronic office, whether the term is interpreted widely or narrowly, is that there is a network which connects computers and other hardware devices within and between offices. There is a corporate system for the new technology rather than units of disparate electronic machines.

Typical applications of electronic mail have already been mentioned. Figure 2.1 showed how a memo text can be drawn up using a word processor and, once the user is satisfied with its structure and content, transferred to all the people requiring the memo 'immediately'. The message will be placed in the **mailbox** of the recipients. A mailbox can be looked on as the computer pigeon–hole belonging to each user and has an 'address' to which the sender forwards the message.

The message might indicate whether any action is required by the recipient. A priority rating could be attached to the memo, and if particularly urgent, the recipient's VDU could flash.

URGENT COMMUNICATION

in order to attract the attention of the user. On the other hand, non-urgent messages can be stored and accessed when required. The system could display

THREE COMMUNICATIONS AWAITING ATTENTION

when the user has completed a job. These messages could be created, checked, sent, read, actioned, and replies returned, without resort to the printed page. Longer documents such as committee minutes and reports which require comment can be prepared and distributed in this way.

With conventional internal mail procedures, the memo will be typed, checked, retyped where necessary, rechecked, photocopied, placed in envelopes, addressed, and put into the internal post system. This will be followed by the response cycle. The internal postal network may take a few hours or even delay each cycle by half a day or a full day. The slow speed in which communications are made within the company could well lose business for that company. The telephone could be used as a quicker alternative to the internal postal system, but telephone calls can be disruptive as they interrupt office work. Although speed is the main advantage of electronic mail, there are other advantages as well:

(a) it cuts down on the amount of paper processed;
(b) it reduces the chances of misunderstandings because it avoids mail crossing in the post;

(c) it cuts down on the 'disturbance factor' that telephone calls produce (interrupting a meeting or some detailed work);

(d) users can look at their mailbox when convenient to them; and

(e) it puts the onus on the receiver rather than the sender, who knows that the mail has been placed in the receiver's mailbox.

Of course there are possible disadvantages as well:

(a) there can be a lack of personal contact and therefore reduced job satisfaction; and

(b) it increases the amount of mail sent and received because of the temptation to create long mailing lists.

Those readers who collect their real mail from pigeon holes might like to look at the contents of the waste paper bin placed next to the pigeon holes – or place a bin there if one does not already exist. The quantity of mail which is thrown in, some unopened, some unread, is often surprising, and might include copies of a memo that you have written.

Electronic mailing packages can have facilities for integrating:

(a) calendar;

(b) diary;

(c) holiday; and

(d) meeting management.

Typically, as users turn on the computer in the morning, they will be presented with a list of their appointments for that day. It is also possible to look at commitments for other days by looking at the personal electronic diary. Other authorised personnel can access diaries of employees in order to locate staff at any time. There will also be a diary for the company, and this will give details of open meetings and events relevant to all employees.

The holiday management element of the package will combine all the individual holiday periods of the employees to produce a holiday chart for the company. Managers may include a requirement that holidays are spread out according to their wishes and ensure that key personnel are not away at the same time.

Meeting management can be particularly burdensome for secretarial staff when members of the group are away frequently, and it can be difficult to arrange times for meetings when members are all free. A package solution may search the electronic diaries of all members of the group and 'pencil in' the first suitable date when they are all available. The system may remind members of the group nearer the date of the meeting. If there are also room management facilities in the package, the system may allocate the room for the meeting. All these features can help in planning the office activities.

A further development is the holding of committee minutes on computer files. Each committee member may be required to read these and 'sign' them for approval. An agenda for the next meeting can be compiled by each member of the committee adding to the agenda if required. Supporting documents can also be held on a computer file and this will reduce the amount of paper that committees produce. Some of this material may be confidential, and therefore it is essential that such systems are able to limit users' access only to files to which they have 'legal' access.

Some office planning systems integrate diary management with an address book of clients' names and addresses as well as internal mailbox addresses. These systems may also have limited file management features, adequate for these planning activities. Letters constructed with the use of the address book will go out to clients using the *real* mail and those for internal recipients will go by electronic mail.

2.7 OTHER FEATURES OF THE ELECTRONIC OFFICE

There are a number of other technologies that may be featured in the electronic office.

(a) Dictation
One possible way of increasing the efficiency of text processing is through the use of dictation machines. Rather than dictating a text directly to a secretary, which requires transcription into shorthand, the text is dictated to a cassette tape and forwarded to a word processing operator for keying-in later. Some firms operate a central pool of word processing equipment, rather like a typing pool. If necessary, urgent text can be dictated directly to the operative or to dictation units using the telephone system. Control is important. Text should be prefixed by department code, author code, and the time and date of the dictation. Once the text has been keyed-in, it could be sent to the sender's mailbox for checking and then transferred to the recipients.

(b) Photocopying and phototypesetting
These may be part of the conventional office. Photocopying can be cheaper and quicker than printing each copy and may give satisfactory results for many applications, especially internal work. The photocopier can be attached to the network and can be programmed by the user on a VDU. The user may specify the number of copies to be produced. Typesetting equipment produces better quality output and can be programmed in a word processing environment. The direct transfer of information through the network eliminates some stages of conventional typesetting procedures which are prone to error.

(c) Facsimile
This can be looked on as the 'photocopying' and transfer of pictures and text from a distance. Facsimile systems, or **fax**, presently use the telephone system. There is no keying-in involved. Just as text can be converted to electronic signals (digitised) and converted back to text, so can pictures, graphs, maps, signatures and drawings, and the technology is such that the quality of reproduction and the reliability of the technology is very good. They are easy to use and the better machines can transfer an A4 page in less than a minute, some in a few seconds. Modern machines have variable transmission speeds, so that the resolution of a complex page can be maintained by a slower scanning speed, in *fine mode.*

(d) Teletex
This publicly available electronic mail system is often referred to as a 'super telex' service, being about 30 times as fast as telex in transmitting data. Text is prepared (and edited) on a conventional keyboard, sent using the public telephone network, and the receiver gets a copy in the form transmitted, that is, markedly better than telex messages and obviously markedly faster than the conventional postal network. It also has advantages over LANs (see below), in that all companies can use it who have paid for the facility, including those in other countries.

(e) Viewdata
Companies may well have access to public or private viewdata computers via a television set with a viewdata receiver. The data for these pages (screens full of information) is transferred through the telephone network. Public viewdata holds 'pages' of information paid for by advertisers or by government information services. Although

viewdata can be used as 'read-only', an information provider may alter pages directly. With some viewdata services, it is possible to call a page of advertised product, read the price information, make the order, and send it through the system back to the supplier.

(f) Teletext (not to be confused with teletex)
This is rather more limited than viewdata. Unlike viewdata which uses the telephone network to transfer data, teletext uses the televised signals. It can be used as an advertising and information medium. In comparison with viewdata, the service is limited by having only about one hundred pages available, but the service is free to the recipient (excepting the initial cost of the adapted television receiver) as there is no telephone charge associated with it.

2.8 LOCAL AREA NETWORKS

Electronic mailing between offices in a building, or between offices in a number of buildings which are in close proximity (usually no more than a few hundred metres) is usually achieved using a local area network (LAN). As approximately three-quarters of a manager's mail is likely to come from internal sources, an increase in the efficiency of its processing can be very helpful to the efficient running of the firm. As we have already discussed, there are significant speed advantages. Furthermore, LANs have a very low error rate. They need not be expensive themselves, but they enable the sharing of expensive resources so that they can be utilised to the full.

An alternative to the LAN, required for longer distances, is a **wide area network**. This normally uses the telephone network which can transmit text as well as voice signals. The telephone network can also be used as an alternative to a LAN, but it may prove far less reliable and is particularly vulnerable to the failure of the exchange itself. Usually the capacities of a Private Automatic Branch Exchange (PABX) are lower and transmission rates slower than a LAN. However, the cable is already installed and the telephone network can be used as a link with the outside world as well as being a provider of internal links.

Users connected to a local area network will normally have their own computer. These may be rudimentary but users may also have access to a 'bank' of very powerful computers which are part of the shared resources of the network. A laser printer may be another shared resource. These shared resources need centralised control to ensure that they are used wisely. This centralised control will include the network microcomputer (or possibly minicomputer) which will act as 'postmaster' for the system. The LAN system will also have a **file server**, which is a hard disk microcomputer system which manages the network, and its disk system will contain the shared programs and data.

The 'ideal' is the ability to include on the network any type of device and different types of each device, be it printer, computer or scanner, in any location. This type of configuration is known as **open systems architecture**.

The best known LAN system is the Ethernet, developed by Xerox. It is a single length of cable, known as a **bus**, to which the equipment is attached. Users can take out data from the bus, just as homes take out electricity from the electricity grid, water from the water network, and so on. Data sent out by a user is *broadcast* and the intended receivers recognise *their* label on the heading preceding the data, which is then extracted. A particular Ethernet LAN can be 500 metres long, but up to five may be joined together allowing up to a total of about 1000 devices on a network of 2500 metres. Figure 2.13 shows a typical Ethernet design. There is a **terminator** at each end of the **Ether**, which is a co-axial cable, not dissimilar to TV aerial cable. Fibre optics cables are more expensive, but are likely to become more popular because this is a quicker medium for transmitting data than a standard bus. All the devices, whether shared or not, are attached to the Ether with a **transceiver**. This establishes a particular address for each port.

One local area network configuration, known as HiNet, is shown as Figure 2.14. A number of workstations are attached to the network (in fact up to 32 micros can be attached in this way) and a 'gateway' links to external services such as a mainframe computer. The network control unit acts as a 'manager' for the network. The operating system and other software and user files are downloaded from the disk servers and file server. The print server is used to spool print files which are printed off on one of the printers attached to the network.

Links with offices further afield require some form of external telecommunications. To use the telephone network requires a modem for the sender and receiver. It could be used for a supplier to get in touch with the retail outlets and send the new price list, for example. The overall design for the office could be similar to that shown in Figure 2.15.

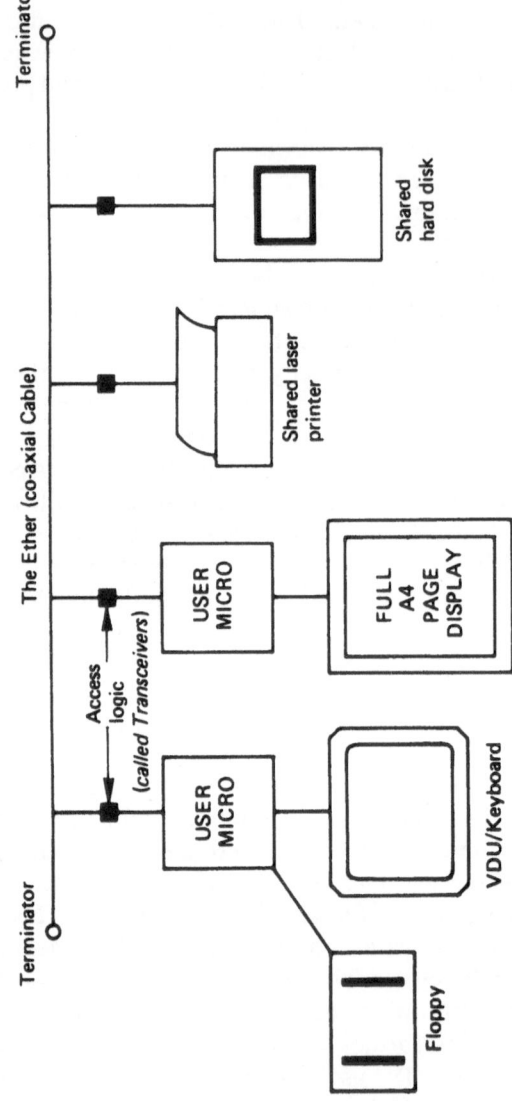

fig 2.13 *the Ethernet design*

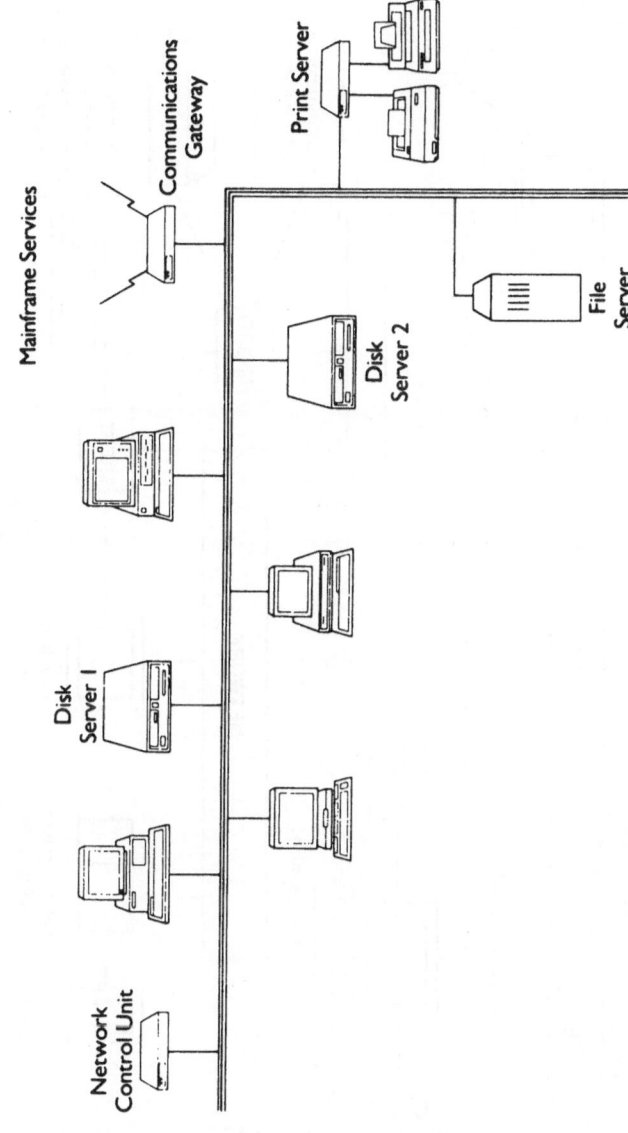

fig 2.14 *HiNet XA (Extended Architecture) network*
Source: Digital Micro Systems

fig 2.15 *the electronic office*

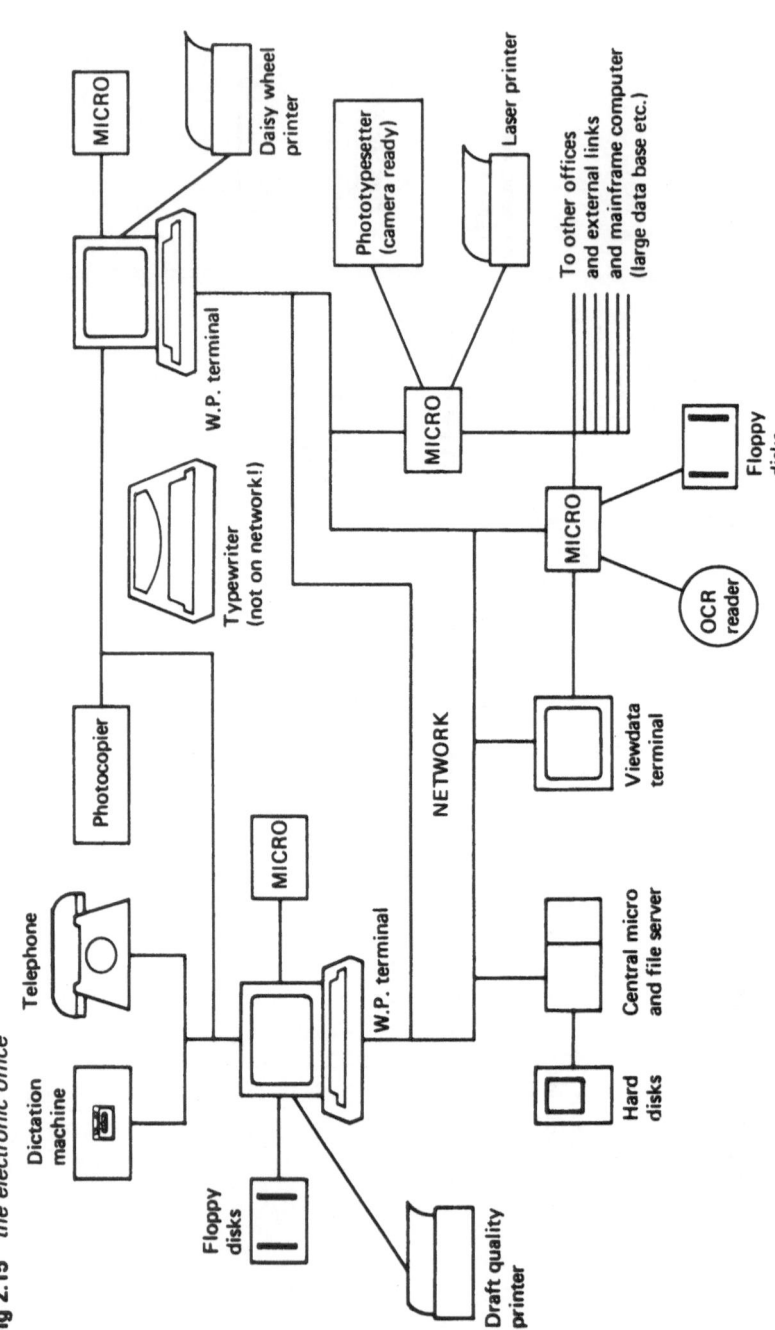

2.9 DESK TOP PUBLISHING

Many systems process more than text and are generally referred to as desk top publishing (DTP) systems. They are aimed at those businesses producing published material that might include newspapers, brochures, reports, magazines, catalogues and so on. These applications require greater sophistication, in particular graphics and multiple column format, than that needed for producing typed pages. Many word processing packages have been enhanced to provide some of the facilities necessary for DTP (though they are not intended to be solely used for DTP), but true DTP systems provide very advanced features. An important aspect of any package with DTP features is a preview facility (true *what you see is what you get*, including figures) allowing the user to examine a document on screen in the exact way in which it will be printed. Particularly important is the ability to control page layout before printing. A normal requirement is to move figures around and change column contents quickly and easily, leaving some items in the same position if requested. It will also alter spacing to a fine degree so that the page has a full 'professional' appearance.

A DTP system is likely to include text handling parts as sophisticated as that of a word processor, although some do not include a spelling checker, mailmerge and thesaurus. On the other hand, they might include features such as instructions on where best to place word hyphenation, which a word processor may not provide. Thus a word processor might be used for text preparation, and the DTP system for final layout, including diagrams, which might themselves have been produced using some drawing package. For this reason, DTP systems need to be able to read files produced in a variety of formats: textual, graphical and image.

A central feature of the DTP system is the scanner, which produces digitised images and is used as an input device for graphics work. The scanning of a colour photograph is complex, but the facility is now available. Some scanners will scan transparencies and negatives as well. A colour A4 image may take less than two minutes to scan. These applications are 'memory hungry', both for main memory and hard disk space; indeed a WORM drive is usually recommended. The problem is due to the amount of data in a colour image. Many businesses will also require an OCR reader for direct input of text. The DTP system will also enable the user to design drawings and place them in the text at appropriate places.

Training is particularly important. It is not reasonable to expect a secretary to jump from word processing to DTP, even if that secretary previously made the leap from typewriters to word processors successfully. It may be that DTP is more the province of skilled typographers and layout people than of even trained secretaries.

Businesses should weigh up the advantages and disadvantages of adopting the DTP solution. A specialist package woud be more appropriate for businesses publishing newspapers, brochures, magazines and catalogues, where a 'professional' quality is important. On the other hand, many applications and many businesses may only require the level of sophistication provided by a modern word processing package. The extra expense of a DTP system, including new equipment such as a scanner, and particularly the extra training required to master the system, could involve high overheads. Further, an over-complex page, using all the features of DTP unnecessarily, can be difficult to read, error-prone and do anything but impress the reader.

2.10 IMPLEMENTING THE NEW TECHNOLOGY

There are many articles claiming increases in productivity of 50% to 500% through the use of the new technology in offices. There is a fear of being left behind and many managers are ready to succumb to the salesman, even though a word processing system is likely to cost at least ten times as much as an electric typewriter. Cost justification is not easy because it is difficult to measure the money gains of quicker communications and more effective management, as managers spend less of their time on ineffective office tasks. But there can be savings in secretarial time as well, particularly with electronic mail systems replacing the internal mail system.

Implementing word processing and other office systems is likely to be a smoother process where staff are consulted and feel part of the decision to 'modernise'. A manager may be assigned the role of part-time or full-time project co-ordinator for the 'office technology project'. Prospective users of the equipment may well be encouraged to go to exhibitions and use equipment provided on a free trial by suppliers or with a relatively small hiring charge. It may be reasonable to allow users to choose the system, if each of the possibilities 'does the job' and falls within the price range.

This process of involving the people who are going to operate and make use of the new technology in decisions about them, is normally referred to as **participation**. It should not only cover choice of hardware and software, but also decisions about the way of working in the department. It is also surely reasonable to look for the involvement and advice of the trade unions, as they are likely to suggest ways of improving working relationships which should avoid the failure of the new technology because of lack of acceptance.

Such procedures are likely to generate enthusiasm and quell the anxiety associated with change. Once the equipment is purchased, it is essential that time and help is provided so that users can adapt to the change in procedures. The complaint from staff has too often been that training is crammed into too short a period. It is not adequate to 'dump' a word processing system on a desk with the manual, even if the manual does have a chapter entitled 'Word Processing in Five Minutes'. It is at least necessary for the trainee to have someone nearby to answer the basic questions.

Installing and configuring the printer and other devices is not always straightforward and should be carried out by the supplier. Your time is better spent on getting to know the package and the system.

One way of ensuring good understanding is for the user of the equipment to draw up a user guide for the system. This will include examples of the uses of the system which are relevant to the company. This can be placed alongside the technical handbook provided by the supplier.

Another useful innovation is the setting up of an *office technology users group* which is a forum for discussing problems and new ideas.

Once the system has been used satisfactorily for a few weeks it is a good idea to return to the documentation manual. Now is the time to pick up the advanced features and other facilities of the system that you know from experience would be worthwhile using.

One problem associated with giving users free choice of equipment is the difficulty of sharing text and passing information between departments. The systems are likely to be incompatible because of hardware and software differences. Even if files are in standard **ASCII** (American Standard Code for Information Interchange) format, there are likely to be difficulties in getting these to 'talk', though ASCII makes such ambitions more likely. DTP systems need to define files in terms of text plus 'mark up', that is, information about layout. A structured generalised markup language (**SGML**) has been proposed, but is still not standard. The sharing of packages is equally difficult, particularly where the microcomputers run on different operating systems. Instead of one company word processing system, there are several, and this also necessitates several training programmes, maintenance contracts, and so on. Even the most 'liberal' of organisations should demand that their departments get at least centralised approval for purchases, even if total standardisation is considered impractical or undesirable.

A possible way to short-cut the training process is to purchase a *dedicated* word processor rather than a *general-purpose* microcomputer with a word processing package. Most dedicated systems are designed to ease the learning process. The dedicated system will have been designed for the purpose of word processing and therefore have features that general-purpose microcomputers will not have. These features may include function keys to move text around, bring in another page of text, or bring in other special routines. These keys can be 'programmed' for each purpose in most microcomputer systems, but it can be a complex process. However, many users who have purchased dedicated word processing systems now wish to look at other computer applications, and face the expense of a second microcomputer system as well as the software packages to implement data management, spreadsheet or graphics applications. In general, a dedicated word processor is most beneficial where it will be used only by a full-time typist/secretary.

There are further problems associated with the first implementations of the new technology. Ergonomic considerations such as the correct furniture, ventilation, lighting, and noise reduction facilities are also important in creating a comfortable and pleasant environment. These aspects were discussed in section 1.6.

Theft is common, and the *portability* of modern equipment can have disadvantages as well as advantages. Users must also concern themselves with the privacy and the confidentiality of information. Text held on the system could be of a personal or commercially sensitive nature and should not be available to the casual observer. A shredder should be readily available to dispose of draft copies of confidential correspondence. This may also cost a few hundred pounds. The opportunity for the 'illegal' access of information is greater to users on a network than where the data is controlled by a personal typist.

Another problem which can occur with the implementation of the new technology is the likely changing pattern of work relationships. Such changes can cause distress and therefore affect attitudes. Typists, who may have had a good relationship with particular managers may be 'pooled' in the word processing department. The term 'VDU operator' may infer a reduction in status when compared to 'typist/secretary'. The trend in many firms is to centralise secretarial and administrative support.

One possible design is that shown in Figure 2.16. This may be more efficient, ensuring more productivity from staff, and is a defensive

fig 2.16 *changing work relationships*

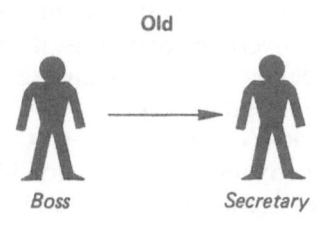

Old

Boss → Secretary

New

Manager

Telephone

Dictating machine

Administrative Secretary

Headset

Typographers

W.P. Operators

measure against sickness and loss of key personnel, but needs to be brought in with care as both the secretaries and the managers may not be happy about the change. It is obviously less personal to dictate letters to a dictation machine than it is to a secretary. These changes may be viewed negatively because of the loss in personal contact and possible loss in status. The result may be an unhappy staff environment with consequent decreases in the quality and speed of work. Further, in a DTP environment, secretaries may feel they are losing status to typographers and layout people.

Some managers feel that word processing relevant to them should stay in *their* office. Dealing with the orders made by a customer, now on the telephone, searching out parts for urgent orders, or the correspondence regarding overdue accounts is, it could be argued, all in the realm of the sales department and many argue that centralising this type of activity is a retrograde step.

An alternative approach is for managers to key in the text themselves. Although many managers do not like this approach because, they argue, 'they are not paid to type', it is likely to lead to an increase in productivity. Having got used to word processing on a computer, they will be more likely to try other applications of the microcomputer. The resistance may well be due to managers fearing that they may 'make fools of themselves'. This fear is not so prevalent now as computers become more widespread in businesses. They are no longer the preserve of the technologist.

Another positive aspect of word processing is that the use of the new technology has proved to be an area where young unemployed people can gain skills which are in demand. Computers are more exciting than typewriters and a great deal of satisfaction can be gained from learning how to use them.

On the other hand the new technology can hardly be said to be greeted by all staff with enthusiasm. As we have seen, jobs and working relationships will change. Change may well be perceived as a negative thing. Offices are labour-intensive and one of the aims of implementing word processing and related systems is to reduce labour costs, even if this is not always the result of such ventures. The fear of unemployment in offices, whether real or perceived, can cause unrest and strike action even where firms implementing such systems stress that the reduction of staff will come about gradually and only through 'natural wastage'.

Nevertheless, the job satisfaction of secretaries who have moved from typewriters to word processors has usually increased, particularly where their implementation has been carried out with care. In these situations, most staff are pleased to develop new skills and rise to the challenge of the new technology.

FILE MANAGEMENT

AND DATA BASE

APPLICATIONS

File management and data base systems help people create, store and access information efficiently using computers. Section 3.1 distinguishes between clerical and computer files. Section 3.2 discusses the basic features of file management systems. These allow the user to: design the record structure; check the data as it is input to the file; store the data on disk; access the data as required; and print it off.

This is followed by a discussion of the types of file management system and how the more powerful data base management systems might be distinguished from them. This distinction has become somewhat blurred in the context of microcomputer packages. Section 3.4 discusses the benefits coming from the use of data base systems. The next section describes distributed data bases, where the data can be held in a number of locations and accessed by users remote from the location where the data is stored.

3.1 CLERICAL AND COMPUTER FILES

A computer can help to manage the data of the organisation. It becomes an *electronic* filing cabinet capable of holding much more data in a much smaller space than a clerical system using paper and cards stored in a filing cabinet. File management packages can access the data conveniently and quickly. This helps in the general day-to-day processing of the company and also enables managers to obtain facts about the company quickly so that they can make vital decisions supported by more accurate and up-to-date information.

There are a large number of file management systems available on microcomputers. A file management package, along with a spreadsheet and a word processor, is often bought with a new microcomputer. Sometimes these three packages are provided 'free' with the microcomputer.

Many file management packages are designed so that the computer files that they support are similar to the clerical files that they replace.

(a) Each **file** will relate to a specific type of data in a specific application area. Firms are likely to have a payroll file, customer file, product file, and stock file.

(b) A file is made up of a collection of **records** containing the same type of information. There will be one record for each product on the product file, just as there would be one card or document for each product on the equivalent clerical file.

(c) Both types of record will include a number of **fields** (sometimes referred to as data items). For a product file, the fields could include a product number, description, selling price, the raw materials needed for its manufacture, and so on.

These three constituent elements, files, records and fields, exist in computer and clerical files. As Figure 3.1 shows, the design of customer and product files can be very similar, whether the medium for holding the data happens to be a floppy disk or a paper folder.

Figure 3.2 shows how the computer and clerical procedures can be similar for a payroll system. The computer and the clerk will both carry out the calculations to work out the gross pay, tax amounts, insurance contributions, and the net pay, which are used to produce the payslip for the employee. For example, the gross this month is calculated by dividing the salary field by 12. The gross this month can be a field on a computer file or one written on the card. The calculation can be performed by the computer, by calculator or by using mental arithmetic. There is no fundamental difference, but in *some* circumstances the computer can be faster, more accurate, more convenient and cheaper.

Effective management is informed management and it is essential that managers can get the facts of their business in a convenient and timely way. This is usually difficult in a manual system, unless the company is a small one with all the data known or readily available to management. The one-man firm is, from this point of view, the ideal. The owner is the manager and knows the company inside out. But if the firm is successful, it will expand and it is then necessary to delegate responsibility. Computers can help to make this process more successful by making the facts available to all the managers that need them.

Many file management systems are very adaptable and yet are simple to use, so that data can be retrieved in a number of ways. A

fig 3.1 *files, records and fields*

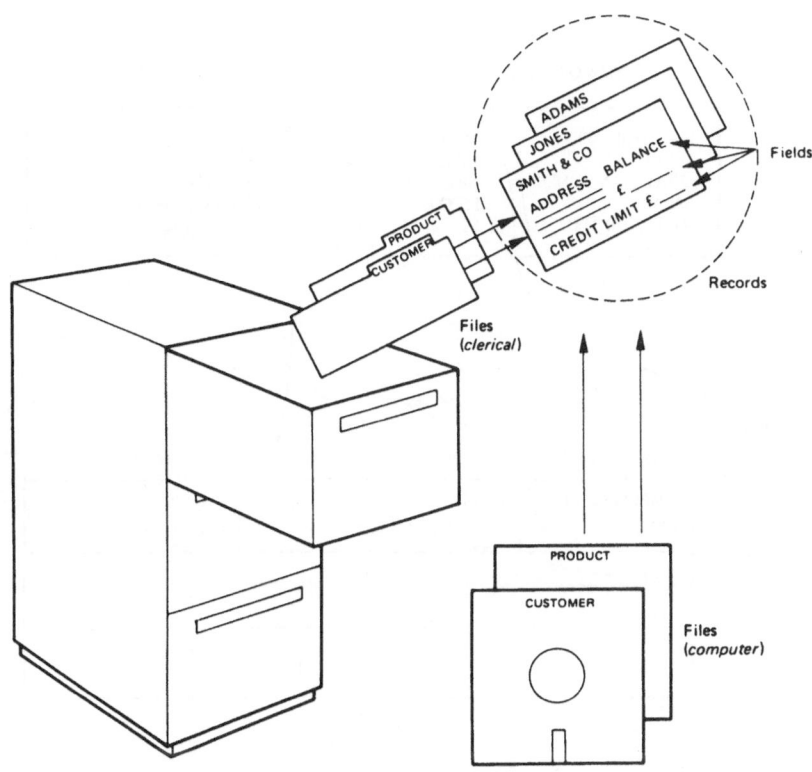

user may wish to look at only certain fields in a record or certain records in a file. This can be very easily achieved using most file management systems. The data selected can then be sorted in a sequence specified by the user and presented on a VDU screen or printed out as a management report.

Some systems will allow the user to look at more than one file at a time. A record from each file may be displayed in a separate window on the screen. A report on sales orders, for example, can require data from the product file (for information about product prices), a stock file (for information about products in stock) and a customer file (for information about credit limits). File management systems that can cater for this degree of sophistication are frequently referred to as data base management systems.

File management systems can be compared in their details by using such criteria as:

fig 3.2 *payroll file (computer or clerical) to payslip*

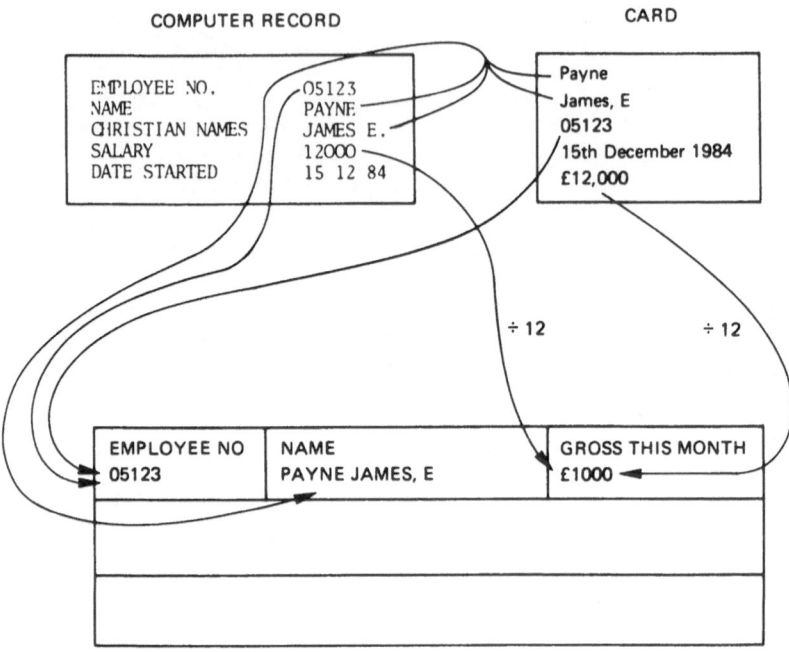

(a) the maximum file size (that is the amount of records allowed per file);

(b) the maximum record size (that is the number of characters per record);

(c) the maximum number of fields in a record;

(d) the maximum field size;

(e) the speed of response in dealing with user requests.

This is the basic comparative data, but there are other important differences, such as the way in which they:

(a) validate data (check that it is accurate) before including it in the files;

(b) store records, for efficient storage and access; and

(c) handle user requests for information in files,

and these aspects will be looked at in the next section.

3.2 FEATURES OF FILE MANAGEMENT PACKAGES

File management systems will allow the user to design the structure of the records (**formatting**); validate the data as it is input to the computer (**data entry and validation**); store the data on disk (**data storage**); allow the data to be accessed in the format required, sorted and selected as required (**retrieval**); and printed off (**reporting**). File management systems may also give the opportunity for users to write subroutines to process the data in a way that is not possible using the standard facilities of the system. These subroutines of the user's own code are frequently called **macros** (or 'own procedures') and many file management systems provide a simple language to enable these to be written. In this section we will look at each of these features in turn.

(a) Formatting
Before data can be entered into a file management system, the user must decide on the types of files and the data to go in them. Data relating to customers is normally put together in a customer file, product data in another, and supplier data in another. This is convenient because it is easier to collect, store, and retrieve data for one area at a time. Applications will use one or more of these files, and for manufacturing companies these could include:

- Suppliers
- Customers
- Personnel
- Departments
- Components
- Finished Products
- Stocks
- Warehouse Locations

In a hospital the files could include:

- Patients
- Medical Staff
- Administration Staff
- Drugs
- Treatments
- Wards

and in a university:

- Students
- Lecturers
- Administrators
- Courses
- Classes

Having decided the range of files likely to be required, the next step is to decide on the data items which will be included in each record of the file. The customer file, for example, will have one record for each customer and each record could contain:

(*i*) customer number;
(*ii*) customer name;
(*iii*) invoicing address;
(*iv*) delivery address;
(*v*) balance outstanding;
(*vi*) credit limit.

A patient's record might contain:

(*i*) patient number;
(*ii*) patient name;
(*iii*) patient address;
(*iv*) next of kin;
(*v*) doctor name;
(*vi*) ward number;

and a course record may contain:

(*i*) course number;
(*ii*) course name;
(*iii*) level;
(*iv*) department;
(*v*) maximum number of students;
(*vi*) full time/part time;
(*vii*) number of years to completion;
(*viii*) course tutor.

The file management system will require details about each of these fields. These details could include:

(*i*) length in characters;
(*ii*) format (numeric, alphabetic, character, yes/no, time or date);
(*iii*) range of possible values; and

(*iv*) password, if it is necessary to prevent illegal access to that data item.

The user must be aware of any restrictions that the file management system imposes in designing the file. These restrictions may include the maximum number of fields per record and the maximum number of characters per field.

Much of the data will be **coded**. These codes will usually already exist in the manual system, and unless they are deficient in some way will normally be carried over on to the computer system. If the coding system is well designed, an item can be identified more conveniently than a description in words. There are a number of coding systems:

(*i*) *Classification coding*, where characters suggest a class, for example:

lxxxx Customer order
13xxx Customer order in Midlands region
1326x Customer order in Midlands region for steel product
  (1=wood product; 2=metal product)
13269 Customer order in Midlands region for steel product
  (including a check digit – see below)

(*ii*) *Alphabetic coding*, which could be designed in a similar way as the numeric classification code above, but each character position will give scope for 26 classes rather than ten (0 to 9).

(*iii*) *Faceted coding*, where each element represents a facet and the code is meaningful, for example:

BSCF01 (BSc, full time, 1st year)
HNDP03 (HND, part time, 3rd year)

(*iv*) *Hierarchical coding*, the most well known of which is the Dewey Decimal system which is a classification system used in libraries. This book is located in Aston Library under:

001.xxxxxxx (Artificial intelligence)
001.64xxxxx (Computers)
001.6404xxx (Microcomputers)
001.6404024 (Microcomputer applications)

Specific application areas would be denoted by adding to this code: 657 (for accounting applications) or 658 (for management applications).

When data is input, it is also important that the data is valid, otherwise the information provided will be incorrect: 'garbage in, garbage out'. Validation routines are discussed under the sub-heading 'Data entry and validation' below. However, the check digit system is related to coding and is therefore discussed here. This digit added to a code makes the overall code self-checking. The check digit has a unique relationship with the rest of the code so that any mistakes due to transferring the number on to the computer will be detected. These errors are usually either **transcription** errors (numbers in the code are copied incorrectly) or **transposition** errors (the correct numbers are written but they have been copied in the wrong order). The **modulus 11** check digit system, shown in Figure 3.3, will detect all of these errors.

The user may also be permitted to specify data items whose contents are calculated by the system. For example, 'maximum customer order' in a customer record could be derived by subtracting the 'balance owing' field from the 'credit limit' field. Many file management systems offer a whole range of **operators** such as addition, multiplication, division, exponential, modulo and percent-age, that can be used for this and other purposes.

As we have seen, the design work necessary *before* specifying the file, record and field details to the file management system, is not a trivial task. The data is logically separated into a number of files, the record structure for each of these is defined, and the length, type, validation rules, and security requirements for each of the fields worked out.

Indeed this aspect is common to many of the applications discussed in this book. Automation applies to only some aspects of the application. There is still much time and effort required to analyse the application area and design the system. Without this effort, the computer application will not fulfil the needs of the users.

Once the file design has been completed, then this design is specified to the file management system. Most of these systems allow the user to create a screen form to set up the data structure. This screen will also be used to enter the data. The system is therefore storing two things: the structure of the data file itself, and the data entry 'form', often referred to as a **mask**. A typical form for a product file is shown in Figure 3.4. Forms should be set up so that data can be entered quickly and conveniently. Again this requires some thought. The data will be entered in the boxes provided. The boxes are shown in **inverse video** (the colours of the background and foreground are exchanged) to make it obvious where data should be entered.

fig 3.3 *Modulus 11 check digit system*

CALCULATING CHECK DIGIT

CODE = 1340 X (WHERE X WILL BE THE CHECK DIGIT)

Stage 1: MULTIPLY EACH NUMBER BY ITS *WEIGHT* AS FOLLOWS

Code	1	3	4	0
	x	x	x	x
Weight	$\frac{5}{5}$	$\frac{4}{12}$	$\frac{3}{12}$	$\frac{2}{0}$

Stage 2: ADD THE RESULTS

$5 + 12 + 12 + 0 = 29$

Stage 3: DIVIDE TOTAL BY MODULUS 11

$29 \div 11 = 2$ REMAINDER 7

Stage 4: SUBSTRACT REMAINDER FROM MODULUS 11 GIVING THE CHECK DIGIT

$11 - 7 = 4$ (check digit)

THE CODE NOW BECOMES 13404

NOTE:- Codes giving a remainder of 0 or 1 will give a check digit of 11 or 10. There are a number of possible solutions to this problem: (a) avoid these codes in the system, (b) use a letter for these check digits (eg A or B), (c) use a two number check digit (eg 01 to 11)

VALIDATING CHECK DIGIT

Stage 1: MULTIPLY EACH NUMBER BY ITS WEIGHT (giving the check digit itself a weight of 1)

1	3	4	0	4
x	x	x	x	x
$\frac{5}{5}$	$\frac{4}{12}$	$\frac{3}{12}$	$\frac{2}{0}$	$\frac{1}{4}$

Stage 2: ADD THESE NUMBERS

$5 + 12 + 12 + 0 + 4 = 33$

Stage 3: DIVIDE THE RESULT BY MODULUS 11 IF THERE IS NO REMAINER

eg $33 \div 11 = 3$ remainder 0

THE CODE IS VALID

OTHERWISE IT IS INVALID

Different colours could also be used where a colour monitor is available.

When defining the record structure, one data item is normally designated the **key field**. This is used to identify a particular record occurrence on the file. A customer number could be used to identify

fig 3.4 *record design and data entry 'form'*

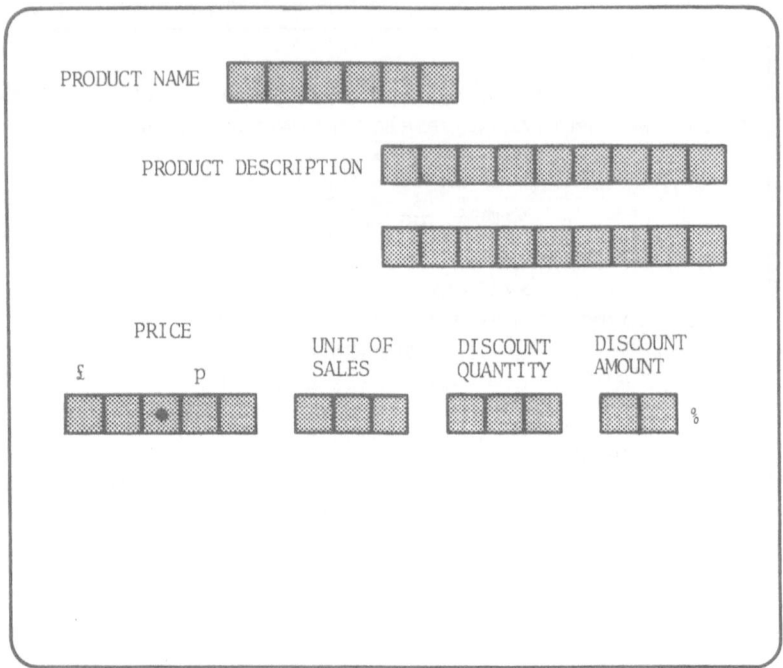

a particular customer's record on the customer file and an employee name could be used to identify an employee's record on the personnel file. The customer number and the employee name are the keys for the two files. They 'label' each record in the file.

Keys are important when retrieving data from files because it is possible to relate the key of the record to its **address** on disk where the record is held. The address of a record locates it on disk, just as the address of a house locates the house in a street. This link between the key and the address on disk storage enables fast access because it is not then necessary to search through the records on disk serially (from the beginning of the file until the required record is found).

One of these quick methods of file access, through an index table, is illustrated in Figure 3.5. The index table holds all the keys of the records in the file and their corresponding addresses. By a simple search through the index, the record address can be found, and the record retrieved.

At some time in the future, it may be necessary to change the data structure of a file. The application may have changed in the interven-

fig 3.5 *locating records 'directly' using an index table*

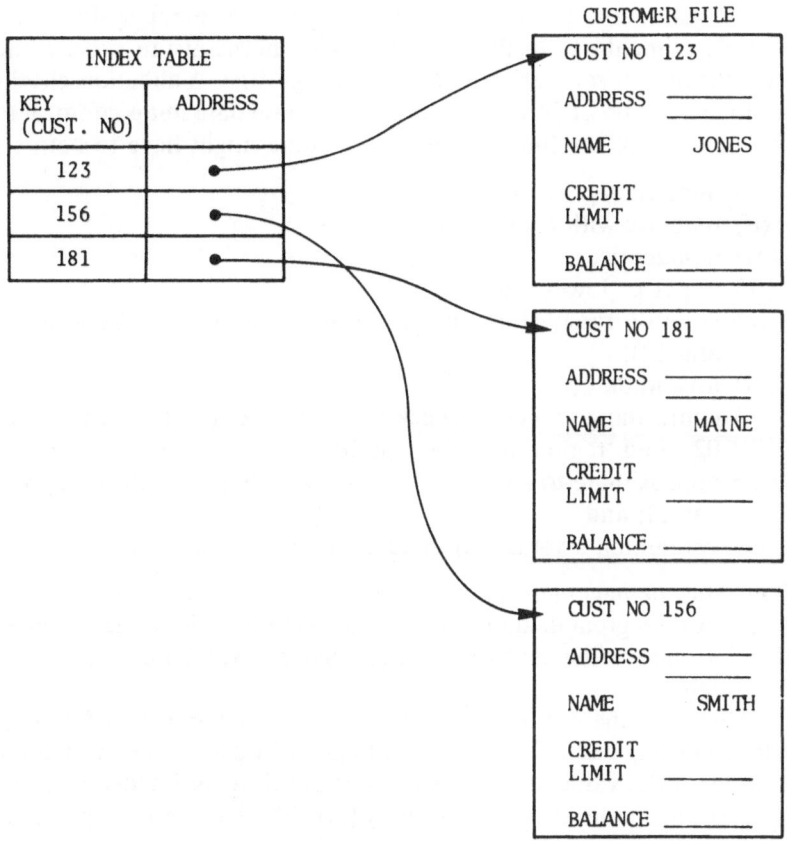

ing period or the user may have designed the system poorly. Many systems make it easy to add or delete fields at this stage; some do not, and prospective purchasers ought to consider this when choosing a system.

(b) Data entry and validation

Assuming that the files have been formatted, the data has to be keyed in and validated before adding to the master files. The purpose of validating data is to ensure that no invalid data enters the data base. This is essential, for 'information' which is incorrect could be damaging to the company. It can have unexpected ramifications where files are shared by other users and departments. Further, once the computer system starts to be looked at with suspicion, it could become worthless, as all the output will be questioned.

The validation routines in some file management systems are rather rudimentary. In this case it may be necessary to process the data through a separate validation package first. Validation checks could include procedures to ensure that certain data items conform to one or more of the following tests. The data might have to be:

(*i*) numeric;

(*ii*) numeric with a check digit;

(*iii*) alphabetic;

(*iv*) upper or lower case;

(*v*) within a range (for example, 'sales area' must be between 01 and 12);

(*vi*) a valid date;

(*vii*) conforming to a cross check (for example, if sales area is 01 or 02, then 'region' must be 'south');

(*viii*) approximate to a value (the value is within, say, 1% of a given value); and

(*ix*) containing a value (the field contains a given value).

Some file management packages do have facilities for this level of validation. A great deal of attention needs to be paid to the design of the data and codes and to ensuring that the validation checks are thorough.

Sometimes the user may want the package to complete a data item when entering data. The system could place 'today's date' in a field or increment the value in a field by one for each record added to a file.

There are a number of ways by which file management packages facilitate data entry. Some present the user with a soft copy form and the user fills in the form for each record. As you can see from Figure 3.4, the soft copy form can look the same as a paper form. The boxes indicate the length of the data items. Once one data item has been completed by the user and the system has verified that this data does conform to the validation rules specified, the cursor will 'jump' to the next entry.

As well as loading the data in the data base in the first place, the users may wish to change the data. The same validation rules ought to apply for updating the data. Some systems will allow the user to **batch** updates. An example of a batch update might be to increase the salaries of all the people working on microcomputers by 5% (as their computer experience makes them 'in demand' elsewhere).

Although most data will be input using the conventional keyboard, there are alternatives. **Bar coding** (used on products in a shop or warehouse) and **character recognition** are the most widespread. There are a number of types of character recognition, such as:

(*i*) Magnetic Ink Character Recognition (MICR);
(*ii*) Optical Mark Recognition (OMR); and
(*iii*) Optical Character Recognition (OCR).

We have looked at OCR systems in Chapter 2. They are usually used to read typed or printed documents as input to word processing systems, though they can read data, such as figures, when printed in one of the acceptable fonts.

MICR is less usual in standard business applications, although it is commonly used in the banking sector (e.g. in processing cheques). It is usually restricted to one line of MICR print per document.

OMR, on the other hand, is frequently used as a way of reading data into files. Figure 3.6 shows an OMR reader inputting marked cards. Similar devices are used for inputting marked forms and forms with bar codes which are commonly used to identify products in a warehouse or shop.

OMR documents include survey response sheets, catering arrangements, order forms, time allocation records and wage time sheets. The form is designed so that the person completing the form marks the options required, usually in HB pencil. The OMR reader recognises these marks and reads the data into the system.

These are methods of scanning documents and reading data into the computer system. They tend to be specific to particular applications and can quicken the process of data entry.

(c) Data storage

Most file management systems require disk storage. Unlike word processing, where the choice of VDU and printer gain emphasis, in a data base environment it is the backing storage which is paramount. Floppy disks are a common choice, but hard disks are faster, more reliable, and have greater capacities. They are also coming down in price. A floppy disk may hold a file of around 5000 records of about 200 characters per record. If this does not seem adequate for the foreseeable future or fast access speeds are required, then a hard disk is necessary.

Even so, the user who has experienced data base management facilities on mainframe computers is likely to be disappointed with the performance and facilities of microcomputer packages. They will seem slower, particularly where a number of files are cross-referenced, and their multi-user capabilities are likely to be limited.

fig 3.6 *Datascan Series 7 Optical Mark Reader*
reading marked documents
Source: Kendata Peripherals Limited

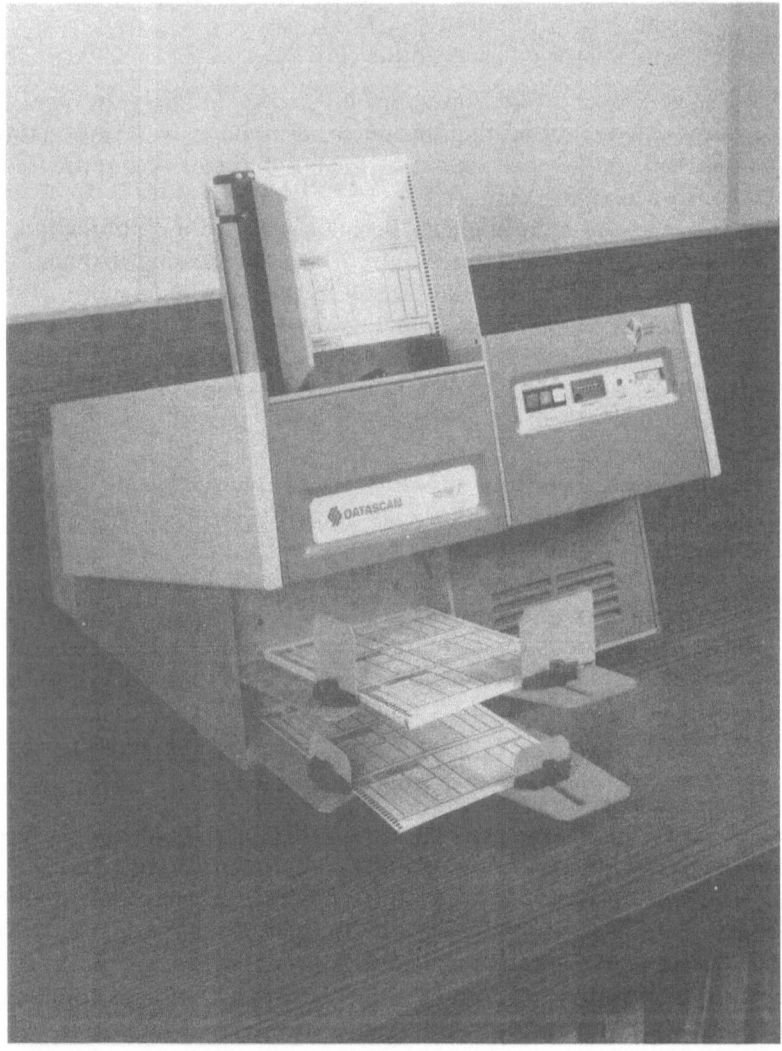

The way in which data is organised for storage will be important for
data retrieval. There are a number of methods of organising files. We
have already briefly looked at the index method (Figure 3.5). Some
systems only offer one method, whilst others offer a number of
methods, and the user must choose the most appropriate when
setting up the particular file.

A second method of file organisation is shown in Figure 3.7. This is called a 'linked list'. In each record there is a pointer which contains the address of the next record. The last record may point to the first record or contain a 'null' pointer. In Figure 3.7 the records are arranged in ascending order of customer number. Sometimes there are a number of pointers set up. Customer records could be joined according to sales areas, customer types, or scales of indebtedness, but there are limits to the number of access paths, for otherwise it would be impossible to store all the links and retrieve the data conveniently. More importantly, the addition and deletion of records becomes a complex job for the computer system, because the maintenance of the correct sequence of pointers is complicated.

Further, the data structures are relatively rigid and awkward to change once the data base has been set up. It also means that users have to be aware of how the data relationships were created because otherwise they will not be able to use the data base efficiently. For all these reasons, the index method of file organisation is more usual in microcomputer file management systems.

A search of the file which is based on the key field is usually the quickest way of retrieving data. Frequently, but not always, the records are sorted in this key sequence ready for creating the file. However, although most searches will be based on this key field, many systems may allow for the inclusion of alternative keys which have to be specified.

Searches of the customer file may be based on customer name as an alternative to customer number. Some systems which set up indexes giving the key field and addresses, may also facilitate the use of alternative keys by setting up other indexes. This is illustrated in Figure 3.8. There is one index table specifying the addresses of records according to customer number, and another according to customer name. The design of the same file using a system of multiple pointers is shown in Figure 3.9.

(d) Retrieval

As we have seen, many users will require processing via the key of the file or via alternative keys. Sorting facilities will be important to enable the output of the records to be made in the order of the alternative keys and therefore in a different sequence from the one in which they are stored. The system may effect this by creating a temporary file in a new sequence.

A more common approach to providing this facility, is either to sort the index, or to create a second or third index in the sequence of the alternative keys. The file can then be read in this new order

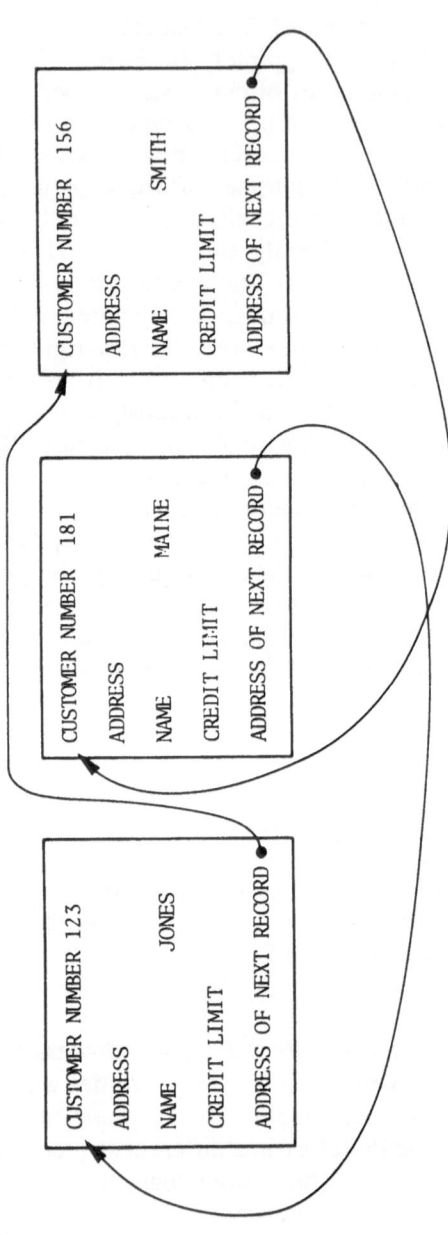

fig 3.7 *linking records – the use of pointers in a list*

fig 3.8 *locating records 'directly' through the use of multiple index tables*

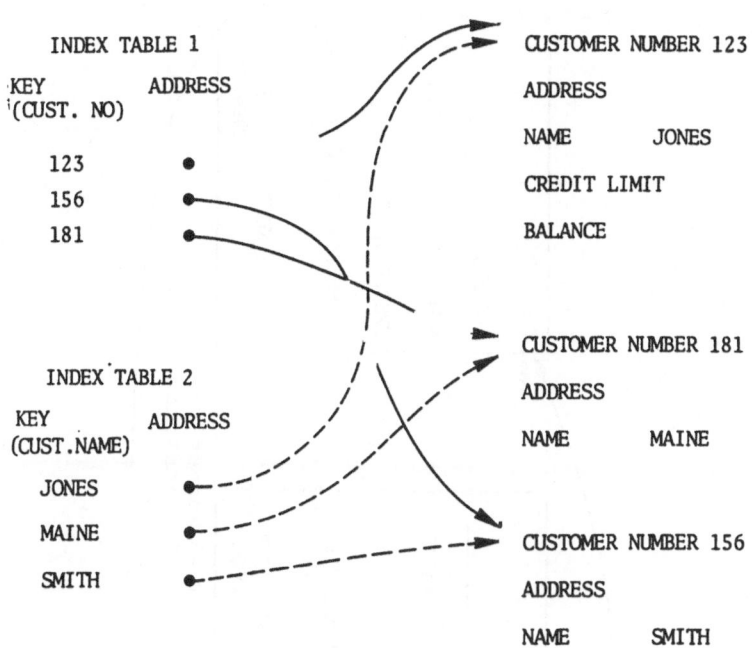

(shown in Figure 3.8). The speed of the microcomputer system in retrieving, deleting, and sorting data is important, as such processes can seem very slow to the user.

Many systems offer **browsing** facilities which list the records in a file in the quickest way possible and allow the user to obtain information on the data base quickly even if the data is not laid out in the most convenient way. This normally means displaying the data as one record per line on the screen.

Some simple searches may be achieved from the user's point of view by processing through a series of menus or soft copy forms. A menu contains a number of options and the user chooses the particular option required. Some requirements will be specified through a series of menus, but this can prove slow and tedious to the trained user, and there should be ways by which the menus can be bypassed. By following the series of menus in Figure 3.10, the user can obtain details of a particular sales representative.

Alternatively, the user can part fill a form and the system complete that form to give the same information (Figure 3.11) as that provided

fig 3.9 *linking records – multiple pointers*

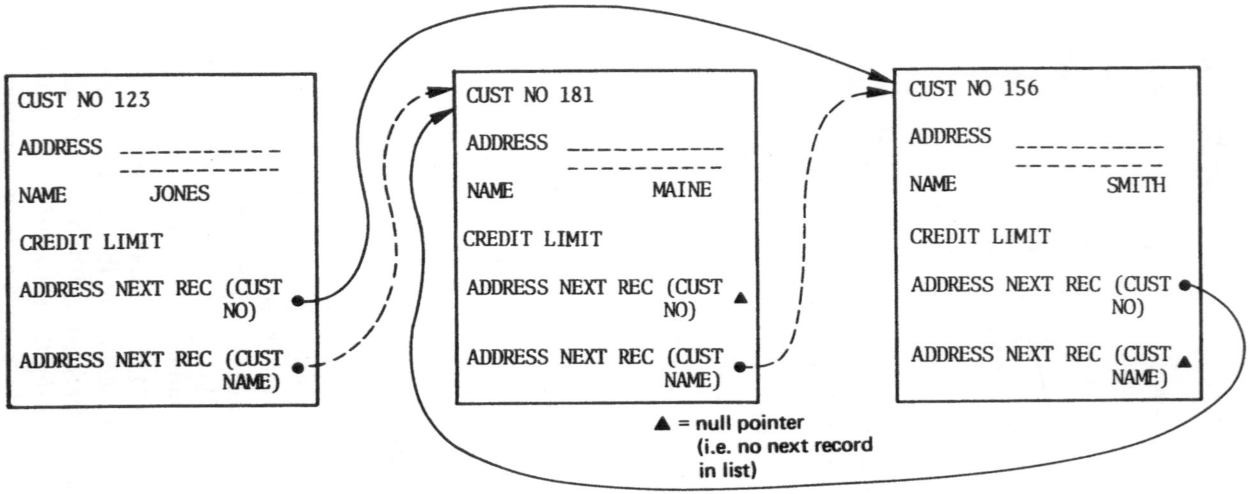

CUST NO 123
ADDRESS ------ ------
NAME ------ JONES
CREDIT LIMIT
ADDRESS NEXT REC (CUST NO)
ADDRESS NEXT REC (CUST NAME)

CUST NO 181
ADDRESS ------ ------
NAME ------ MAINE
CREDIT LIMIT
ADDRESS NEXT REC (CUST NO) ▲
ADDRESS NEXT REC (CUST NAME)

CUST NO 156
ADDRESS ------ ------
NAME ------ SMITH
CREDIT LIMIT
ADDRESS NEXT REC (CUST NO)
ADDRESS NEXT REC (CUST NAME) ▲

▲ = null pointer
(i.e. no next record in list)

fig 3.10 *enquiry through menus*

SALES SYSTEM

WHICH AREA
1. NORTH
2. SOUTH
3. MIDLANDS
4. EXIT
? 2

Menu Level 1

SALES SYSTEM

WHICH REP
1. LONDON
2. HOME COUNTIES
3. SOUTHERN
4. EXIT
? 3

Menu Level 2

SALES SYSTEM
SOUTH REGION

SALES FOR REP: R. JONES (SOUTHERN)

WEEK	SALES	EXPENSES
1	5,400	3,000
2	7,200	3,000
3	6,000	3,000
4	3,500	3,030
TOTAL	22,100	12,030

Report

fig 3.11 *enquiry through forms*

1. Form display

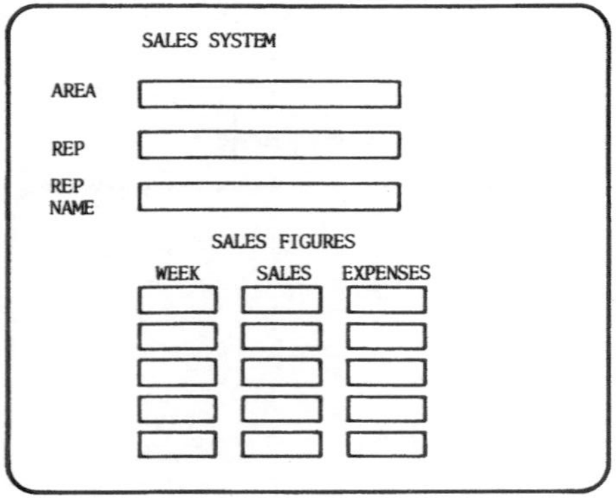

2. Part completed by user
   using one of keys (rep or rep name)

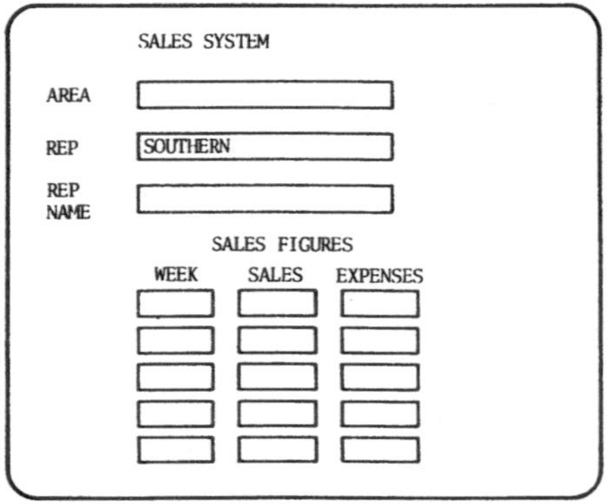

or

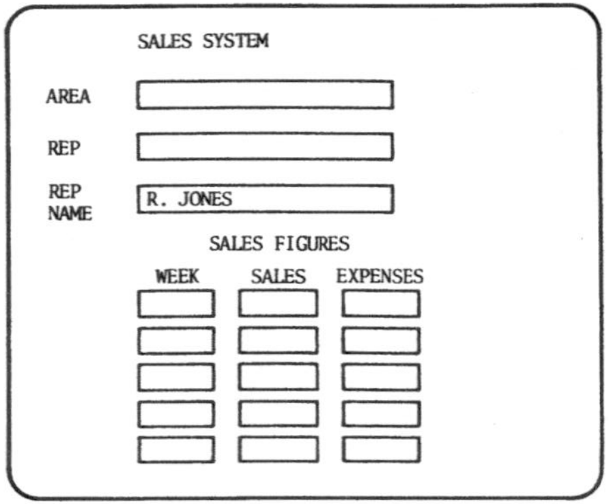

3. Result - completed form

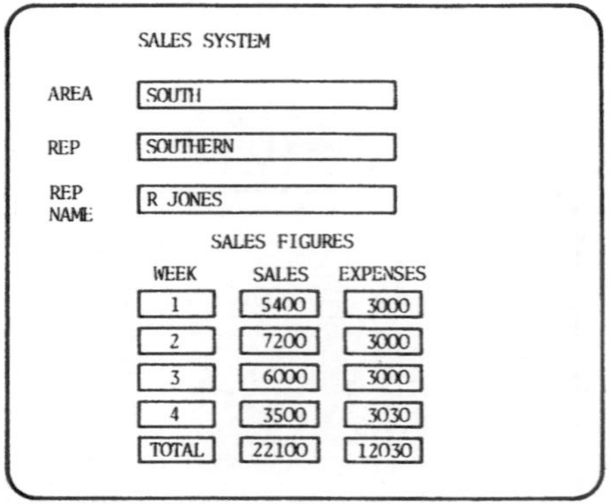

using the menu-driven system. This method can be used to simulate the manual paperwork system that the computer system replaces, as the forms can be similar to the clerical forms. The use of a light pen may speed up the process of 'form filling'. A light pen can be held by the user against the screen and the form completed.

The system may display the results as a report rather than as a completed form (see Figure 3.10 – report). Some systems offer the users a number of alternative ways to obtain their information requirements.

Frequently the user will wish to select records from a file, and the process of selection is such that totally menu-driven or form-driven systems prove inadequate. A typical request could be to find out how many of the more expensive men's suits produced (over £50) have a non-standard colour. Statement (a) selects those records from a file where the 'cost' field is more than 50, and where the 'colour' is neither grey nor black, and statement (b) adds one to the total of non-standard products where this is applicable.

(a) **IF COST GREATER THAN 50 AND COLOUR NOT 'GREY' OR COLOUR NOT 'BLACK'**

(b) **THEN ADD 1 TO NON-STANDARD-COLOUR-TOTAL**

Another request could be to select from a customer file those customers who live in the North East region, to sort them in ascending order of credit balance, and to display the results on the monitor. Many systems offer the user a range of conditional operators in order to select data from a file. These include:

- (*i*) equal to;
- (*ii*) greater than;
- (*iii*) less than;
- (*iv*) greater than or equal to;
- (*v*) less than or equal to.

These operators are the Boolean operators and their meaning can be changed with **NOT**; a search can be based on comparisons linked by **AND**s and **OR**s. Data can be altered ready for printing by the use of:

- (*i*) add;
- (*ii*) subtract;
- (*iii*) multiply;
- (*iv*) divide;

and frequently other operators, such as:

   (i) sum;
   (ii) minimum or maximum;
 (iii) average;
 (iv) to the power of:
   (v) square root;
 (vi) round to whole number;
 (vii) standard deviation;
($viii$) sine, cosine, etc.

Many microcomputer file management systems have a query language based on the SQL language developed by IBM. This has a SELECT – FROM – WHERE – ORDER construct. Thus: SELECT the specified field or fields FROM the specified file or files WHERE the following conditional operators apply and sort the result according to the ORDER of the following fields. For example:

      SELECT NAME, AMOUNTOWING
      FROM STUDENTFILE
      WHERE AMOUNTOWING GREATER THAN 0
      ORDER NAME

may produce the following list:

NAME	AMOUNTOWING
Atkins D.F.	115.80
Bell J.J.	100.00
Smith P.	550.00

We will discuss SQL in more detail in the next section.

One feature common on microcomputer file management systems is the ability to select records where only part of the item value required is known using wildcard characters (mentioned already in the context of word processing systems). Thus 'DAVI*' for a surname will retrieve DAVISON, DAVIES, DAVIDSON, and DAVIS. There may be search strings based on the middle of the name such as '*avi*' which would pick up AVISON, DAVISON, AVIS, and many others. Some may be sophisticated enough to retrieve 'sounds like' data such that 'DAVIS' will also pick up 'DAVIES'. This is known as a **phonetic** search.

(e) Reporting
Most file management and data base packages offer facilities for setting up and printing reports using the data held in the data base. The reports could be displayed on the VDU as well as printed on

paper. The principles of report layout, extracting data and performing calculation routines to produce totals, are largely the same. Differences may occur in the 'style' of output, for example, the way colours, light intensity, and blinking values are used on the screen or the way the screen is split up into several windows.

Users may wish to set up a number of screen and report layouts for each file. These can be called in by name when required.

On each hard copy or VDU page will be the headings which help the reader understand the contents of the report and give other information such as the date (or week number) when the report is printed and a page number. This type of information is usually provided in the report **header** and **trailer** which is printed on each page of the report.

The **main body** of the report will consist of the raw data which is extracted from the data base. The user may extract only a few of the fields held in a file (or files), or only a few occurrences of the fields chosen (according to some selection criterion).

The last part of designing a report is to set up the various total fields. These will include the **subtotals, grand totals** and other information which summarises the report. Some systems will make these calculations when printing off the report. There may also be **control breaks**, which divide similar sub-groups of records. At a control break the user may require a new page. An example of a report layout is given in Figure 3.12.

Many systems include a **report generator**. Reports may be set up by following a series of questions and answers. Standard reports, for example a list of records or a list of selected items from records in a file, should be very easy to set up using such a facility.

It may be possible to use this facility to create a report using data from a number of files on the data base. For example, an invoice can be created from a **PARTS** file (containing part numbers and prices) and a **CUSTOMERS** file (containing customer numbers and parts delivered). The two files will be linked by a part number. In this way it is possible to read the price of a part that a customer has ordered, and therefore compute the invoice value.

Some complex reports may have to be set up using users' own procedures to be run each time the invoices are due to be printed, because the report generator does not cater for the level of complexity required.

(f) Macros
The ability for users to set up their own procedures is not available on all file management packages. The facility can serve two purposes.

fig 3.12 *report*

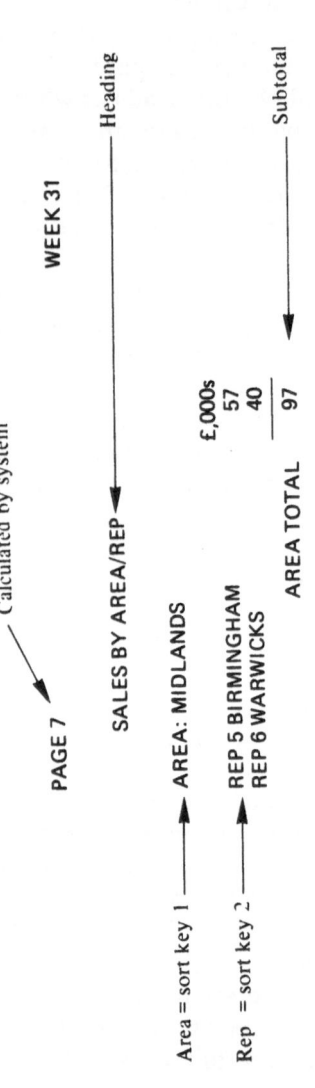

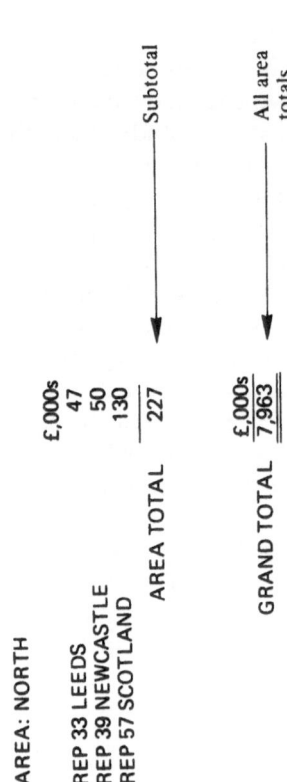

Calculated by system ──→ Heading

PAGE 7   WEEK 31

SALES BY AREA/REP

Area = sort key 1 ──────→ AREA: MIDLANDS

                                              £,000s
Rep = sort key 2 ──────→ REP 5 BIRMINGHAM   57
                         REP 6 WARWICKS   40
                                                  ──
                              AREA TOTAL   97 ──── Subtotal

Could have page break here

AREA: NORTH

                                              £,000s
                         REP 33 LEEDS   47
                         REP 39 NEWCASTLE   50
                         REP 57 SCOTLAND   130
                                                 ───
                              AREA TOTAL   227 ──── Subtotal

                                              £,000s
                             GRAND TOTAL   7,963 ──── All area
                                              ═════   totals

First, the particular package may not have the commands that the user requires and therefore it is necessary to write 'own code' in order to process the data in the way required. Secondly, it allows the user to set up subroutines which can be run again and again without having to key in the instructions each time. This avoids tedium and reduces the possibility of making errors. The particular language will vary with the system, but it should be easy to use and therefore should not be a conventional programming language like Cobol or Fortran, although interfaces with these languages may be available as well. Even so, writing own macros is not an easy task and most command structures will take a few weeks to master. There may, for example, be a hundred commands and functions at the user's disposal. This provides the necessary power, but reduces the speed with which the system can be learnt.

Typical commands for this facility might include:

(*i*)	**IF . . .THEN . . .**	which will perform the functions where the logical expression is true;
(*ii*)	**ELSE**	perform another set of functions or . . . ;
(*iii*)	**GOTO . . .LABELNAME . . .**	where the program carries out the statements following the location marked by a label;
(*iv*)	**MENU**	where the user can set up a menu of alternatives which the operator follows.

The logical expression may contain the logical operators and functions discussed in the section on 'retrieval' above.

An example of a use of a macro would be to effect the rules when assessing the credit limit of a customer. This might be expressed in English as: 'Only increase the credit limit of a customer with a good credit record, that is one who has never exceeded his limit without permission. The credit limit should never be increased by more than 50 per cent at any one time.' This type of logic could not be expressed in one statement, but would require four or five statements; these could be recorded as a macro, and executed with one command on future occasions when a request is made to increase the credit limit of a customer.

Figure 3.13 shows the main menu of one file management system. It has four major elements:

fig 3.13 *the main menu of the Delta 4 file management system*
Source: CompSoft plc

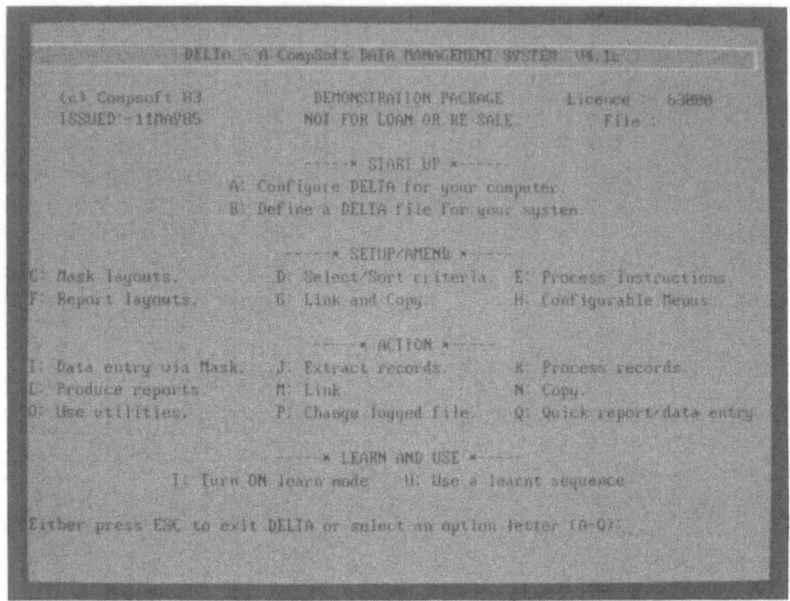

(i) **STARTUP**	which includes the options to define the printer and VDU characteristics to the software and define a file to the system;
(ii) **SETUP/AMEND**	which includes the options to set up a mask of the record layout on to the screen, state criteria to select and sort records from a file, set up reports, and set up user-defined menus;
(iii) **ACTION**	which includes options to enter data on to a file and to print out reports; and
(iv) **LEARN AND USE**	which includes options that will help the user who is unfamiliar with the system to learn how to use it.

3.3 TYPES OF FILE MANAGEMENT AND DATA BASE SYSTEM

The distinction between file management systems and data base management systems has become blurred. It could be argued that a file management system is a data base system with limited features, but then most suppliers would claim that their product is a 'data base system'. It is more useful to suggest that a file management system allows the user to read and update only one file at a time. Thus a dentist's practice may have a file of patients and a file of product information and these can be accessed separately. There is no link between them and this may not be a requirement, both files being necessary but applications using them separately.

A data base system will allow users to use more than one file. For example, if the dentist's system were based on a data base management package, it would be possible to output a report giving a list of patient information from the patient file and including in the report information from the product file. This would be used to find out which products the patients required for their treatment and the cost of these products (and therefore the treatment). Most systems on microcomputers are advertised as data base systems and many enable users to link 50 or 100 files and more. Indeed many microcomputer packages have all the features of some mainframe systems.

Disk storage technology on modern microcomputers has improved greatly. The floppy disks on modern micros are designed to have four times the storage capacity of the previous 'generation' (about three or four years). Some systems use a high density flexible disk having a capacity of three-quarters of a megabyte (750 000 characters) or more. Hard disks, having a capacity of 20 to 40 megabytes and upwards, are also available with these computers.

There are many data base packages available on microcomputers. Some have been designed specifically for microcomputers: or for microcomputers running on a particular operating system. Some packages are based on data base systems that have proved successful on minicomputers and mainframes. Users who are used to data base systems on larger machines are likely to notice a degradation in performance, although limitations in their facilities, in terms of limitations in the maximum number of fields per record, the maximum number of records per file, the number of files that can be linked together, or in their security provisions have been greatly reduced.

As we have seen, whereas file management systems usually only operate on one file at a time, data base management systems are more sophisticated, allowing a number of files to be related in one request. Thus a manager may construct a report using data from a number of files in the data base. A query could also be constructed so that, in order to answer it, data needs to be supplied from more than one file. Thus, in order to answer the query:

GIVE CUSTOMER NAMES OF CUSTOMERS ORDERING PRODUCT RANGE A?

access is made to the product file (in order to search for the product numbers in product range **A**), then a search of the order file is made (to obtain the customer numbers of those customers ordering these products), and finally a search of the customer file is made (to get the names associated with these customer numbers).

Frequently microcomputer data bases have query languages which are much easier to use than the equivalent mainframe system. Microcomputers have been sold to the general business user rather than to computer professionals, and so this is perhaps not surprising. Data can be input using a question-and-answer session with the user. Alternatively, data can be entered by means of setting up a table or filling a VDU 'form'. Rarely is the user required to have an in-depth knowledge of computers or any knowledge of a conventional programming language.

An SQL-based query could be:

```
SELECT NAME,DEPARTMENT,BALANCE
FROM STUDENT,DEPARTMENT
WHERE STUDENT.NAME=DEPARTMENT.NAME
AND AMOUNTOWING GREATER THAN 0
ORDER NAME
```

The **NAME** and **AMOUNTOWING** can be obtained from the **STUDENT** file, but the **DEPARTMENT** of the student has to be found by searching the **DEPARTMENT** file. The match on the **NAME** of the student will give his or her department. This is illustrated in Figure 3.14.

SQL has become a standard query language on mainframe computers and now microcomputers. It is used by end users and computer programmers. It is not a particularly easy language to master, but it is powerful. Some systems may have SQL and other more easy to learn user interfaces. As it is a 'standard' to some extent, applications running on one system can be 'ported' (that is transferred) to another system. For example, an application can be prototyped (a limited version of the application written and tested on a small computer) and then transferred to the main business computer when it is working. Alternatively the microcomputer can be connected to the mainframe and files on that computer transferred to the microcomputer for manipulation there.

fig 3.14 *joining records*

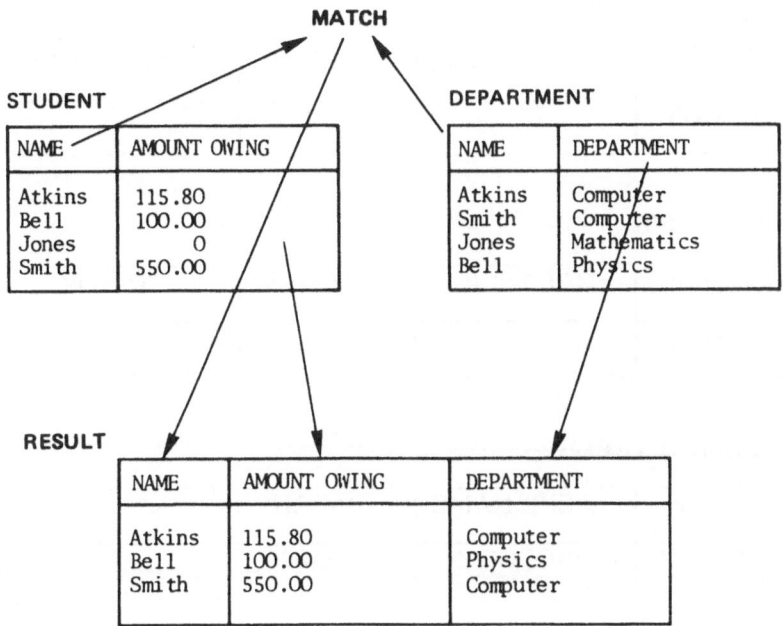

Another query language is Query by Example (QBE), which is very similar in use to the query by forms example shown in Figure 3.11, except that the user completes a query table to stipulate the selection criteria by putting ticks or P (for print) on those items required to be output (see Figure 3.15). To link more than one query table, the user places an example value in each occurrence of the common field (say 'name' in the SQL example) and the results are displayed in a table which itself can be edited, saved and printed.

It may be possible when entering data into what appears to be a single form to update multiple related files at the same time. Thus, if a woman changes her name after marriage, this can be effected on all files that use that name. Such sophistication requires good integrity features in the data base system.

Data base management systems will normally allow a number of users and applications to have different views of the data. Users may regard some data as important and ignore others, and restructure the data to reflect the emphasis that they place on it. An accountant may view company data in one way, the sales team in another, the stock

fig 3.15 *QBE example*

DEPARTMENT

NAME	DEPT. NAME	HEAD	STAFF NOS
SMITH	P		

STUDENT

NAME	BALANCE	COURSE	TUTOR
SMITH	P		

RESULT TABLE

NAME	DEPT. NAME	BALANCE	
SMITH	BIOLOGY	£1076	

department in a third way, and top management, interested in the company's five-year plan, in yet another. All these 'views' should be achieved without duplicating data on disk.

Another approach is for packages to include **data modelling** features as well as having an integral data base management facility. In this type of system, when users set up their data model, the users name the files and the system draws boxes around these names. The next step is to show the links between the files (known as entities), and so the data structure is set up. The simple model – usually referred to as an **entity–relationship diagram**, is shown as Figure 3.16. It has three file types and the hierarchy implies that a **COURSE** can *consist of* many **MODULES** and a **LECTURER** can *teach on* a number of **MODULES**. This structure, with files and links between them, is drawn by the user interactively, usually with the aid of a mouse.

Once the structure has been drawn in this manner, the system sets up the file definitions with the help of the user. The file definitions for the three files drawn in Figure 3.16 are defined in Figure 3.17. Complex data relationships between a number of files, found in the real world, can be designed and set up using such a package. It therefore helps the user in the design work which is assumed to have

fig 3.16 *entity-relationship (E–R) diagram*

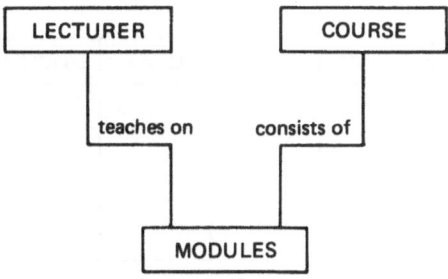

been done, and done well, in most data base systems before beginning to use it.

It is possible to query the data base using various selection criteria such as:

SELECT RECORDS IN MODULE WHERE M-NUMBER IS GREATER THAN 311

An expression can be constructed consisting of a number of Boolean operators for selecting records in a file (for example =, <, > for equals, less than and greater than), and operating on the results (for example +, -, /, >? for plus, minus, divide and maximum of). The expressions can be complex, with logical ANDs and ORs and NOTs. Associations between files are already set up by the system, so it is possible to ask questions such as:

WHAT IS THE LECTURERS DATE OF BIRTH WHO TEACHES MODULE A

or

WHAT COURSE INCLUDES MODULE A

These systems can therefore be used by users and data processing people as a data base design package, data base management package and as a prototyping tool.

Prototypes are developed as trial versions of the system – to test various possibilities – and once the users are satisfied with the design of the prototype system, it could be used as the basis for the mainframe version. Alternatively if the limitations of the microcomputer hardware are not important (in terms of memory size, speed, and a limited multi-user facility) the prototype could 'become' the operational system, when the users are satisfied with the results provided by the prototype (see also section 7.3).

fig 3.17 *file definitions for E–R diagram in fig. 3.17*

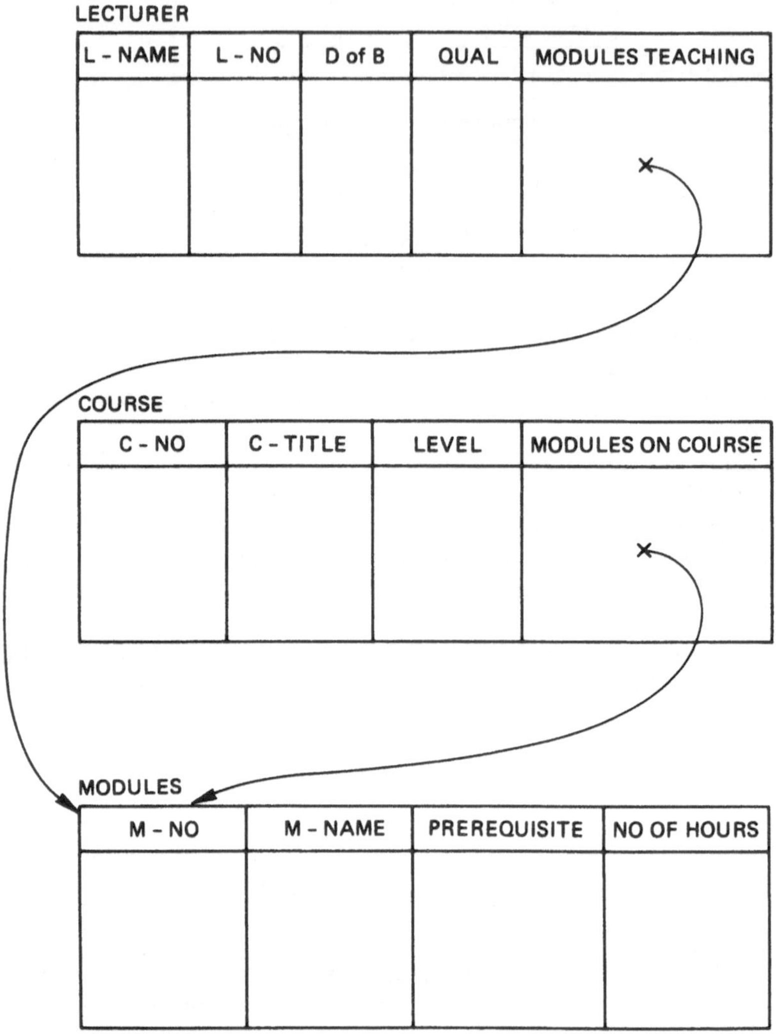

LECTURER

L – NAME	L – NO	D of B	QUAL	MODULES TEACHING

COURSE

C – NO	C – TITLE	LEVEL	MODULES ON COURSE

MODULES

M – NO	M – NAME	PREREQUISITE	NO OF HOURS

3.4 FUNCTIONS OF A DATA BASE SYSTEM

A data base is an organised and integrated collection of data. There needs to be a powerful piece of software which will handle the many accesses to the data base. This software is the data base management system. As we have already seen, some microcomputer systems are file management systems rather than data base systems, but the best systems will help users achieve many of the following:

(a) reduce data duplication and inconsistency and consequently increase its shareability;
(b) increase the integrity of the data;
(c) increase the speed in implementing systems;
(d) provide a management view of the organisation; and
(e) improve the standards and security of the systems developers.

Prospective purchasers of data base systems are advised to look at a number of systems to see how they measure up to these requirements, if possible running some of their own applications.

(a) Reduce data duplication

Organisations have for some time been putting large amounts of data on to their computer systems. Frequently the same data was being collected, validated, stored and accessed separately for a number of purposes by a number of departments. Sometimes the data is collected at different times and validated by different validation routines, and therefore different systems could be inconsistent. This 'data redundancy' is costly and can be avoided, or at least reduced, by the use of a data base. If the data is collected only once, and verified only once, there is little chance of inconsistency.

Businesses using a data base system on a mainframe computer have frequently achieved the aim of reducing data duplication. Data is shared between departments. However, where departments have bought their own microcomputers, the problem of data duplication has frequently increased. This need not be a permanent feature. With the use of personal computers, the sharing of data can be achieved by a multi-user system, a network of microcomputers sharing the data base on a hard disk, or a distributed data base (discussed in section 3.5).

(b) Increase data integrity

In a shared environment, it is crucial for the success of the data base system to control the creation, deletion and update of data and to ensure its correctness. Furthermore, with the possibility of a number of users accessing the data base, there must be some control to prevent failed transactions leaving the data base in an incorrect state. Although these aspects represent challenges, they also represent an opportunity to increase data integrity significantly. As we have already discussed, the data should only be collected once, and therefore it will pay users to ensure the data is as reliable as possible. The software chosen should therefore be able to thoroughly validate all data that is entered into the system.

(c) Increase speed in implementing systems

Systems ought to be implemented in less time, since the data for some applications may already have been collected for another purpose. Accessing the data will also be easier because this will be handled by the data retrieval/query language and the report generating facilities of the package. A lot will depend on the ease with which a particular data base system can be learnt and used.

(d) Provide a management view of the organisation

Many of the applications discussed in this text relate to processing basic data such as sales orders, costs and expenditures . . . the processing of the low level operational data of the firm. This is not an unreasonable emphasis because most microcomputers are used for this type of processing. In many organisations, middle management and top management are not getting the benefits from the expensive computing resource that it has sanctioned.

Managers are now aware of the need for a corporate view of their organisation. Such a view requires data from a number of departments and divisions. With decision-support systems using the data base, it becomes possible for problems previously considered solvable only by intuition and judgement to be solved with an added ingredient, that of information. This will obviously require a powerful package capable of using data from a number of files and providing reports on a regular basis and others of a 'one-off' nature.

The requirements of management in decision-support systems can usefully be summarised in two phrases: *management by exception* and *management by summary*. Most of the detail will not interest the manager, who will be much more concerned about the unusual, for example parts that are not available, or customers in bad debt. Management will also be interested in the overall results, to check that policy is being followed. Many data base systems now available on micros have the facilities to provide these types of information, so that management may make better decisions armed with better information.

(e) Improve standards and security

With many data base systems on microcomputers, it is possible to impose standards for file access and update and to impose good privacy and security features. Improved standards may well prove to be the greatest benefit to the organisation of using data base systems.

These standards include routines to ensure that the data base is never 'lost'. Thus, if disks are destroyed, there should always be available a backup from which the data base in its current state can be recovered. It should not be necessary to backup the whole data base frequently, but there should be a backup of the data base plus a record of changes made since the time of the last complete backup.

Again, there must be proper mechanisms to control access by unauthorised users. These could be looking for confidential business information or seeking confidential information about individuals. On the other hand, they may be 'hackers', very often people who have fun breaking into confidential systems, proving that security systems can be broken. Simple password systems aiming to prevent access into the system are sometimes not good enough for data base systems. There may be a requirement to allow access into a data base, but not a particular file, record, or data item. This requires a degree of sophistication only recently becoming available in microcomputer systems. Some users may be permitted to read a file (look at its contents), but not update it or delete a record. It should be possible to store information about unsuccessful attempts to read data: for example, what the unauthorised user was attempting to read. There is also a range of products which enable the user to hide the contents of a file using encryption techniques. Encryption writes information on a file in code on disk to make it unreadable without the reverse process of decryption.

If there is a great deal of data sharing, then it is usually best to employ one person (or more) to assume the responsibility for ensuring that good standards are devised and followed. This is the role of the **data base administrator (DBA)**. This may become a full time task for one or more people in the organisation. The DBA should be prepared to discuss aspects of data use and storage with managers and user staff. Where data is shared, there may be conflicts and the DBA should help to resolve these by applying a department-wide or even a company-wide perspective, rather than that of one person or power group. The DBA will help train people and help them with technical difficulties. Users will probably be grateful for such help, no matter how 'user friendly' the data base system.

Other aspects of data sharing include the privacy, security and integrity of the data base. The protection of data on the data base is normally the responsibility of the DBA. On liaising with the users, he or she may help them implement privacy locks at the file, record, or item level. This should ensure that the data is not accessed by unauthorised users. The DBA may be regarded as the custodian of personal data, as required by government legislation relating to privacy and data bases.

The DBA may set standards for copying files. Rapid recovery from failure is essential where a number of users need access to the data base. In a very serious situation, such as a fire, hardware and software replacement is usually easy, but it is also necessary to have reliable and up-to-date backup files. A company's data is a major resource and must be protected. For example, if the accounts details were lost, it might be difficult for the business to survive.

A recent problem with regard to security is that of **viruses**. These are programs which attempt to damage other programs or data covertly. A disk coming from another user can contain a virus which will spread through your own disks so that, for example, spurious messages or figures appear on the screen or, at worst, files are lost. A defensive action, but the wrong one, is to attempt to restore from backup files. It is the wrong move because the data on the backup files will also be lost. It is important, therefore, at the first sign of a virus, to run a program which is an antidote to it. A number of programs are available which will detect and eradicate a number of the most common viruses on any particular machine. These programs should be run regularly, as they should detect a virus, even if its existence is not obvious to the user, before it does too much damage.

In fact, files are much more likely to be lost by operator error (such as deleting files by mistake or over-writing them with other information), software errors or unreliable hardware. The policies and procedures set by the DBA, for example in giving users access to only that data necessary to fulfil their jobs, obtaining software only from reputable sources, the full testing of applications software and the regular running of virus protection programs, should prevent loss of data by viruses or any other means.

Although some writers argue that it is the users' job to ensure the accuracy of any data admitted on the data base, and that the DBA's concern lies only with its security, it is advisable that he or she sets standards for data validation which will help to maintain the integrity of the data base. This is reasonable because data created by one user may be used by others. Without the DBA, there will be no incentive, or security net, to ensure that the data is correctly validated.

Much of the information about the data base and the activities of its users will be documented by the DBA. Even though documentation is not a popular task, it is essential that it is done, and that it is done well. It must be up-to-date, so that changes are reflected in the documentation.

Although, therefore, it may well not be necessary to employ programmers and systems analysts in a microcomputer environment, where there is widespread data sharing the role of the DBA is vital. Many small firms have allocated the task to one person on a part-time basis and found that it is necessary to make the role full-time. Where data is shared in a network the role becomes particularly critical.

3.5 DISTRIBUTED DATA BASES

Sometimes shared data can be distributed in a number of locations or a number of machines in the same location. In one arrangement, each computer system stores the data which originates at that location, but the data can be accessed by users at other locations. Thus the data related to the sales office remains in the sales office but can be accessed by others. This means that not only is the data base distributed, but so is the intelligence of the system. The users at different locations are not just terminal users. They have intelligent machines with software to perform general data processing as well as software to access the data base.

With personal computers on most office desks, it seems reasonable to link the 'data base' on each machine so as to avoid duplicating the collection, validation and storage of data. It also avoids the necessity of having to access the corporation mainframe, where such a machine is available. This may be deemed undesirable because of time delays, expense, and the dependence on the data processing department.

In order to ease the possibility of sharing the data, it is preferable for the data base software to be standard, and possibly the microcomputers should be the same model. There also needs to be a reference to which all users can refer. This will contain information regarding the data at each site, how it can be accessed, integrity controls, and who is responsible for giving permission to use the facility. The data base administrator will be the human reference point, and the written directory of information about the data base ('data about data') is normally called the **data dictionary**. Most data base systems will keep the data dictionary up-to-date.

Most application packages will set up and use data provided by the local data base facility. However, there is also a need to access the data bases of other departmental computers through the network. The user will need to have access rights to these other systems. In the

fig 3.18 *distributed data base*

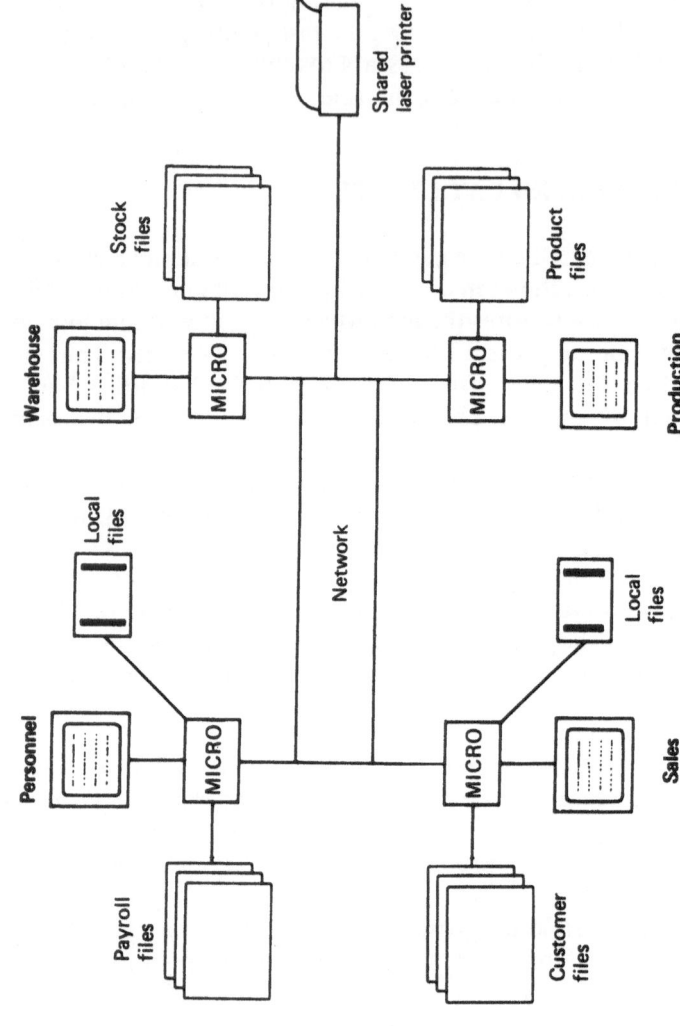

fig 3.19 *central data base*

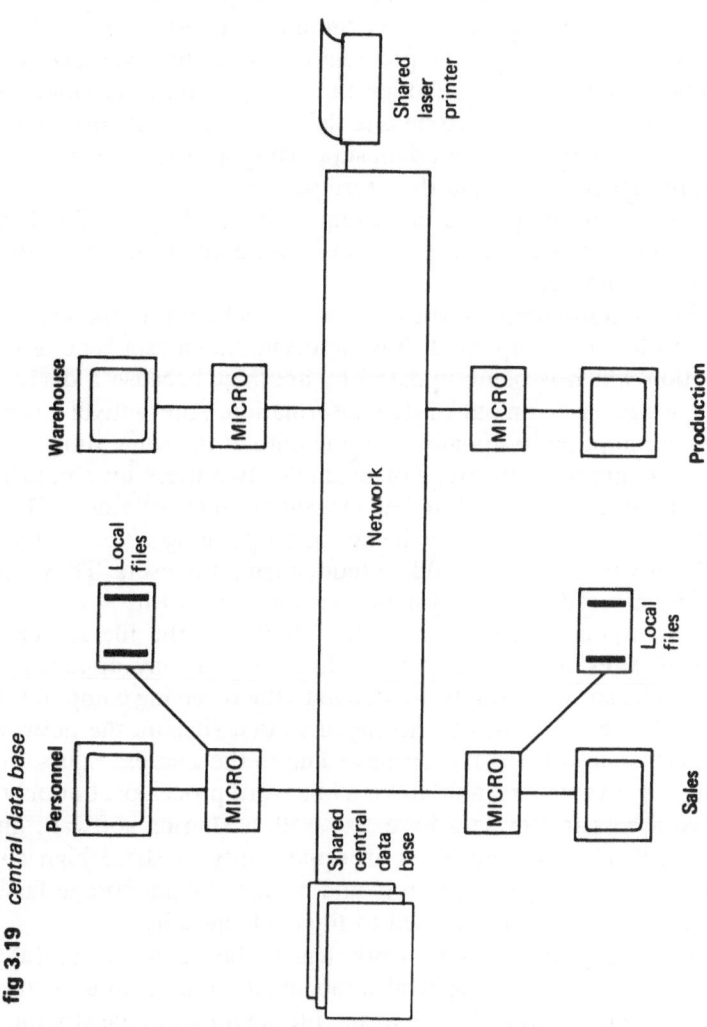

configuration shown in Figure 3.18 there is no notion of a central computer. In an alternative approach, shown as Figure 3.19, a microcomputer with a data base could be part of the network for the use of all users and therefore be seen as a central data base.

Although the basic concepts of a computer network were discussed in the context of mailing in the previous chapter, the advantages of a local area network can accrue at least as much from file sharing. The operating system will have to be one that supports a network, and it will have to be particularly good on supporting security features so as to prevent illegal access, and therefore perhaps a breach of any data protection act or company secrets requirements. It must also have good backup facilities in case one user accidentally destroys data belonging to another.

Another requirement is the ability to lock out users when a particular file is being updated. It is important that a user is not given information which is being updated by another, because a decision could be made based on out-of-date information. Alternatively, users could be attempting to update the same data at the same time. This would cause great confusion. For example, two users may both be attempting to allocate the last few remaining items of stock. These facilities should be provided by the network operating system, but the way it deals with locking should be hidden from the users. They only need to be assured that the system does take care of it.

Another aspect of a network is the ability for the file server to provide all sites on the network with a copy of any applications software. The software will be loaded in to the receiving computer on request. The network may be arranged so that sites on the network can receive application software according to their access rights. For example, all sites may be able to load in a word processor, but only a few have access to the data base. As well as sharing software and data, a network gives the users an opportunity to share high cost components, such as laser printers and powerful data storage facilities. These can therefore be used to their full capacity.

The extra expense of a network has to be assessed carefully. Setting up the network is a specialist job and it requires time spent on writing and extra hardware such as the file server and tape streamer. The latter is used for backup.

If a network is envisaged, its planning ought to start before the computers are purchased, even if the network is not going to be installed for some time. Otherwise there may be compatibility problems later. The data base software ought to be the same for all users and this system should be implementable on the network when it is installed.

SPREADSHEET

AND

FINANCIAL MODELLING

The electronic spreadsheet is said to have sold more microcomputers than any other package and has a wide number of applications. Yet the concept is simple; a spreadsheet is a matrix on which calculations can be performed. Section 4.1 looks at the spreadsheet concept and section 4.2 at the features that might be expected in any spreadsheet package. The next two sections look at how a spreadsheet might be created to represent an application and how to print the results. Section 4.5 discusses problems that are associated with spreadsheets. Their limitations could well be solved by a financial modelling package which originated on large mainframe computers but is now available on some of the larger microcomputers. These are discussed in section 4.6.

4.1 THE SPREADSHEET CONCEPT

Managers may spend 20% or 30% of their time preparing budgets. The traditional method of preparing these is to use a very large spread of paper, known as a spreadsheet or worksheet, which is divided into columns and rows, creating a matrix pattern. An example is shown as Figure 4.1. Here the columns are headed by the months of the year and each row is allocated a particular expenditure type. In the example the expenditure types are salaries, rent, electricity and gas. The rightmost column is used to hold the total for the year of each expenditure type. Thus the total on the salaries row is the sum of the individual months' salaries. At the bottom of each row is the total expenditure for each month. The **cell**, that is a particular row-and-column coincidence, at the bottom right corner, is

fig 4.1 *basic spreadsheet (expenditure for year)*

	J	F	M	A	M	J	J	A	S	O	N	D	TOTAL
Salaries	20	20	20	25	25	30	30	30	30	40	40	40	350
Rent	40			40			40			40			160
Electricity	15				18				4				37
Gas		10			10			15			20		55
Total Expenditure	75	30	20	65	53	30	70	45	34	80	60	40	602

the sum of all the expenditures for all the months. This will be the same as the sum of all the expenditure types.

This particular spreadsheet could be developed to include income as well as expenditure, and therefore to include overall projected profit figures. This is shown as Figure 4.2. The profit figure for each month is calculated by subtracting the expenditure total from the income total. The creation of this type of spreadsheet could be done clerically unless the calculations are complex or the amount of data is large.

Some of the advantages of the computer are apparent even when setting up the spreadsheet, for the calculations can be complex and building a useful model will be time-consuming, but they become much more obvious when changing the contents of part of the spreadsheet. Let us assume that the figures are those projected for next year, and increased fuel costs are announced. Say, for example, the price of gas is raised by 10% and the price of electricity by 12%. This requires the expenditures on gas and electricity to be altered and the total fields to be altered as well. This is a laborious task by hand. Repeated changes become very time-consuming, monotonous, and error-prone. However, these changes are easily carried out by a computer spreadsheet package.

Much of the data of a company is likely to be held on a number of spreadsheets. They are a convenient way of setting up all sorts of charts, records and tables including profit and loss accounts, sales forecasting, budgeting charts, breakeven point analyses, cheque book registers, mortgage repayments, inventory valuation, exchange rate charts – in fact anything with a rows and columns format.

As we have seen, changes may be forced on the manager as circumstances change. But the manager may also want to see what will happen if elements affecting the company change in the future. What will happen if interest rates rise?; if labour costs rise?; if taxes rise?; if the company stops selling one of its range of products?; or if sterling falls against the dollar?

fig 4.2 *basic spreadsheet – expenditure, income and profit for year (created using Microsoft Excel)*

	JAN	FEB	MAR	APR	MAY	JUN	JUL	AUG	SEP	OCT	NOV	DEC	
SALARIES	20	20	20	25	25	30	30	30	30	40	40	40	350
RENT	40			40			40			40			160
ELECTRICITY	15				18				4				37
GAS		10			10			15			20		55
TOTAL EXPENDITURE	75	30	20	65	53	30	70	45	34	80	60	40	602
INCOME A	25	25	25	25	25	25	25	25	25	25	25	25	300
INCOME B	25	25	25	25	25	25	25	25	25	25	25	25	300
INCOME C	10	5	7	9	15	30	1	0	0	0	0	0	77
TOTAL INCOME	60	55	57	59	65	80	51	50	50	50	50	50	677
PROFIT	-15	25	37	-6	12	50	-19	5	16	-30	-10	10	75

It is in answering these **what if?** questions that the computer spreadsheet is particularly valuable. If the user decides to change the contents of one cell, the package will automatically make all the changes necessary to the other cells which are affected by that change. The results will be displayed quickly and accurately. The user may want to specify other 'what if' questions as a response to the first change. Again, this is easily accommodated by a computer spreadsheet. The user can therefore see the degree of sensitivity of the model to changes in one or more variables and is not restrained in experimenting by having to do the calculations by hand.

Such a complex series of changes could not be carried out by clerical means. People would be spending all their time on making calculations. Traditionally the effects of possible changes were guessed at, or only one or two tested. Alternatively, the task was given to specialists, typically in the firm's operations research department, or given to systems analysts to design a computer system. This had two main problems. First, it would take time to develop the system and to receive the results. The second problem was that the requirements had to be predicted. With computer spreadsheet packages, the managers carry out the research and see for themselves the effects of any change that they might make or which might be forced on them. They are not likely to be inhibited from trying a number of alternative solutions to a particular problem.

The paper spreadsheets could be very large, but computer spreadsheets are capable of being much larger. A typical spreadsheet package has a maximum of 16 384 rows and 256 columns, which is over 4 million cells in total. Many are much larger than that, so that capacities of many millions of cells are common in business spreadsheet packages.

Obviously a very large spreadsheet cannot be held in the main memory of a 512k or one megabyte computer. It may be possible to purchase memory boards which will extend the main memory of a computer to four megabytes or more. Alternatively, some packages will hold part of a large spreadsheet in memory while the rest of it is stored on disk. This is using virtual memory, a concept discussed in the previous chapter. This will slow down processing if the part of the spreadsheet needed is not currently in memory, since chunks of the spreadsheet will have to be swapped in and out of the computer memory. This process is handled automatically, but memory speeds are much greater than disk speeds.

Unless the spreadsheet is very small indeed, the whole spreadsheet cannot be displayed on the screen at any one time. The standard screen is 80 characters wide. If each cell is, say, 8 characters across, then only 10 columns can be displayed on the screen. The screen will therefore show only the few rows and columns that are of particular interest at any one time. The section it displays can be changed conveniently. The screen acts as a magnifying glass does when it is moved around a newspaper which is being read by a long-sighted reader. The reader knows that the rest of the page exists, even though only that part under the magnifying glass can be read at any one time. The screen is a **window** of the spreadsheet as shown in Figure 4.3.

fig 4.3 *VDU screen as window on spreadsheet*

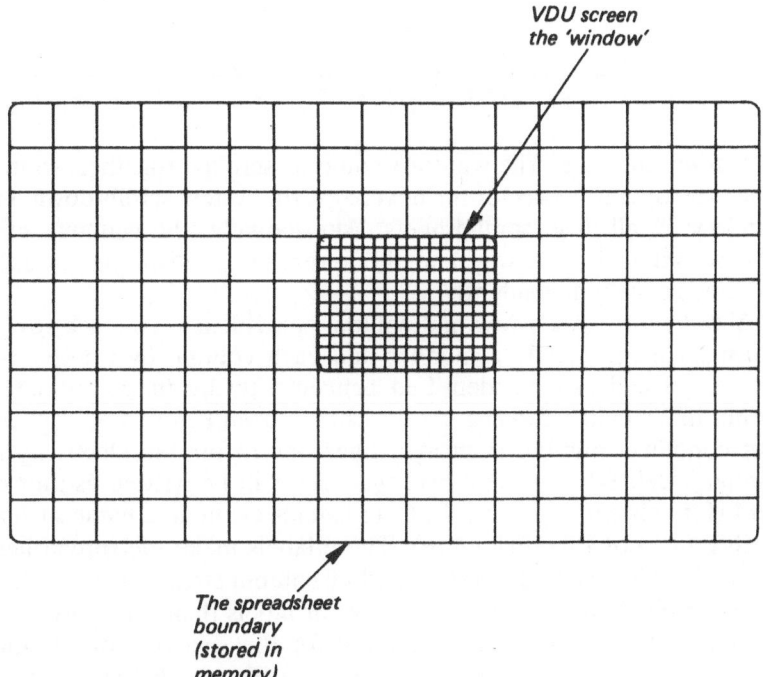

VDU screen the 'window'

The spreadsheet boundary (stored in memory)

Some packages will allow users to display many windows, each from a different spreadsheet. The idea is similar to that described in Chapter 2 where we discussed word processing systems which were capable of handling a number of windows, each displaying text from a different text file (see Figure 2.9). In the same way, each window can hold a separate spreadsheet for comparative purposes. Figure 4.4 shows two windows each showing the same type of spreadsheet for

fig 4.4 *two windows*

	JAN	FEB	MAR	APR	MAY			JAN	FEB	MAR	APR	MAY
SAL	10	10	10	10	10		SAL	12	12	12	12	12
RENT	5						RENT	8				
GAS		3			3		GAS		3			5
ELEC		4			4		ELEC		4			6
RATES	10						RATES	11				
WATER	1						WATER	1				

two different years. The windows could be scrolled together, so that when the operator asks for the next page, the system scrolls down one window on all 'live' spreadsheets. Alternatively, the windows may not be linked in this way and the spreadsheets displayed in each window move independently.

A cell represents a row and column coincidence. As each row is normally identified by a number and each column by a letter (or letters), a cell can be identified conveniently by its co-ordinates, rather like a map reference. As we can see from Figure 4.5, each cell can contain a number such as a figure of 15 for the electricity in January (cell B4). In some packages 'B4' will be written as r4c2 or c2r4 (for column 2 and row 4). Cells can also contain a name such as RENT (A3) or PROFIT (A10). These labels make the spreadsheet readable. Most spreadsheets will allow column sizes to vary so that, for example, cell width can be larger for labels than for figures.

Cell widths can usually be ignored for the specification of titles which could go across a number of cells (see Figure 4.6). The package will facilitate this by having a 'title' option. The titles can be **protected** so that they do not get overwritten later by mistake. The *default* cell width is likely to be around eight characters. Like other types of package, the default values should represent the value required by most users, but they should be capable of being changed easily, either for a particular occurrence, or globally, that is, throughout the spreadsheet.

Figure 4.6 also shows the **status line** and the **option line**. The status line will give the user information such as the present position of the

fig 4.5 *row and column references*

	A	B	C	D	E	F	G	H	I	J	K	L	M	N	O	P	Q
		Jan	Feb	Mar	Apr	May	Jun	Jul	Aug	Sep	Oct	Nov	Dec	Tot			
1	Month																
2	Salary	20	20	20	25	25	30	30	30	30	40	40	40	350			
3	Rent	40			40			40			40			160			
4	Electricity	15				18				4				37			
5	Gas		10			10			15			20		55			
6	Total expenditure	75	30	20	65	53	30	70	45	34	80	60	40	602			
7	Income A	25	25	25	25	25	25	25	25	25	25	25	25	300			
8	Income B	25	25	25	25	25	25	25	25	25	25	25	25	300			
9	Income C	10	5	7	9	15	30	1	0	0	0	0	0	77			
10	Profit	-15	25	37	-6	12	50	-19	5	16	-30	-10	10	75			

Row (numbers)

Column (letters)

Spreadsheet window

VDU screen

Cell p5 (or r5c16 or c16r5)

fig 4.6 *options and status line*

Option line

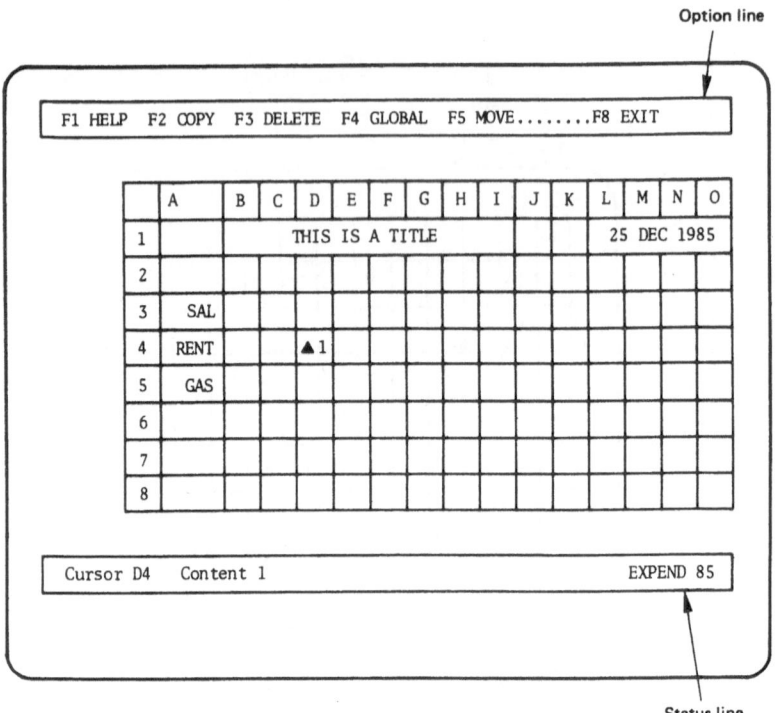

F1 HELP F2 COPY F3 DELETE F4 GLOBAL F5 MOVE........F8 EXIT

	A	B	C	D	E	F	G	H	I	J	K	L	M	N	O
1				THIS IS A TITLE								25 DEC 1985			
2															
3	SAL														
4	RENT			▲ 1											
5	GAS														
6															
7															
8															

Cursor D4   Content 1   EXPEND 85

Status line

cursor in terms of a row and column number, the present contents of that cell, and the name of the spreadsheet. The option line contains a list of the command options open to the user. Some packages combine these in one line or two at the bottom of the display. Others display the options open to the user only at the time that the user presses the *help* function key.

Figure 4.7 shows the spreadsheet (sometimes called a worksheet) and menu style of the Lotus 1-2-3 package. At the top left-hand corner is the cell where the cursor is positioned (A1). The column letters and row numbers are marked in inverse video for ease of reference. There are seventeen options on this first level spreadsheet menu. Figure 4.8 shows the screen with three spreadsheet windows.

Most packages will also allow the user to add and remove columns and rows so that, for example, a new row can be squeezed in or an old one deleted easily. This could be very useful if, for example, a user creating a daily expenditure spreadsheet has forgotten that the year

fig 4.7 *Lotus 1–2–3 spreadsheet layout and menu*
Source: Lotus Development (UK) Limited

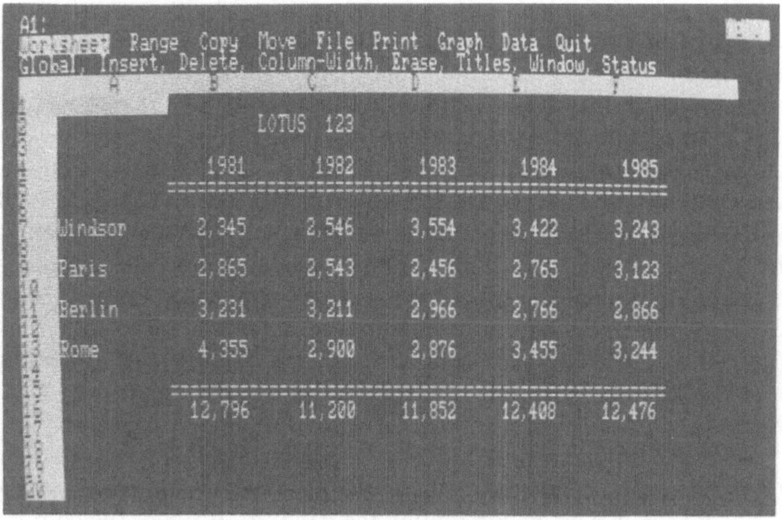

fig 4.8 *Lotus 1–2–3 spreadsheet with three windows*
Source: Lotus Development (UK) Limited

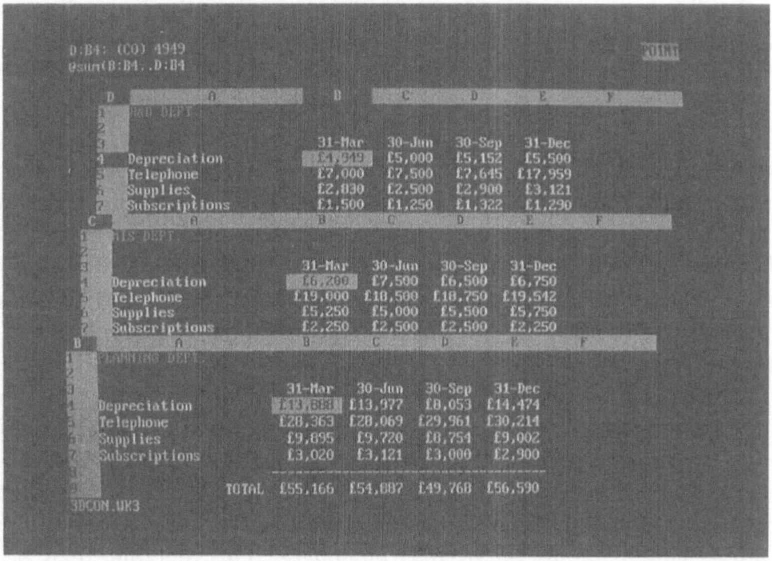

happens to be a leap year and February has 29 days, or that a product is no longer stocked and need not be included in the spreadsheet.

The contents of a cell can also be specified by a formula. This facility gives the electronic spreadsheet the ability to reflect the effects of one change on the rest of the spreadsheet. Referring again to Figure 4.5, although the total expenditure for January (**B6**) contains 75, in fact it is specified by the formula **B2+B3+B4+B5** and the package derives the contents from the formula. If the user changes the contents of **B3** from 40 to 50, the contents of **B6** will automatically be changed from 75 to 85 and the contents of other cells will also be updated where they are affected. **B10** will be changed from -15 to -25 and **N10** from 75 to 65. When defining the contents of a cell as a formula, the contents of any cell referenced in the formula could also be derived by a formula, though never a name or other text (which would not make sense). Thus profit (**B10**) will have the formula (**B7+B8+B9−B6**). As we have seen, **B6** itself contains a formula.

When setting up a spreadsheet, the replication feature saves much laborious work. The **replicate** command avoids writing the formula **C7+C8+C9−C6** when completing the cell **C10**. Instead, the contents of this can be replicated relatively from **B10**, so that it adds **C7** (not **B7**) and **C8** (not **B8**) and **C9** (not **B9**) and deletes **C6** (not **B6**) to arrive at **C10**. Replication uses **relative** referencing: whereas an absolute reference refers to a specified cell location, relative referencing refers to a cell location relative to another (r1c1 refers to the first cell on the spreadsheet whereas relative r1c1 refers to the cell 1 row down and 1 column to the right from the present position (the conventions change according to the particular spreadsheet package).

This feature was used extensively in the drawing up of the spreadsheet in Figure 4.5. For example, the total profits for all the individual months can be replicated from **B10** in this way. A salary increase could be reflected in the monthly salaries figure from January to December, and again on the total expenditure figures across the board. As we shall see, by defining an area for replication, it is possible to replicate a series of rows and columns elsewhere in the spreadsheet.

Operations are frequently carried out on *areas* or blocks. This process has already been mentioned in the context of word processing. It refers to the dividing of the text, or spreadsheet *file* into a section or sections. As shown in figure 4.9, areas in the spreadsheet context can be a set of rows and columns, forming a rectangular shape, which are to be treated *en masse*. The rectangle can be a

fig 4.9 *valid and invalid area definition*

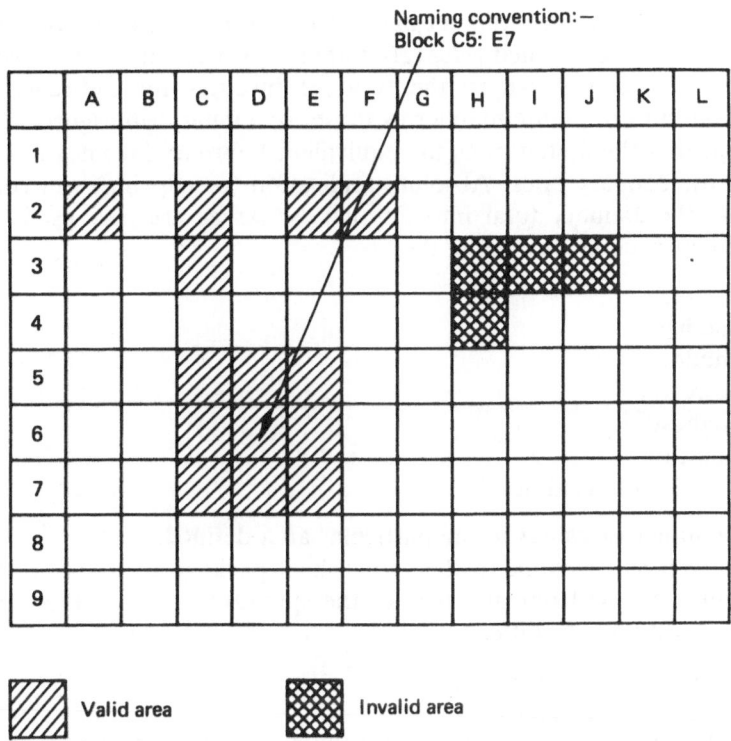

Naming convention:−
Block C5: E7

Valid area   Invalid area

number of rows and columns, one column and a number of rows (or vice versa) or one column and one row (in other words, one cell).

As can be seen in the figure, blocks are defined by the boundaries of the top left cell and bottom right cell (for example, **C5:E7**). If the user wants to add up a column, this can be achieved by the formula (A1+A2+A3+A4+A5+A6), but the area can be defined as (A1:A6) and, by using a SUM statement, have a formula SUM(A1:A6). On many systems the area (or block) can be defined by **marking** it. This is achieved by putting a mark at the beginning and end of the area, operating on it then or naming it for future reference. Some spreadsheet packages support different colours on the screen so that it is possible to **paint** areas of the spreadsheet, where different colour text could have different meanings. For instance, automatically calculated totals could be placed in a different colour from data which is entered by the user. This is obviously useful for highlighting areas of the spreadsheet(s).

Having defined the area, it can be used for replication and copying. The area can be copied *relatively* rather than absolutely. A typical example is shown where the total of incomes for February is calculated in the same manner as those for January (in Figure 4.5), except that the system uses the equivalent February incomes rather than the January ones. Absolute replication (or copying) will copy across the January total into February's. Areas are also used for functions such as evaluating the

(a) mean;
(b) median;
(c) mode;
(d) lowest;
(e) highest;
(f) sum; or
(g) standard deviation

of a number of values in the particular area defined.

As well as functions in the spreadsheet package to facilitate the copying of cells from one part of the spreadsheet to another, the system will have facilities to:

(a) blank off cells or areas;
(b) delete cells or areas;
(c) edit a formula or text to correct them without rewriting the cell;
(d) format, to change the column width;
(e) move, to move the contents of a cell;
(f) insert a row or column (shifting others as necessary);
(g) locate a particular value in a cell; and
(h) lock or protect cells to prevent their accidental deletion.

4.2 FEATURES OF SPREADSHEET PACKAGES

The first section discussed the features available in all spreadsheet packages. Of course, packages will differ according to ease of use, speed of operation, quality of documentation, on-line 'help' facilities, the operating systems and computers that can run them, memory required, and so on. These aspects, discussed in earlier chapters, are important when choosing any package and are equally important in choosing spreadsheet packages. Some packages have tutorial disks so that the user can set up and change an example spreadsheet and this helps ease of learning, as it does any type of package. In this section we discuss the differences between spreadsheet packages which are particularly important for this application.

(a) Size

The size, in terms of the number of columns and rows, varies greatly between packages. The early systems were typically capable of holding 16 000 cells, eight characters wide. These systems were run on computers with 32k to 64k memory, with floppy disk storage. With 512k memory being normal, and much larger memories available, and hard discs with 20 or more megabytes of storage, a much larger spreadsheet size, frequently many millions of cells, is possible. Potential users should be aware of the difference between the theoretical maximum of the spreadsheet which is quoted in the 'glossies', and the actual maximum of filled cells available before running out of memory. The difference is caused by some packages using up memory of the computer for cells which are blank, which is obviously a waste of memory.

(b) Windowing facilities

Windowing facilities will also be enhanced if the system is designed for a large memory. Many users will want to display separate parts of the same spreadsheet or two or three different spreadsheets on the VDU at the same time. This enables spreadsheets to be compared. For example, the user may wish to work on spreadsheets containing the trading figures for the last three years along with the projected ones for the next year and a summary sheet for the last three years. This will require five windows and this is possible in some packages. This amount of windowing *can* be confusing to the user.

An advanced feature of some packages is the ability to change one of these detail spreadsheets and *automatically* alter the summary spreadsheet accordingly.

Alternatively the different windows may contain the results of different 'what if' questions for a particular spreadsheet, which is obviously useful for comparative purposes.

Another feature available in some systems is the ability to *join* spreadsheets or to form a spreadsheet from two others where they *intersect*, that is, contain similar cells. These operations are similar to those available on many file management systems. The process of merging spreadsheets is frequently referred to as **consolidation**.

(c) Manual option facilities

These enable users to switch off automatic calculation whilst entering data. It is useful where the spreadsheet is a large one and there is a lot of data to be entered. Calculating the implications of each item of data entered will slow the process of data entry, and cause irritating pauses, and it is usually better to wait until all the data has been entered before switching the system back to automatic mode. In some systems part of the spreadsheet can reside in disk if main memory is full. Calculation can be particularly slow in these systems because disk accessing speeds are much slower than memory addressing.

(d) Validating routines

Routines are available on some spreadsheet packages, which also helps data entry to the spreadsheet. This data validation is usually fairly rudimentary, such as ensuring that no alphabetic data is entered for a range of cells defined as numeric. However, some spreadsheet packages may be quite sophisticated in this way and have the kind of validation routines available in file management packages (discussed in section 3.2).

(e) Protecting

Protecting a range of cells may also avoid errors on data entry. This is sometimes also called locking or holding, and it prevents the contents of a cell or an area of cells being overwritten by new data. Titles and cells containing formulas are often automatically locked by users once they are satisfied that their contents are accurate. These cells then become read-only unless they are unlocked. It will still be possible to copy from the cells but not into them. Obviously the facility to unlock cells is important as well.

It may also be possible to hide columns and cells. This is similar to the security measures available in file management systems. To protect individuals' privacy or business secrets, some cells or areas are not displayed to users who cannot provide the appropriate passwords to gain access to them.

(f) Rounding

The rounding of numeric fields will normally be carried out by packages, so that an item of data entered as 3.67 is rounded up to 4 on the cell itself. Most systems, whilst displaying '4', will actually hold the more accurate 3.67 in memory, and it is this more accurate figure which is used in calculations. This can look odd, where two columns, say 3.67 (displayed as 4) and 3.62 (displayed as 4) are added up and the total is displayed as 7 (3.67 and 3.62 will be rounded down to 7).

(g) Cell display

Alternative cell displays, such as retaining the decimal point, can be used to avoid the possibility of the *apparent* rounding errors discussed above. Cells containing numbers are usually right justified and those containing names are usually left justified, although these defaults can normally be altered conveniently. Most packages will also have the option of centring on a cell. Other display alternatives include *percentages, scientific notation,* or *currency symbols.*

(h) Sorting

The sorting of rows and columns is facilitated on most spreadsheet packages, although this may be limited to a single row or column. This limitation may be overcome by carrying out a number of sorts, one after the other, but this is obviously rather tedious.

Although the sort 'key' will be a single row or column, it is important to encompass the whole spreadsheet (or the relevant part) in the sort. In Figure 4.10 (a), the total sales of the four salesmen (B5:B8) needs to be sorted, but the whole area of (A5:B8) is marked, otherwise the results will be as Figure 4.10 (b) which is incorrect, and not Figure 4.10 (c) which is the correct version.

(i) Graphic display

Graphic display facilities which are available on some packages permit the display (and printing) of the spreadsheet graphically. These facilities may be fairly rudimentary, for example, many packages will display a set of numeric values as a bar graph (as shown in Figure 4.11). It may be necessary to widen columns to hold these charts. Alternatively the figures may be scaled up or down as appropriate. For example, one asterisk could represent the number 10, two asterisks the number 20, and so on.

The more advanced graphics such as pie graphs, bar graphs, and area graphs, displayed in a number of colours, which are discussed in Chapter 5, may be available on some spreadsheet packages and in integrated packages, containing a spreadsheet. As can be seen in Figures 4.12 and 4.13, these can be very impressive (unfortunately the colour effect cannot be reproduced here). These are discussed further in Chapter 7. In any case, most spreadsheet packages will produce files which are capable of being read by other packages and make use of their graphics capabilities.

fig 4.10 *sorting spreadsheets*

	A	B
1	TOTAL SALES OF SALESMEN	
2		
3	NAME	TOTAL SALES
4		
5	HENRY	561
6	BILL	306
7	JIM	411
8	DAVE	303

(a) Original

	A	B
1	TOTAL SALES OF SALESMEN	
2		
3	NAME	TOTAL SALES
4		
5	HENRY	561
6	BILL	411
7	JIM	306
8	DAVE	303

(b) Incorrect sort (B5:B8)

	A	B
1	TOTAL SALES OF SALESMEN	
2		
3	NAME	TOTAL SALES
4		
5	HENRY	561
6	JIM	411
7	BILL	306
8	DAVE	303

(c) Correct sort (A5:B8)

fig 4.11 *basic graphics facilities*

```
                    SALES £,000s
        NAME      AMOUNT
        DAVE        7      * * * * * * *
        BILL       10      * * * * * * * * * *
        TOM         1      *
        DICK        4      * * * *
        BOB         6      * * * * * *
        HARRY       3      * * *
```

(j) Operators

The range of operators provided by many systems for devising formulas can obviously contain symbols for addition, subtraction, division, multiplication, and exponential. Many systems also provide *logical operators*, so that the user can set up cells with conditional statements (being true or false). For example, using an **IF** statement, if the contents of one cell is a positive number then the contents of another cell may be **PROFIT**, and if a negative number (or the previous statement is false), then the contents of that cell is **LOSS**. The logical operators:

   (*i*) greater than;
   (*ii*) less than;
  (*iii*) equal to;
  (*iv*) not equal to;
   (*v*) greater than or equal to;
  (*vi*) less than or equal to

may be provided, along with **AND** and **OR** which facilitate combining the logical operators. These operators could be used to calculate the bonuses of staff. For example, if sales targets are met, then bonus is 5%, if sales targets are doubled, then the bonus cell contains 10%, and so on.

(k) Functions

Functions can also be used when defining a cell. These functions can usually be applied to a number or a formula. Such functions available in many systems include:

fig 4.12 *Lotus 1–2–3 bar graph formed from spreadsheet*
   Source: Lotus Development (UK) Limited

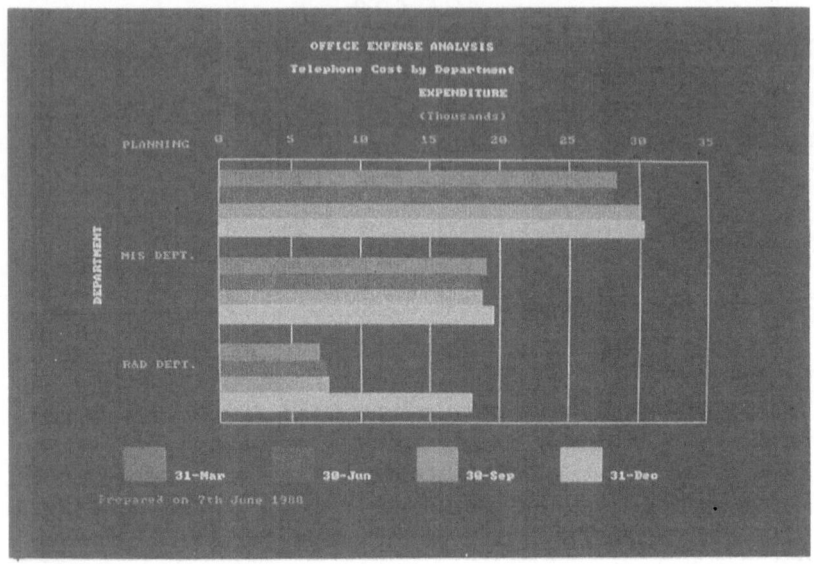

fig 4.13 *Lotus 1–2–3 spreadsheet and associated graphical display*
   Source: Lotus Development (UK) Ltd

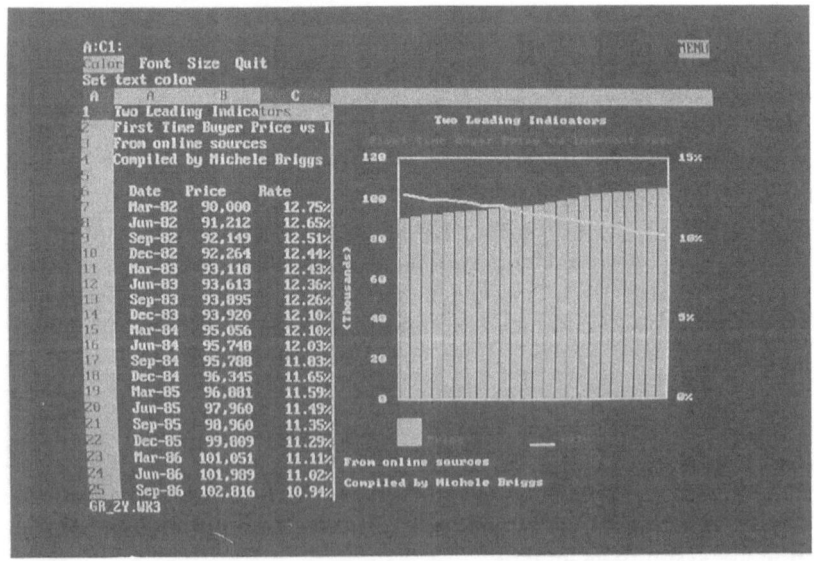

Absolute value
Average value of an area of cells
Average value of an area of non-zero cells
Cosine
Count (the number of values in a range)
Depreciation (allowing for the decreasing value of an asset)
Exponential
Future value (calculating how much money today will be worth in
the future at a given rate of compound interest)
Internal rate of return (the interest rate of cash received as return
on investments, used to compare investment decisions)
Logarithm
Lookup (where the system locates that value in the column to the
right or row below nearest to a given value)
Maximum value in an area
Minimum value in an area
Net present value (of an amount – future income, for example – at
a specified rate of interest)
Number of entries (in a given range of values)
Pi (which returns a decimal approximation of pi to, say, 16
significant digits)
Sine
Standard deviation (of cell values in an area)
Sum (of the cell values in an area)
Square root
Tangent
Variance

A typical spreadsheet has 144 functions built-in, and others could be
added by creating user-defined macros. It may be possible to extend
this range with user-defined functions. These can be held in a *library*
and called in when required.

(l) Logical statements
These can be made by using the operators and functions, such as:

> IF r5c8 GREATER THAN r8c8
> THEN r9c8 EQUALS r5c8
> ELSE r9c8 EQUALS r8c8

A further sophistication available in the more powerful spreadsheet
packages is the ability to refer to **external spreadsheets** by name. Say

there are external spreadsheets called **INCOME** and **SALES**, then the following adaptation of the above formula is possible:

IF INCOME.r5c8 GREATER THAN SALES.r8c8
THEN r9c8 EQUALS INCOME.r8c8
ELSE r9c8 EQUALS SALES.r8c8

If the user had used labels instead of row and columns to identify cells, then these statements become 'English-like'.

Of the functions in (k) above, the lookup function is particularly interesting because, whereas the others require calculation relating to a value or a set of values, lookup implies some **goal seeking**, a function required frequently by managers as they look for a best fit or in order to be able to form a good fit through a series of iterations.

Whereas the lookup function is seeking a 'best fit', the process of goal seeking can describe the more complex process by which the user may set a goal to one value and the system alters other dependent variables until this goal is met. In other words, the user sees the value of a variable that will produce a particular desired effect. For example, let us say that the user wants to achieve a goal, such as a particular sales turnover figure. The user may then set in motion a process of modifying other variables such as advertising and personnel costs until the turnover goal has been reached.

'What if?' analysis is somewhat different from goal seeking. It begins with a strategy to see what would happen: goal seeking begins with a desired result and analyses how to get there. The more complex goal seeking calculations are usually in the realm of the financial modelling packages rather than the spreadsheet (see section 4.6). Spreadsheets are frequently referred to as **decision-support** systems, but it is only when given the power of goal seeking that the term is really merited.

4.3 CREATING THE SPREADSHEET

On calling the spreadsheet package, the system will usually ask the user whether to call in a blank spreadsheet or one from file. The blank spreadsheet might be headed by the columns **A** to **Z**, **AA** to **ZZ**, and **AAA** to **ZZZ**, depending on the number of columns permitted, and the rows from 1 to 256, or greater, again depending on the maximum size of the spreadsheet. These column and row numbers can be deleted ready for printing, but they are useful while working on the spreadsheet. The user is also likely to put a meaningful title to the spreadsheet and to put headings to the columns and rows. Usually only about 8 columns and 20 rows are displayed on the screen. The cursor will point to the first cell (A1) and will be moved to change the **active** or current cell.

The titles and headings can be **fixed** on the screen so that they appear on the VDU screen no matter on which part of the spreadsheet the user is working. This is not to be confused with 'locking'. The latter stops the contents of cells being overwritten.

The user may complete the cell with a number, text, or formula and move the cursor to the next cell. Movements to cells are usually made by using the arrow keys on the keyboard. Larger movements can be made by, for example

(a) an arrow key plus shift; or
(b) control and another key,

but the actual method will depend on the particular spreadsheet package used.

Most packages will also allow control to pass to the:

(a) first (top left) or
(b) last (bottom right) cell in the window (one VDU page)

and

(c) first (top left) or
(d) last (bottom right) cell of the overall spreadsheet,

and the system may allow the user to:

(e) scroll (move) one window left, right, up and down; or
(f) go to the first or
(g) last cell in a row or column.

A final way of moving the cursor is through the **GOTO** command or its equivalent, for example:

GOTO AD12 (or r28c12)

or to a named cell, such as:

GOTO TOTAL

and the cursor will move to that cell. This internal *name* for a cell should not be confused with the text in a cell, which represents the contents of a cell. The name can be used as a reference instead of a row and column number. It may be possible to request the system to display these names (or the formulas) on the screen as a separate window on the screen and to scroll these independently.

Another way of making reference to cells is relative to the present cursor position, or another named cell, and some systems allow the user to search for cells based on the user's own logical criteria, such as

GO TO NEXT CELL WITH CONTENTS GREATER THAN 34564.

As well as giving the user the opportunity to complete the cell, the system will also enable the user to correct or change the contents of cells. Sometimes the easiest way is to delete the old contents and replace them with new. Alternatively, **editing** facilities will be provided which permit the changing of part of the contents. This will be particularly valuable where the content is a long formula or conditional statement.

As well as giving users the opportunity to copy the contents of cells elsewhere, the facility will exist to move the contents of a cell, leaving the original cell blank. As we have seen, operations are frequently carried out on *areas* or blocks, and this can be used as the basis for replication and copying.

We have discussed the use of the arrow keys on the keyboard for spreadsheet applications. The function keys may also be used by the package. They may well be used to specify the commands, rather than having to type out the full command name, as well as getting on-line help or leaving the system.

4.4 PRINTING AND SAVING THE SPREADSHEET

Printing is usually a simple task in most spreadsheet packages and can be invoked by a print command, perhaps one of the function keys. However if the spreadsheet has, for example, 500 columns, it will be impossible to print it off in one piece of paper. For that reason the printing routines may also make use of the *area* concept. Before printing, the user defines a block to be printed. It may be necessary to print off a number of areas and use adhesive tape to form the large printed spreadsheet. Some systems will automatically print off one section per page without the user having to specify the areas separately.

In Figure 4.1 the spreadsheet rows and columns numbering system has been deleted before printing. This is achieved by one command in most packages or a switch (on or off). They have been retained in Figure 4.5 although they would not normally be retained.

Some systems offer printer options such as boldface, underline and italic: features which are standard with word processing packages. Similarly spooling facilities may be available so that a print file is created, and then printed out whilst another spreadsheet is being created or updated.

For users who tend to use spreadsheets regularly, the purchase of a printer which can handle large paper widths may be appropriate. Printers designed for word processing applications may only facilitate 80 or 110 column paper. Some printers have a carriage that can accommodate 132 columns or more and these may be a useful purchase when used for spreadsheet applications. Another possible answer to the problem is to use a printer which can print in compressed type, so that, for example, 230 columns can be printed in a '132 column' printer.

Many systems have *sorting* facilities so that partial or entire rows and columns of text or numbers can be sorted before printing. The names of salesmen (headings on the spreadsheet) or their sales figures could be used as *keys* for sorting purposes. They can be sorted in ascending or descending order, ready for printing. Figure 4.10 showed a small spreadsheet before (a) and after (c) sorting on total sales.

Filing, or *saving*, the spreadsheet is also usually a simple matter. Again it is usually possible to save part of the spreadsheet by defining an area of the spreadsheet to be saved. The file can be retrieved at a later time or day by using the same name as that under which it has been filed. As for any other file, it should be backed up on another disk to protect against loss.

4.5. PROBLEMS WITH SPREADSHEETS

There are a number of potential problem areas with the use of spreadsheets. Two obvious 'traps' are rounding and truncation. Rounding may not matter where 60p has been rounded up to the nearest pound, but it does matter where £5560 has been rounded up to £6000. Truncation errors can be avoided by increasing the column width. The problem is that computer printout often looks 'official' and people take it for granted that it is correct. Truncation could lead to a completely incorrect spreadsheet, which is assumed to be correct, and important decisions could be made on the basis of this incorrect 'information'.

As with any other application discussed in this text, spreadsheets must be checked thoroughly. This will require a detailed knowledge of the problem area so that the model does reflect the real interactions. Such tasks as coding the correct formulas is obviously very important, as one incorrect formula might be reproduced throughout the model.

Further, the live data must be validated. The use of invalid data will also produce incorrect results – 'garbage in, garbage out'. Again, even if only one data element is incorrect, this can have very widespread repercussions elsewhere if it is the basis for a formula or used in replication. Furthermore, one error which has been identified may lead to a complete loss of trust in the whole model.

As with other applications, it is important to keep a copy of a spreadsheet as it is being developed. If there is a disk failure or somebody pulls the electric plug out inadvertently, all the changes made since the last copy was taken will be lost. For this reason it is best to copy the file on to disk at regular intervals.

It is very easy to assume, because a package solution is adopted, that developing the model will be a simple matter. In fact this is often far from the case. Users must familiarise themselves with both the mechanics of the package and the application area, and 'marry' the two. The application may not be a row-and-column type, in which case spreadsheets are unlikely to be appropriate. Spreadsheet packages have many applications so that they are generalised. This means that for any one application, they may be difficult to use.

If a spreadsheet is required for one purpose, say budgeting, it might be possible to purchase a spreadsheet designed specifically for that purpose, which could be much easier to learn to use. On the other hand, application-specific software is likely to be very difficult to adapt for other purposes afterwards.

Another area where choice of software is important is where the user requires special facilities such as graphics output. The most sophisticated graphic output may be available by using an integrated package (see Chapter 7) or by using spreadsheet packages which are designed to communicate with specific graphics packages. Some spreadsheet packages also have a programming language facility which means that users can create their own report formats or menus.

Many users will be tempted to choose packages capable of handling the very largest spreadsheets, and ensure that their computer memory size has been expanded through memory boards to cater for them. But huge spreadsheets may be difficult to use and to interpret, and take a long time to effect calculations and to save. The application may be best expressed as a series of spreadsheets which can be consolidated when required.

4.6 FINANCIAL MODELLING PACKAGES

The distinction between financial modelling packages and spreadsheet packages is often said to be blurred, but there are fundamental differences:

(a) Spreadsheet packages are only as old as microcomputers, indeed they are said to have 'sold' most early microcomputers; financial modelling packages stem from mainframe computer systems and many microcomputer financial modelling packages are based on a mainframe package.

(b) Spreadsheet packages are aimed at users who are not familiar with computers; although financial models could be set up by managers, they are more likely to be set up by, or with the help of, data processing professionals or operations researchers who have been trained in the use of computer systems. The reason stems from the fact that financial modelling is likely to be complex and individualistic, often customised for specific jobs. Spreadsheets are usually general purpose. It is difficult to keep track of complex analysis in spreadsheet programs; financial modellers are designed and tested to perform a particular set of complex routines.

(c) Spreadsheet packages are traditionally aimed at small businesses or departments within larger businesses which require facilities to handle their financial analyses; financial modellers are aimed at large corporate planning departments, and deal with the consolidation of large spreadsheets. Financial modellers can therefore handle very large spreadsheets and can process them relatively quickly, because they run on large powerful machines. Even so, because of the large amounts of data to process, a typical run can take an hour or two.

(d) All spreadsheet packages cater for two dimensions and some are able to cater for three or four; modellers may cater for a larger number of dimensions. Figure 4.14 shows the cost/sales/revenue figures for a number of products, with the month adding the third dimension. A fourth dimension could be added by, say, area or company.

fig 4.14 *three-dimensional spreadsheets*

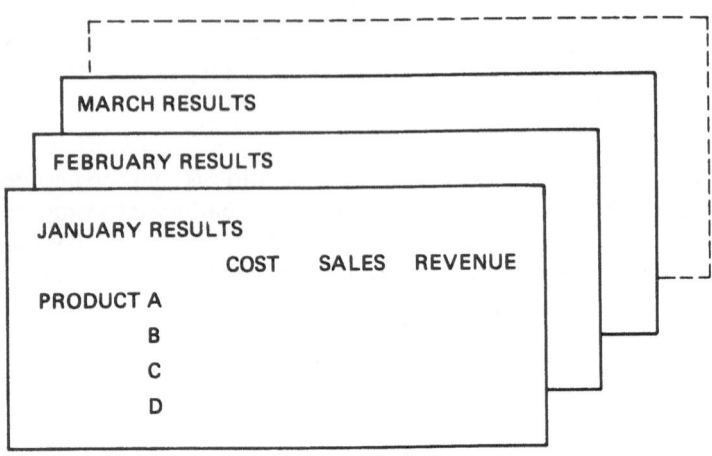

(e) Spreadsheet packages are aimed at users who are not familiar with financial analysis; financial modellers are aimed at professional financial planners who might wish to use the sophistication, complexity and the amount of work that a financial planning package can handle. Thus the goal seeking possibilities and the sheer number of calculations plausible in a modelling package will not usually be feasible in a spreadsheet.

(f) 'What if?' questions can be asked of a spreadsheet package and the results calculated dynamically. The effects of alternative courses of action can be determined immediately and the user informed of the results (**interactive** mode); financial planning systems usually require a complete run through the programs before any results are given (**batch** mode).

(g) Generally, a financial modelling package will keep its data, its logic (the formulas for calculations), and the report specification in different files. The formulas are included in the program run, whereas the formulas in a spreadsheet are held in the cell. Financial modellers can include these formulas in complex arrangements, for example, in a loop which has to be executed a number of times.

By comparison with conventional microcomputer spreadsheet packages, therefore, financial modelling packages require knowledge and experience of both financial applications and computer systems, and need greater time to develop the model, sometimes many man-weeks. Further, they may *seem* slower to execute because they do not calculate results dynamically and handle very large data sets. However, they are usually far more powerful, being able to simulate a very large and complex financial model.

It is therefore difficult for spreadsheet users to migrate to financial planning systems even though their application may need these extra capabilities. Similarly, mainframe users migrating to microcomputer spreadsheet packages may also find the transition difficult because they are so different.

Most financial planning systems require the modeller to know in detail the requirements of a particular application so that the system can be pre-programmed. This allows a very complex set of procedures to be incorporated into the particular run where these are required. The procedures need to be specified in the correct logical order, and the end result will be similar to a computer program in most systems, with line numbers and

IF/THEN/ELSE/
ENDIF REPEAT/UNTIL
ONERROR

and other procedures normally associated with a computer programming language. The particular application run will then go through a **compilation** process. This is a process which gets the program ready for running. If there are statements that the package does not recognise, these compilation errors will be reported so that they can be corrected. Once corrected, the execution of the model and the production of reports, sometimes with graphics, can be done on a regular basis.

The system can then be used to model data presented to it from a separate data file. Unlike spreadsheet programs, the data, the logical rules and the report formats are kept as separate files on disk. The same set of data can therefore be applied to different models, and different sets of data applied to the same model. This means that different interpretations of the business can draw on one file of data, and different files of data can be applied to one interpretation of the business.

The logical rules will refer to meaningful data names, like **PURCHASE PRICE,** so that a formula could be:

PROFIT = SELLING PRICE – PURCHASE PRICE.

The equivalent spreadsheet rule may have to be expressed in a rows-and-columns format, for example:

$$G15 = F15 - B15.$$

Once the financial planning run has been developed to this stage, it could be used by non-experienced people if the analyst has put in simple screen prompts for the user to respond to at appropriate times. But these have to be pre-programmed. Some packages are sold along with a library of pre-programmed applications, and all the users then have to do, assuming the applications follow the expected patterns, is to supply their own data. These models might include:

(a) balance sheet;
(b) lease versus purchase analysis;
(c) mortgage calculation;
(d) breakeven analysis; and
(e) depreciation of assets.

A feature of financial modelling packages, which is not always found in spreadsheets, is the ability to consolidate files or parts of files. Thus the monthly results can be consolidated to form the yearly results at the end of the financial year. Similarly, departmental models may be consolidated to form the corporate model, used for large-scale planning and modelling. Conversely, if the microcomputer is linked to a mainframe, it will be possible for a department to extract that part of the large company spreadsheet relevant to that department. It will also be possible to input that part of the company spreadsheet, relevant to the department, into the mainframe files for organisation-wide analysis.

Another feature of many financial modellers is **goal seeking**, which was mentioned in the context of spreadsheets, but is more general in a financial modelling package. Here, a particular target is specified, and the system can be programmed to inform the user which are the required values that associated variables must achieve to satisfy that goal. It may suggest alternative strategies to achieve the goal. This multi-variable goal seeking facility is rare in spreadsheets.

Spreadsheets and financial modelling packages should not necessarily be seen as competitive products. Spreadsheets are usually best for quick analysis, whereas modelling packages provide greater power and sophistication. In any case, as we saw in the previous chapter when comparing file management and data base packages, the distinction between spreadsheet packages and financial modelling packages is also becoming blurred as the power of the microcomputer increases with larger disk space and memory size and faster processor speed, and the competitive motivation of suppliers leads them to attempt to provide all the facilities that might be required by users.

CHAPTER 5

BUSINESS GRAPHICS

Business graphics systems can be used to convert an indigestible set of facts and figures into a graphical form which can be easily assimilated. This may be a freehand sketch or one of a number of formal graph types. Graphics can be used in a report or in presentations. The media for the former will be the printed page or VDU screen, and the media for presentations might include photographic slides and overhead projector transparencies. An overview of business graphics is given in the first section of this chapter, along with a discussion of the special hardware that might be required. Section 5.2 introduces the formal graph types: bar charts, pie charts and line graphs.

With more people who are not computer professionals using computers, there is a growing need for better human-computer interfaces. The icon interface, or to be more exact, Window, Icon and, depending on the text, either Mouse and Pull-down menu or Menus and Pointers (WIMP) interface, is particularly suited to casual users. The WIMP interface is easy to use and gets rid of much of the computer jargon which is a feature of many operating systems and application packages. This interface, discussed in section 5.3, uses graphics techniques as much as text.

The final section briefly describes a specific technique in graphics, that of computer aided design (CAD). Although this facility is used most in specialised applications such as architecture and engineering, it is used in business applications, such as flowcharting, production routing, and product design. It can also be used as a basic technique for animation, which can help to make presentations more interesting and thereby 'sell' the message better.

5.1 **WORTH A THOUSAND WORDS**

The conversion from statistics to pictures by computer graphics packages is one of the growth areas of microcomputing. Trends or comparisons of predicted and actual results, difficult to see in a set of statistics or computer print-out, can be illustrated quickly using a series of charts. These can be set up side by side. If one way of presentation proves unsatisfactory, an alternative way of displaying the data graphically may prove suitable. Different graphics techniques may be appropriate to each set of data. Different graphics techniques, displaying the same raw data, may also be appropriate for each type of audience as distinct points are highlighted. Alternatively, it may be appropriate to present the same data in a number of ways on the same screen (or page when printed out). In this case, it will probably be necessary to rescale the graphs to fit them on one screen.

Most graphics systems will also have the facility to rotate diagrams through their axis. A chart, such as the frequency histograms shown in figure 5.1, may be rotated by steps that can vary from 90° at worst or by 1° at best. The most sensitive will be required in many computer aided design applications. A 90° rotation will change an upright bar chart (Figure 5.1a) to a sideways one (Figure 5.1b). Graph axes can also be scaled manually or automatically.

In the best graphics work, the quality of the VDU and the printer are particularly important, and the computer memory requirements are large. The VDU screen consists of a collection of horizontal lines called **rasters** and each of these lines is composed of dots called **pixels** which are picture elements. The basic addressable space is an area addressed by the numbers of the raster and the pixel in that line, that is, its x and y co-ordinates. Pictures are created by turning particular pixels on or off. The higher the **resolution** (picture definition), the greater the number of pixels available on the screen. A screen may have a quarter of a million or more pixels.

This requires a large computer memory, for the screen is a display of part of the computer's memory. Further, where colour graphics are involved, each x-y co-ordinate is not only set to on or off, but set to particular colours. Hence colour graphics are very demanding on memory, as well as requiring a more expensive colour monitor. A minimum of 512k memory is normally required for business graphics.

Until recently, the quality of colour monitors available for microcomputers has been rather poor. High resolution colour monitors are now available, and many packages – not only specialist graphics

fig 5.1 *90° rotation of bar chart*

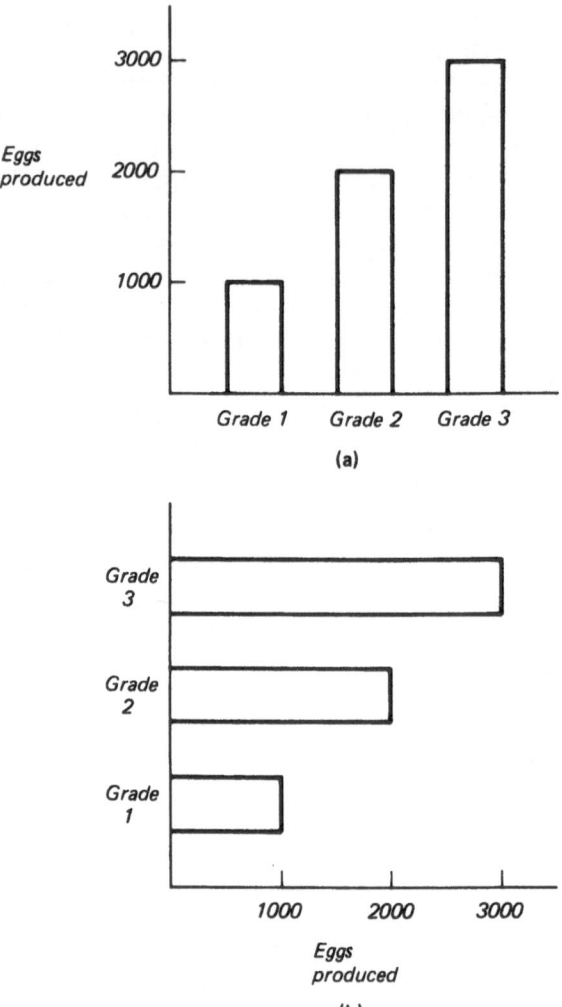

packages – make use of colour. Colour monitors therefore are no longer 'luxuries' and good colour monitors are sometimes essential for graphics work.

A daisy wheel printer is of course unsuitable for graphics work, as it can only print the characters on the daisy wheel. Dot matrix printers can be used to set up the graphics output in the same way that a VDU does, but they print the dots rather than display them.

They can be used for graphics work, although the quality will be less good than that produced by laser printers or graphics **plotters**. Plots are continuous, so that a circle looks like a circle, rather than a series of stepped lines approximating a circle. A plotter is much more suited to graphics work than is a dot matrix printer, and many are capable of printing in a wide variety of colours on paper or on overhead projector transparencies. The results are sharp and clean.

Figure 5.2 shows a typical hardware configuration for graphics work. The histogram which is shown on the VDU is printed out on the plotter (to the right of the photograph). A mouse is often used for drawing and other graphics work, and this is shown in the foreground.

fig 5.2 *HP Vectra Q 5/16 designed for CAD/CAM*
applications with graphics plotter
Source: Hewlett-Packard Limited

Graphics facilities will frequently be used in the production of reports. The writer (or designer) should be aware of the facilities available in the package and the equipment, so that when constructing reports the best use is made of these.

Graphics facilities will also be required in presentations. Conventionally, overhead projector transparencies will be used as the medium for presentations, and many printers and plotters can produce pages of projector transparencies as they can pages of print.

The graphics may be presented using photographic (35mm) slides. The best photographic output requires a camera connected to the system: photographs of VDU screens are not ideal because of glare and the curvature of the screen. Alternatively video tapes can be produced with computer graphics output. The level of graphics required to produce some of these outputs are available on some statistics packages and some integrated packages (see Chapter 7), as well as stand-alone graphics packages.

Whereas bar charts, pie charts and line graphs are ways of presenting numeric data graphically, **presentation graphics** frequently consists of graphic displays of non-numeric data. The subject matter to be displayed may be that relating to selling a product, describing a firm, or relevant to a lecture topic. Presentation graphics concerns the production of slides (either 35 mm or transparencies for overhead projection) allowing text, pictures and graphs, and charts and tables to be displayed, frequently in colour. Many of these slides might include a standard logo or heading. Some packages will enable sets of slides to be produced which are built up in layers so that the user can show how a result is achieved. Other facilities might include speaker notes which are prompts for the speaker and are therefore not displayed. The package may also number the slides automatically.

Another possibility is to use video images. It is possible to connect a video screen directly to the computer and integrate video images with other microcomputer packages. Thus a particular display may contain the sales figures of a leading salesman presented using a graphics package, along with a photograph of the salesman which is captured using a linked video camera. Another use of similar equipment is product information, obtained from a data base system, displayed along with a photograph of the product.

Thus, because applications vary so much, presentation graphics packages may be likened to a 'toolbox' of facilities. The raw data and text used as a basis for each slide may be 'imported' from other packages, such as data base and graphics systems.

Presentation quality is important: to impress and amuse as well as to communicate, and users should be aware that some skill is required to ensure that the facilities are used effectively, that is that the slide says what you want it to say. Some packages do provide sample slides designed by professional artists which can be adapted for particular uses.

Figure 5.3 illustrates further hardware that might be required for presentation graphics, as it is capable of producing high-resolution 35mm slides and prints. The latter may be used in a book or report.

fig 5.3 *typical presentation graphics configuration, including IBM PC computer, Digital Research Presentation Master Application Package, and Polaroid Palette outfit for reproduction of slides*

Source: Digital Research Inc.

Presentation graphics may call for freehand drawings, and many packages allow the user to draw pictures on the screen. By moving a light pen or joystick, or by dragging a mouse, it is possible to make shapes and to alter them. Once the user is satisfied with the drawing, it can be stored on disk and recalled later. To help the artist, a facility normally exists to use a grid on the screen, though it will not be shown on the final version.

We have already described a light pen and mouse when discussing other applications. A joystick is a handle, very like that on an aeroplane, which can be moved left and right and up and down. The cursor on the VDU will move in a similar direction. It therefore serves a similar function to the light pen and mouse, although most people find the mouse the most convenient of these alternatives.

Graphics packages will normally allow the user to change the scale, move, copy or delete part of the drawing. This is achieved by **marking** part of the drawing by enclosing that part in a marking circle. This is similar to the procedure of marking part of a text or spreadsheet for moving, copying or deleting. Once part of the drawing has been marked, its size relative to the rest of the drawing can be changed by using a facility known as **zooming**. It performs the same function as a zoom lens on a camera: to increase or decrease the scale. Parts of the drawing that have been marked may be copied a number of times or moved within the design. Other operators available in these packages include the **smoothing** of lines and circles drawn in rough. By bringing in colours or shades, such systems become very powerful design tools as well as being useful in presentation graphics.

Freehand drawing presents one possibility. At the other extreme, are packages which allow the user to construct a flowchart or other chart from a library of a hundred or more standard symbols which can be brought in 'off the shelf'. These standard symbols are known as **icons**. They can also be created by the user and added to the library. The icons can be drawn in freehand, but are formed more frequently by using the operators provided by the system. These operators will draw regular arcs, arrows, boxes, cylinders, and so on. Each of these can be in different sizes. Different foreground and background colours are also available. Icons, as part of the WIMP interface, are also used in some systems as a way of communicating to users. This topic is developed in section 5.3.

Graphics applications are growing in business microcomputing. They started latest (at the turn of the 1980s) amongst the microcomputer applications discussed in this text. The reason for this late start lies in the complexity and, until recently, expense of providing graphics facilities. These facilities require a great deal of computer memory and, for most applications, an expensive printer and colour monitor. A special graphics card, which is usually necessary to support graphics facilities on microcomputers, represents another 'add on' cost to the buyer. This will be plugged into one of the computer's expansion slots. However, graphics facilities are now within the range of most business microcomputer users, and have become a 'standard' application, as have word processing, spreadsheets and file management, as well as graphics for particular purposes, such as maps for transport companies, and so on.

5.2 THE BASIC CHARTS

Almost all business graphics packages offer three basic ways of presenting numeric data such as distances and sizes graphically. These are bar charts, pie charts and graphs. There are many variations on these basic techniques to 'input numbers and output pictures'. Some of these will be discussed in this section.

Most systems will give the user the possibility of scaling the values so that they more conveniently fit into the limitations of the graphic technique used and the scope of the VDU and printer. In some packages this will be done automatically by the system. There may also be routines in a package which will attempt to layout the graphical output in an aesthetically pleasing way on the VDU or page. Some packages which are available will *choose* the most appropriate graph type for the set of data to be presented. Of course it is possible to override these defaults.

Although graphics systems are designed to produce graphical images, it is important that they are also flexible in their display of text, providing a variety of fonts and font sizes. Text elements of graphs may include main headings, subtitles, the scales along the axes, the names of each axis, or those for labelling.

(a) Bar charts

In a bar chart each bar length relates to the proportional value of that entity. The simplest form of bar chart is a row of parallel bars showing a particular value on one axis (for example, production or sales volumes) and time or category on the other axis. The **frequency histogram** shown in Figure 5.4 is of this type. Here, the vertical axis is used to mark four warehouses, and for each of these four warehouses the horizontal axis shows the frequency in thousands of each of four items of stock.

fig 5.4 *frequency histogram (created using Wing Z)*

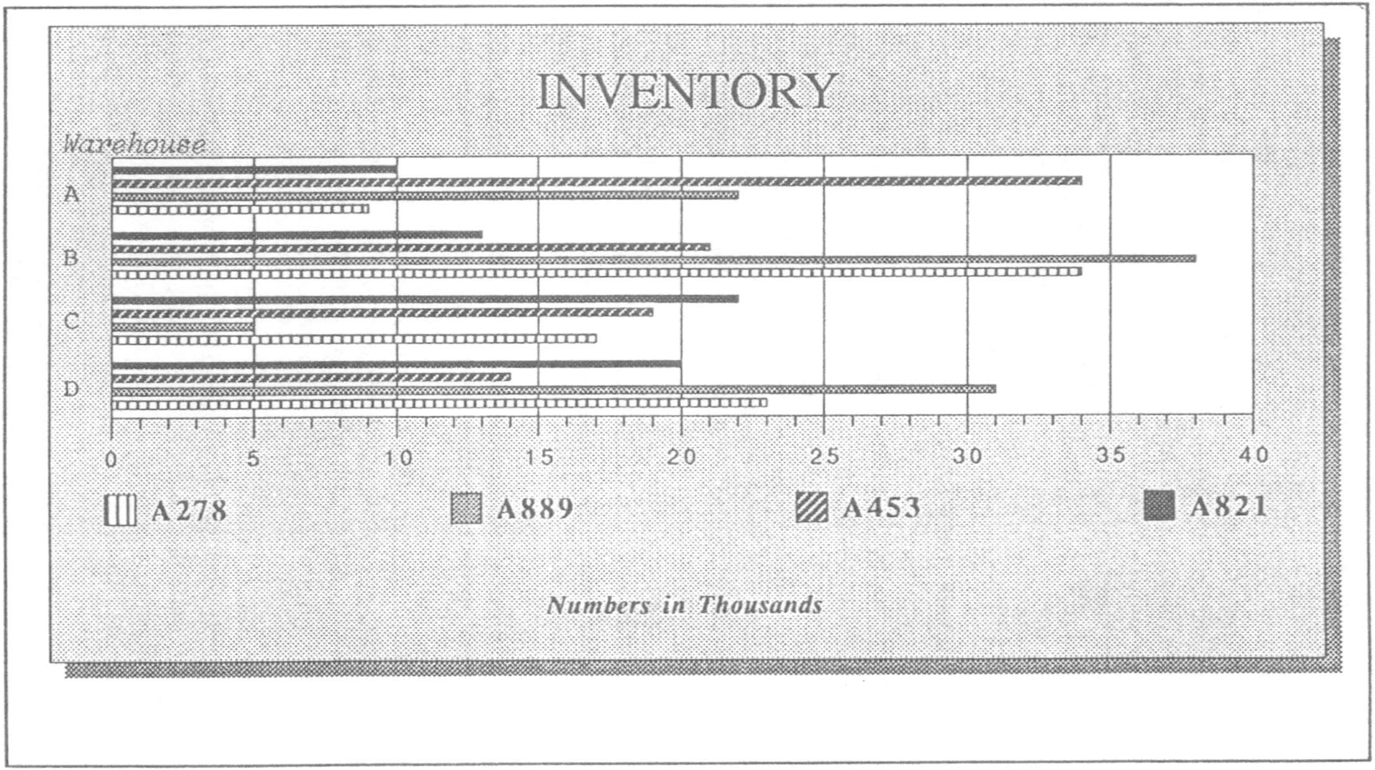

Figure 5.5 shows comparative volumes, that of predicted production targets with the actual volumes. The shading patterns enable comparisons to be made readily. Shading can also be used to separate categories within each bar to illustrate, for example, how the total production figures are made up of their component figures represented in layers. Another use of differential shading in a bar chart is to highlight a particular feature, such as low production due to a strike in the car plant.

fig 5.5 *overlapped combination bar chart*

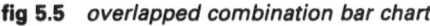
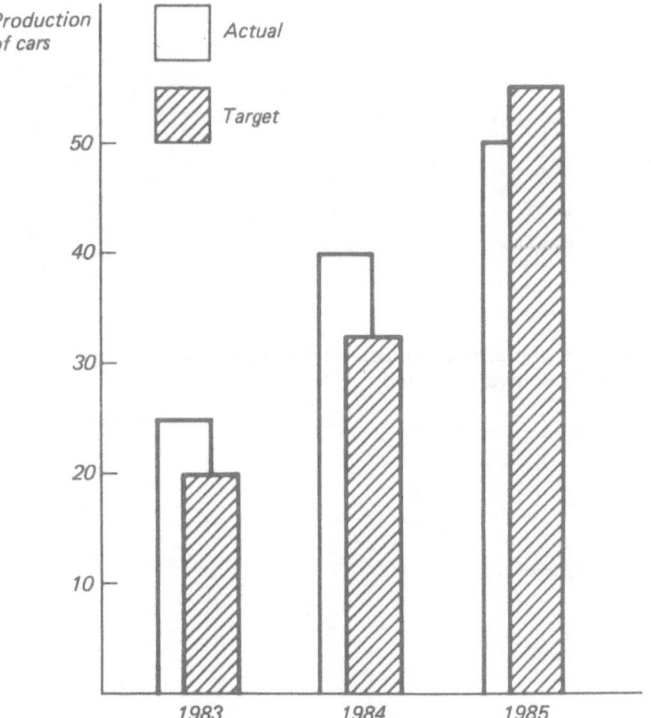

Packages are likely to provide a number of shading patterns as well as colours. Colours can be 'painted' by the user on to parts of the chart (if a colour VDU and plotter are available). Figure 5.6 shows this type of bar chart comparing yearly figures for four towns for a period of five years.

Three dimensional diagrams are more complex, and not all business graphics packages support them. Examples are given in Figures

158

fig 5.6 *comparative bar charts*
Source: Lotus Development (UK) Ltd

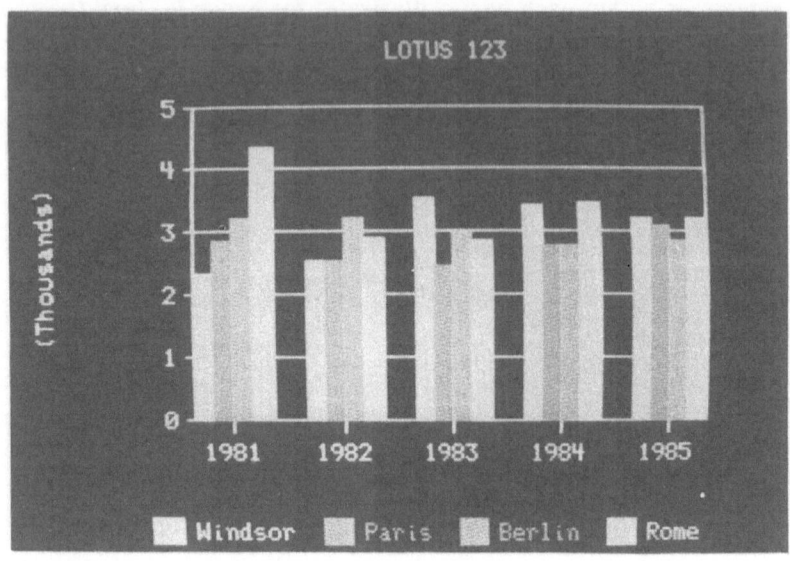

fig 5.7 *three-dimensional graph (produced on dot matrix printer)*
Source: Mercia Software Limited

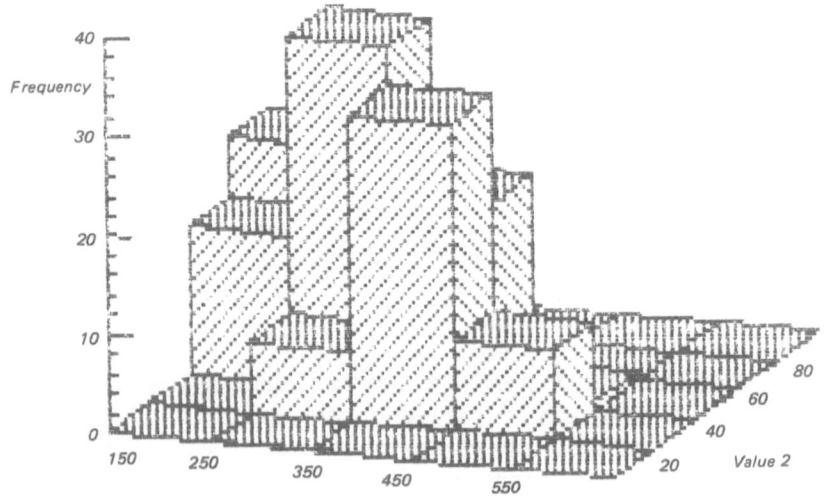

fig 5.8 *three dimensional graph and figures produced on laser printer (created using Wing Z)*

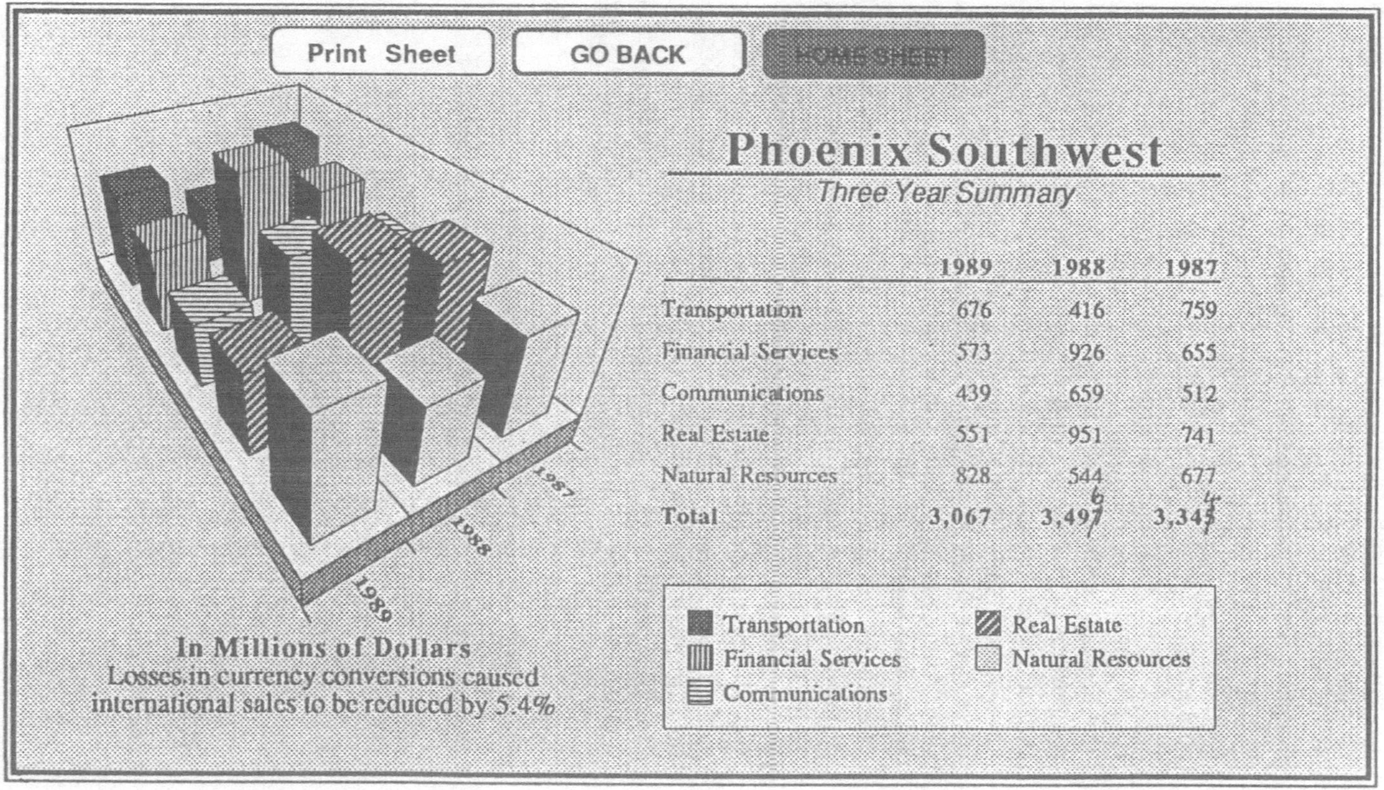

Print Sheet   GO BACK   HOME SHEET

Phoenix Southwest
Three Year Summary

	1989	1988	1987
Transportation	676	416	759
Financial Services	573	926	655
Communications	439	659	512
Real Estate	551	951	741
Natural Resources	828	544	677
Total	3,067	3,497	3,345

■ Transportation   ▨ Real Estate
▦ Financial Services   ▢ Natural Resources
▥ Communications

In Millions of Dollars
Losses in currency conversions caused
international sales to be reduced by 5.4%

5.7 and 5.8. These charts have to be designed well, otherwise problems do occur. For example, values of the second variable have to be larger than the first, otherwise the latter will be obscured. Further, the software and hardware have to be good enough to distinguish between the various elements by good boundary definition. Without good design and facilities, these charts can be very confusing.

(b) Pie charts
The basic pie chart is shown as Figure 5.9. Each slice corresponds to the portion (a percentage) of the 'pie' that the variable takes, so that the total effect is a comparison of the parts to a whole. If one portion has a value of 50%, then it will take a half slice of the pie (180°). The slices can be shaded or coloured and a key indicates the class of each slice. Alternatively, the class to which each slice belongs is indicated in the slice itself.

Segments can also be **exploded** to emphasise particular values. This is shown in Figure 5.10. This figure also shows the exploded pie chart on the screen plotted out. The various graph options are shown to the left of the VDU display as icons, rather than words.

A pie chart can only show one range, and therefore does not prove useful for all situations. However, a pie chart is easy to construct and the information presented easy to understand, and a series of ranges can be shown on a series of pie charts, as illustrated in Figure 5.11. A number of techniques are used in Figure 5.12 to highlight sales figures for a particular region.

fig 5.9 *basic pie chart with key (produced on plotter)*
   Source: Mercia Software Limited

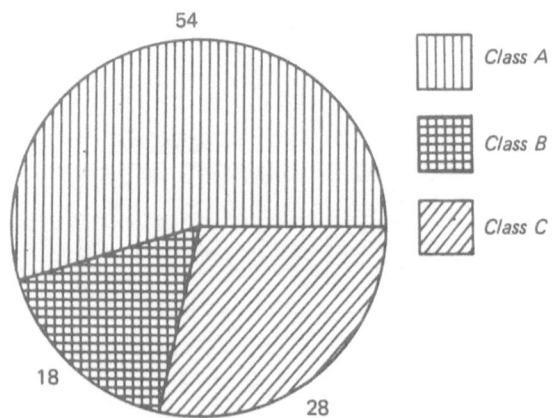

fig 5.10 *exploded pie chart displayed and plotted on Penman Products' Penplot*
Source: Penman Products Limited

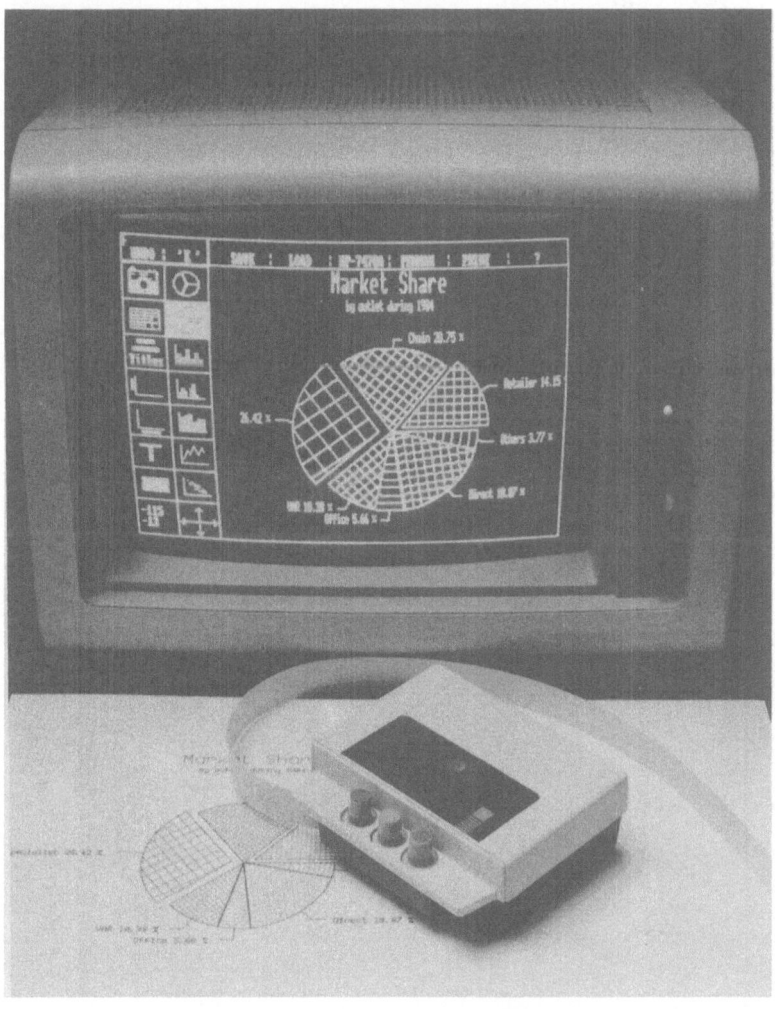

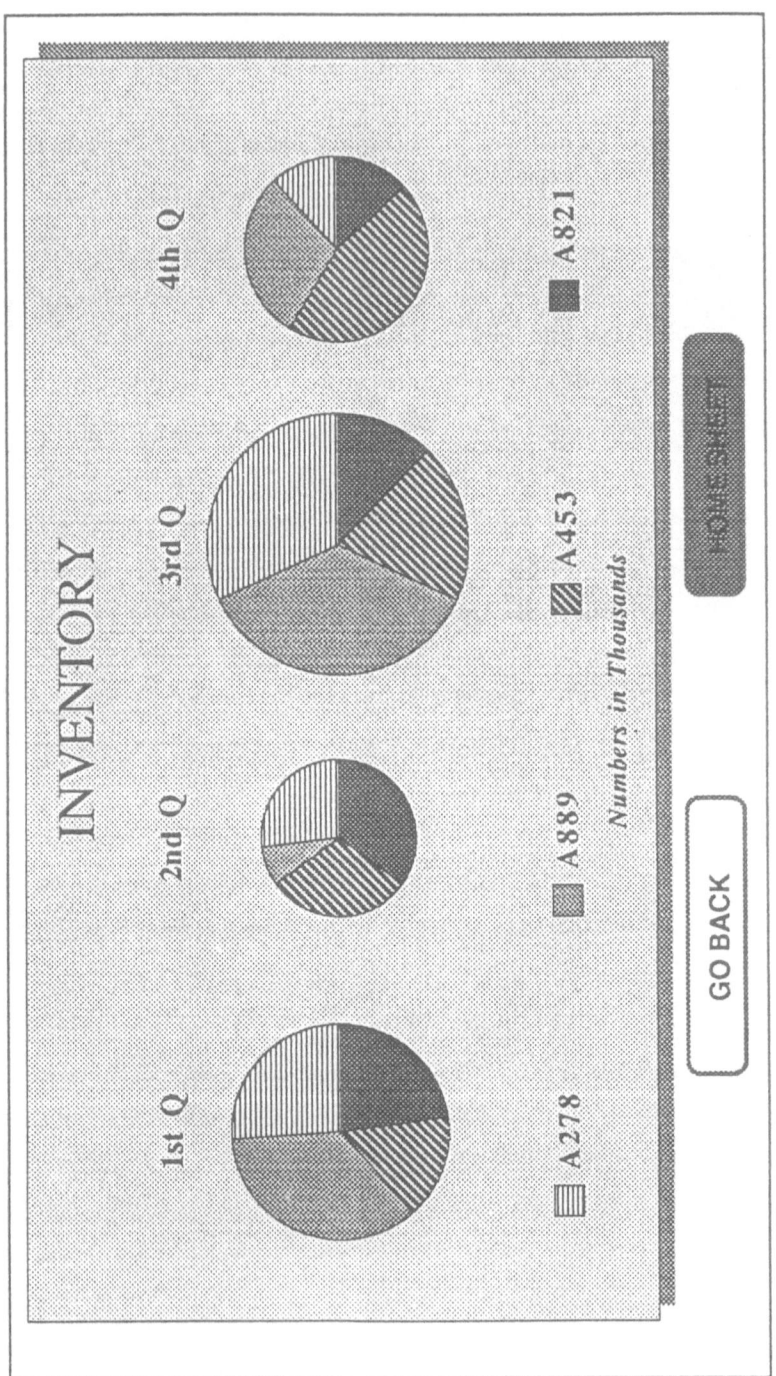

fig 5.11 comparative pie charts produced on laser printer (created using Wing Z)

fig 5.12 *the use of different techniques to highlight sales figures (created using Wing Z)*

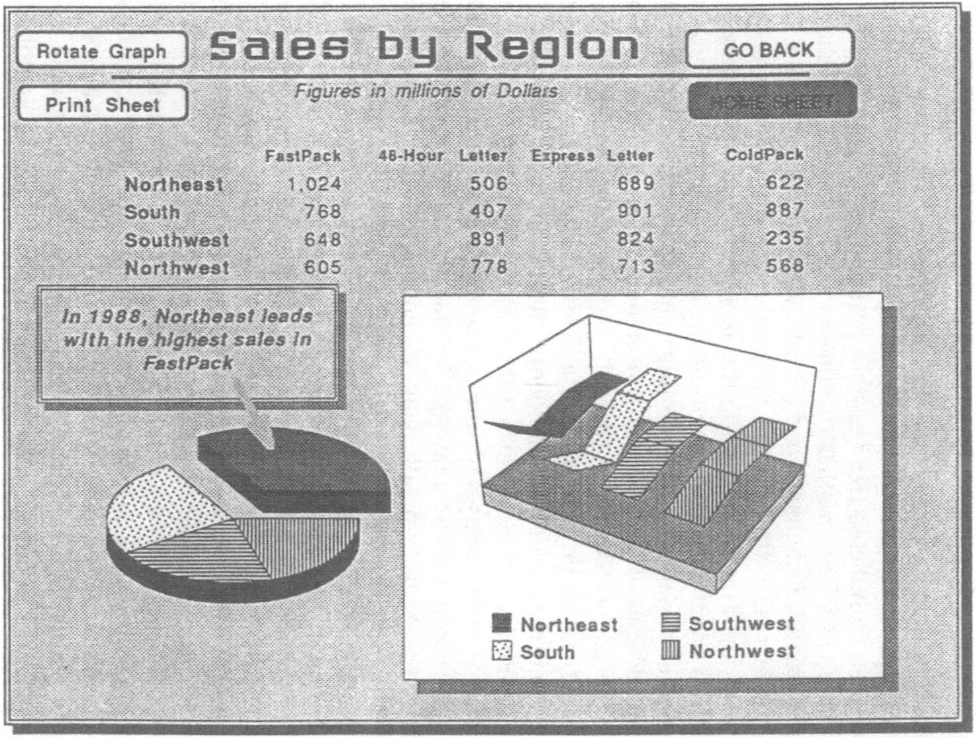

(c) Line graphs and other charts

There are a number of types of graph. The most well known is the simple line graph, particularly useful in showing a trend over time. Figure 5.13 shows the change in cost over time. The **scattergraph** gives the individual plots (Figure 5.14), and the line for Figure 5.15 was formed by **smoothing** plots into a general tendency. By showing the tendency and the actual plots, recordings which do not correspond to the tendency can be highlighted. The combination of scattergraph and line graph can also be used to show the difference between a predicted trend and the actual plots (Figure 5.16).

There may be more than one line on a chart. Figure 5.17 shows the interaction of demand and supply curves. Demand and supply volumes react with price in different ways. According to economic theory, their interaction marks the likely price and production figures (shown by the dotted lines). In Figure 5.18 each line represents different variables within the price and production axes. By use of distinct types of line, the different trends are clearly seen. A number of alternative line types (dotted, dashed, emboldened, and continuous) can be brought in from a 'pool' of line settings, in the same way that there will be a number of shading patterns available.

Figure 5.19 shows a layer (or area) graph where the total of all values is seen, along with the amounts for each component of the total (represented by a layer). The stacked bar chart can be used to show the same type of data, excepting that the layer graph is continuous over time, the bar chart is stepped. It is also possible to have a mixture of line graphs and bar charts incorporated into one diagram (see Figure 5.20). Figure 5.21 shows the high and low (**HiLo**) points, joined together. In this case the high and low temperatures for each day in a particular week are shown as a hilo plot.

As we have seen in many of the examples used, once a graph has been drawn it is necessary to clarify its meaning. Labels and titles should be added to the graph. Each axis of a graph should be given a label. Step or tick marks on the line might also help the reader to gauge the values of a bar or line. Labels should also be added to the data points in the figures, where appropriate. Some data can be emphasised to enhance the meaning of the graph, by emboldening, and other facilities. The meaning of each layer in a layer graph or segment in a pie chart can be illustrated by a key. All this type of labelling and emphasis ought to be provided by the graphics package as standard.

Figure 5.22 shows a plotter which outputs text on overhead transparencies, and graphs of various kinds.

fig 5.13 *basic line graph*

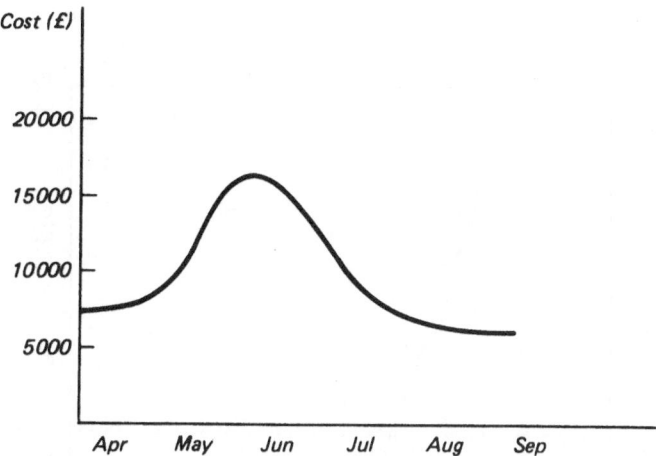

fig 5.14 *scattergraph (produced on plotter)*
Source: Mercia Software Limited

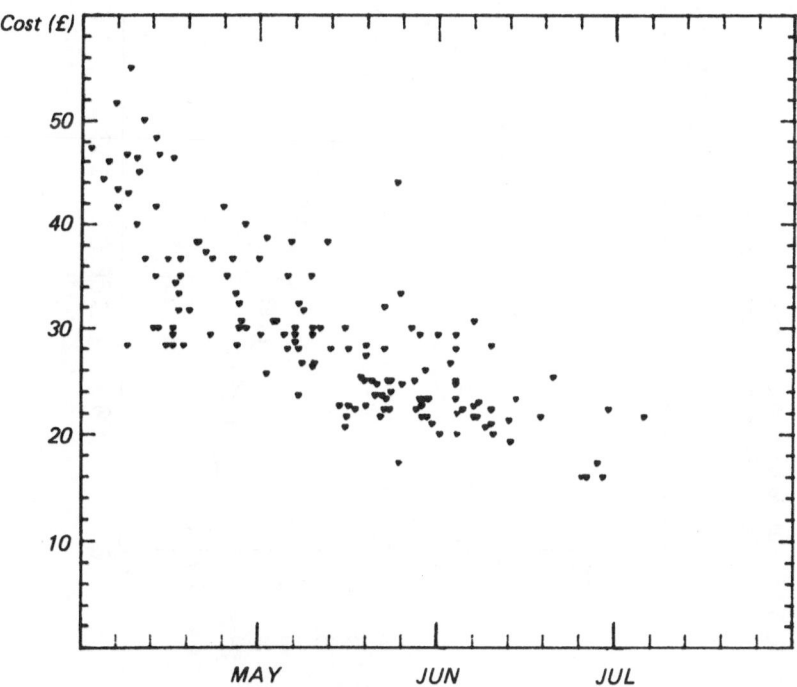

fig 5.15 *individual plots and trend*
Source: Penman Products Limited

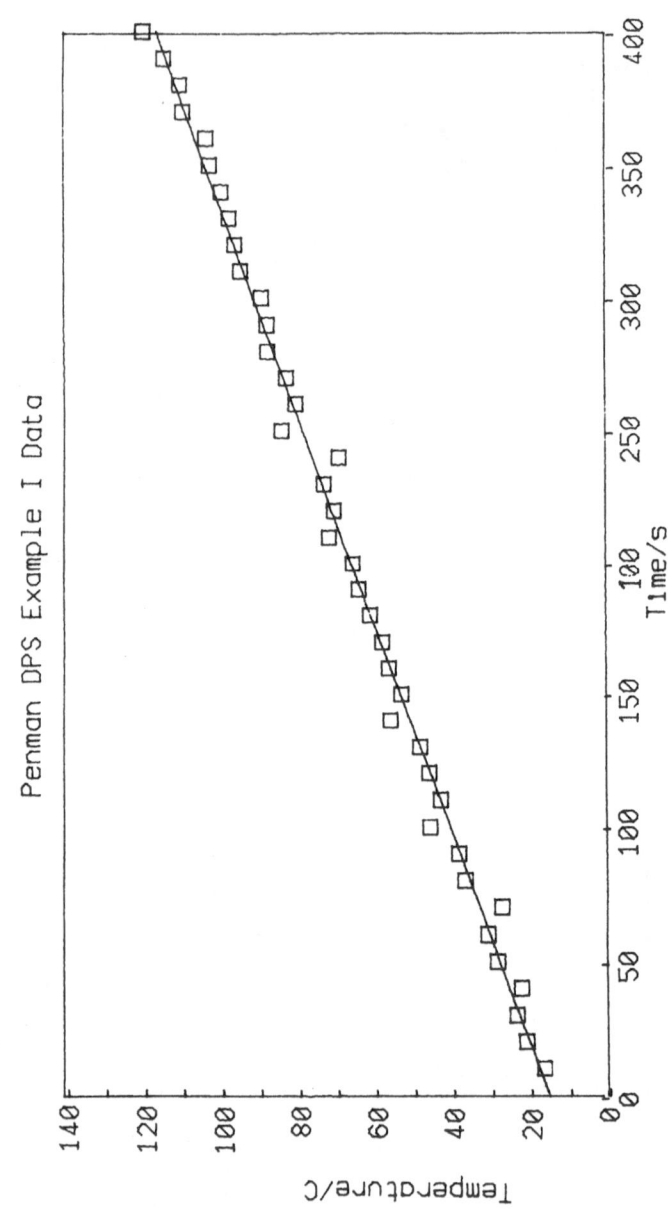

Penman DPS Example I Data

fig 5.16 *observed v. predicted, highlighting plots against trend*

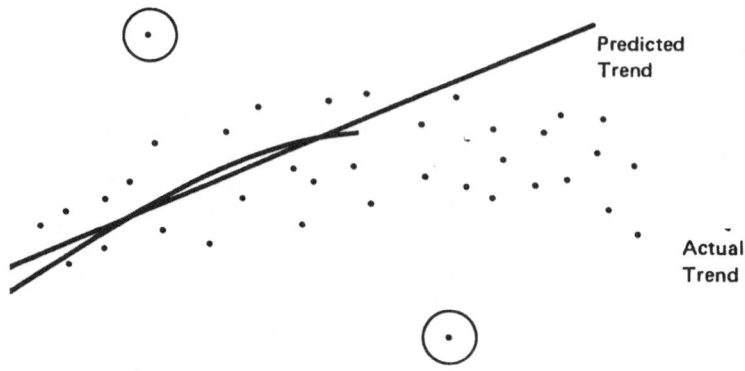

fig 5.17 *demand and supply curves*

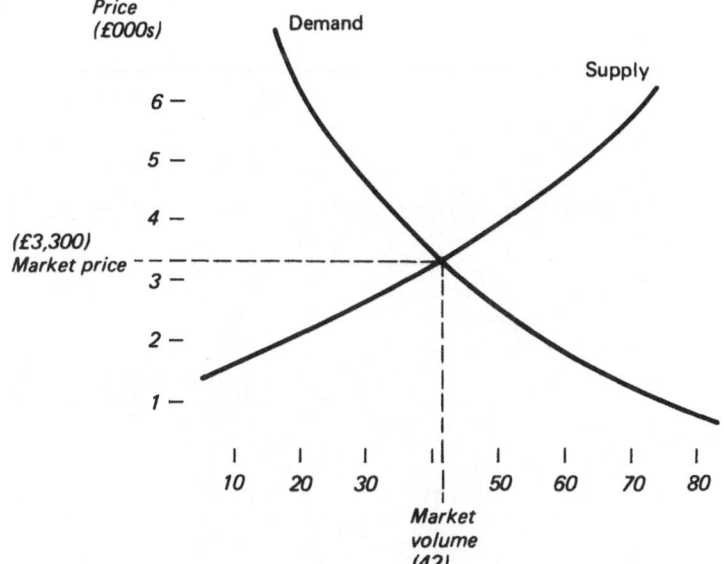

fig 5.18 *alternative line types*

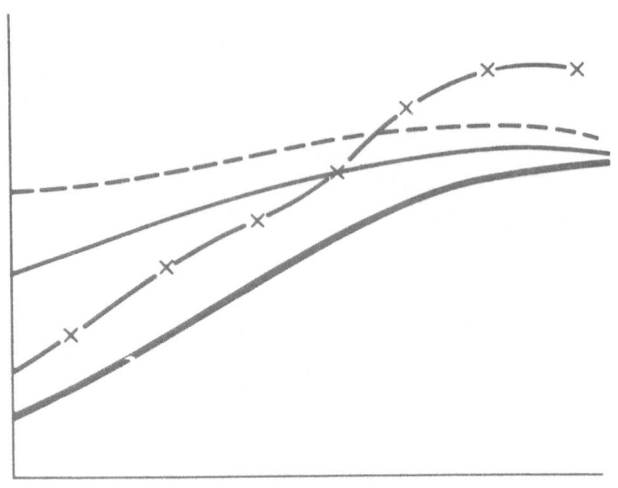

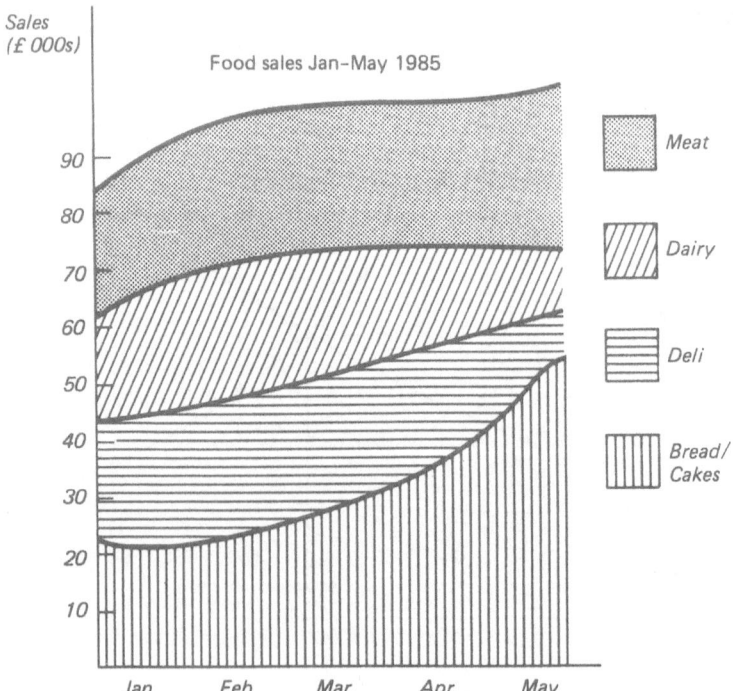

Sales
(£ 000s)

Food sales Jan–May 1985

Meat

Dairy

Deli

Bread/
Cakes

90
80
70
60
50
40
30
20
10

Jan   Feb   Mar   Apr   May

fig 5.20 *combined bar/line graph*

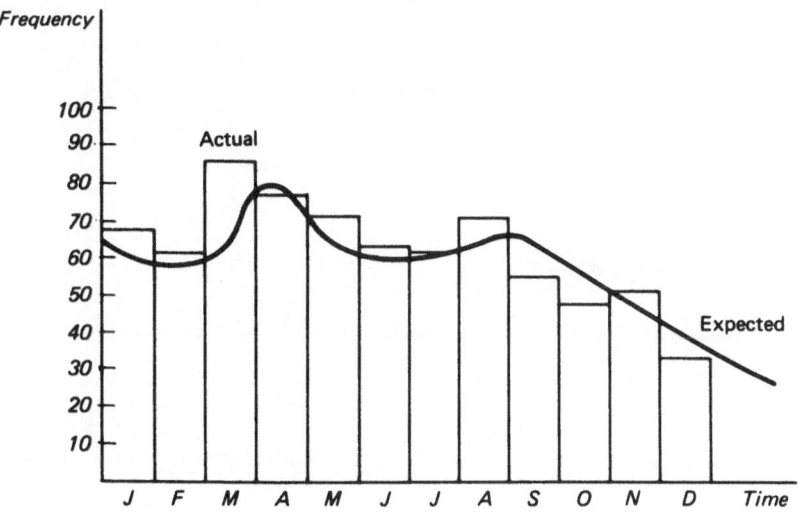

fig 5.21 *HiLo diagram*

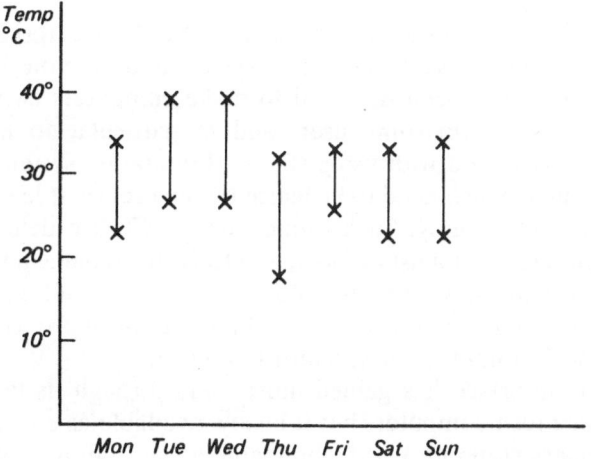

fig 5.22 *HP 7440 plotter with graphics output*
   Source: Hewlett-Packard Limited

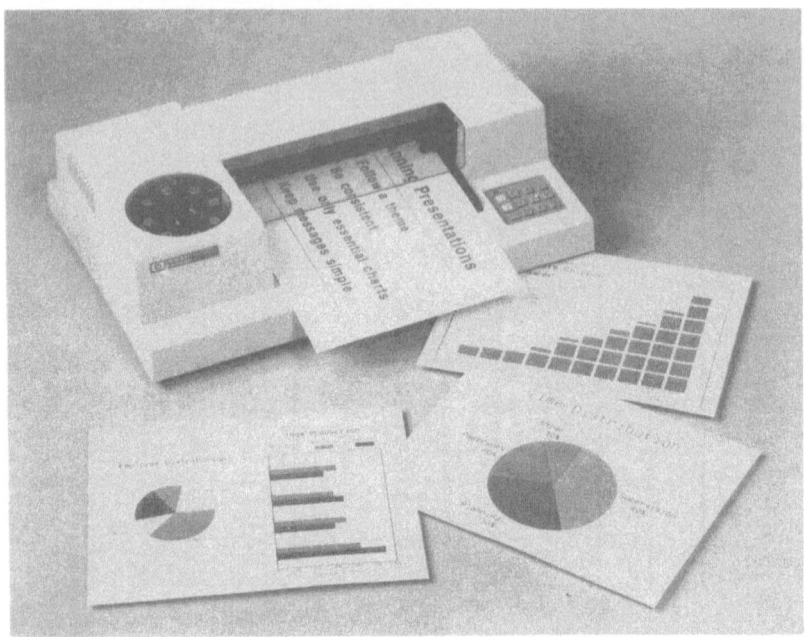

5.3 ICON (WIMP) INTERFACE

The icon user interface was developed by Xerox research and implemented on the Xerox 8018 Star system and then on the Apple Lisa system. It has been designed to make computers easy to use, especially for the first-time user, and in particular to avoid the difficulties associated with using standard operating systems. These use commands, which need to be learnt by the user or at least require the manual to be handy. Such commands as **DEL** (for delete a file), **DIR** (for directory, or a list of files), and **REN** (for rename a file), may be straightforward for the trained user, but difficult for others, particularly where there can be a hundred or more commands available with a number of variations on each.

The icon interface has gained most users through its use on the Apple Macintosh computer, but it is now available as a standard on some business computers and obtainable as an option on others by purchasing the software as an extra. Whereas the 'computer expert' may choose the conventional operating system, non-computer professionals may prefer the WIMP interface.

Icons represent only one aspect of the WIMP human-computer interface, the environment being:

• Windows	• Windows
• Icons	• Icons
• Mouse or	• Menus
• Pull down (or Pop up) menus	• Pointers

The idea behind windows is to allow users to work on parts of a number of applications. By assigning to windows (and therefore compartmentalising) each file or design, parts of a number of systems can be viewed at any one time. Windows can be moved around the screen and window sizes can be changed in order to concentrate on one part of the system but keep in view other parts of the system. If the particular part of a file, such as a page in a text, is not in view, then the window can be scrolled through. In their normal work, people will be 'doing' more than one thing at a time, and windows parallel this possibility on the screen. However only one window is *active* at one time, the other jobs are 'there in waiting', to be chosen once the user finishes with the active window. Whereas windows in a word processing system will allow the user to work on two or more texts or two or more parts of the same text, windows in the operating system environment could enable the user to work on two or more entirely different applications.

The basic analogy of the WIMPs interface is that of the **desk-top**. Pictorial symbols or icons of all the features of the desk-top are provided on the computer screen. There are filing cabinets, waste paper baskets, documents, and 'in' and 'out' trays.

By using a hand-held mouse which can point to one of these symbols, the user can ask for the action implied by the symbol (store, throw away, and read). The equivalent operating system commands, such as **WRITE** file name, **DELETE** file name, and **READ** file name, have to be typed in on the keyboard.

In some systems, these commands can still be typed on the keyboard when using a WIMP system, but where such an environment is available, most people find it easier to point the mouse and click rather than to type in a command.

The mouse can be used to carry out functions such as deleting files by pointing to the original file, clicking, moving (or 'dragging') it to the waste paper basket icon and clicking again. There are alternatives to the mouse, such as the light pen, joystick and touch sensitive screen, but the mouse is less tiring on the arms and more flexible than most of the alternatives . . . and has proved to be the most popular.

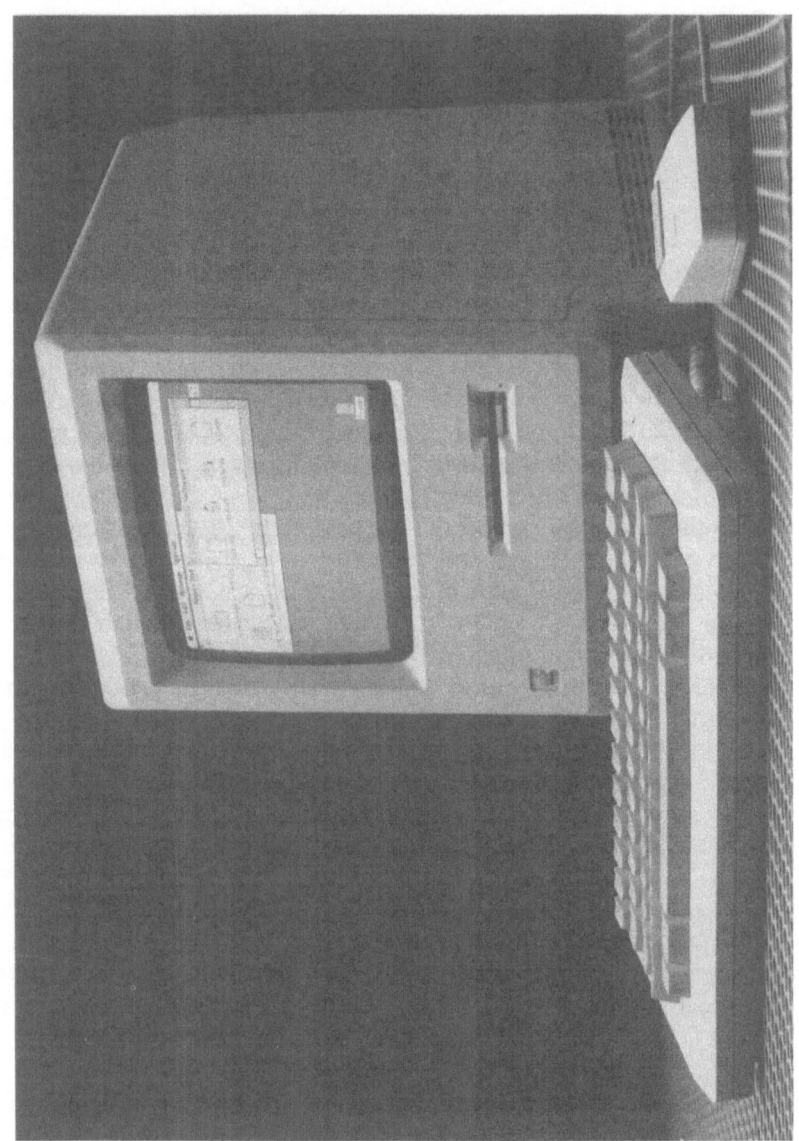

fig 5.23 *windows, icons and mouse*
Source: Apple Computer (UK) Limited

Figure 5.23 shows a Macintosh screen, keyboard and mouse. At the top of the screen is a menu line giving four options. There are two windows displayed. The one on the left shows the user files that are held on the disk in the disk drive. Each of these files is named and described through an icon. The report file (bottom left), for example, looks like a sheet of typewritten paper. Superimposed on this window to the right is a window describing the software available. This includes a set of utilities (to give the time and date for example), MacPaint (for screen design), and MacWrite (a word processing package). At the bottom right of the screen is a rubbish bin (named 'trash') which is used for throwing away or deleting data or a text. The arrows which are seen at the bottom right of the window will be pointed to in order to scroll on more details of other software packages available, because not all the icons (and package names) can be shown in the window at one time.

Having chosen a particular icon using a mouse, there may be a number of further options available to the user. For example, if the user points to a file symbol and registers that choice by clicking the mouse, there may be further options – open a file, close a file, read a file, write a file, and so on. These further options are usually displayed as a pull-down menu. This list of options is pulled down by the user. In some systems, the menus are designed to 'pop up' rather than pull down. The user then chooses the option required, again by pointing and clicking the mouse.

The user may wish to run a conventional application program. After choosing the program from a menu using the mouse, control will leave the WIMP environment until that program has finished. Some programs, such as the word processor, file management system or spreadsheet bought as part of the WIMP environment, may follow the same style as the WIMP operating commands and it may be possible to convert other packages to this style.

Although the WIMP interface is generally regarded as a much friendlier and easier way for users to get the best out of their computer and package, there is a contrary view. Such systems tend to be inflexible and many experienced users would far rather use a conventional command language. Further, and this is true of graphics in general, although pictures are often quoted as being worth a thousand words, many people find it difficult to think pictorially, and are much more used to words and numbers and can interpret these better than pictures. Furthermore, it is difficult to convey some information pictorially. A file containing sales data for the Midlands in 1986 could have a file name of SALES/MIDLANDS/1986. This conveys the meaning of the contents of the file to the user, but it would be difficult to represent this meaning graphically.

More important in a microcomputer environment is that these systems do use a considerable amount of the computer's memory, and applications that can run under a standard operating system environment may not run in a WIMPs environment unless memory is extended. Lastly, processing in a WIMP environment can be slow and therefore irritating to the more experienced user.

5.4 COMPUTER AIDED DESIGN (CAD)

Application-specific graphics, for computer aided design for example, tend to be complex and are only likely to be available in a specialised package for use by specialists. These applications are therefore outside the scope of general business graphics. However, CAD represents an established area for computer graphics and is used in many business applications such as flow-charting a series of processes, production routing, floor design (Figure 5.24) and product design, as well as more well-known applications such as integrated circuit design and design aids for architects and engineers.

It is more established than conventional business graphics because there are vast savings to be made and therefore the applications justified the high expense of earlier graphics systems, which were based on a minicomputer or mainframe computer. However, though many applications are still so 'hungry' for memory and speed that they lie outside the scope of microcomputer applications, many CAD applications are possible using the larger microcomputer systems.

CAD packages offer commands to draw a line, plane, arc, circle, and 3-D designs such as cubes and cylinders, insert holes, and so on. A detail of a design may be built up on a screen, and once satisfactory, reduced in scale and incorporated into the rest of the design at the right place. This design can be saved as an icon for other drawings where appropriate. In some applications an icon can represent a material or part type. These can be stored and then displayed as elements in the construction of a bill of materials for production processes or for product design. Thus libraries of symbols can be created, to be re-used for a particular drawing type or for a number of applications. Some symbols may be built in with the package.

As with most applications discussed in this book, the computer system gives users freedom to change their mind. An architect's drawing, for example, can be changed easily – a 'soul-destroying'

fig 5.24 floor design (created using Dreams)

process in a hand-drawn design. A useful feature is the 'undo'. This enables the user to go back to the previous state, if he does not like the change. Some packages offer a multiple undo, that is the ability to go back several changes. This feature is likely to be 'memory hungry'.

Amongst many special features, the application package must be able to rotate designs about an axis, change their scale, zoom in and out, produce mirror copies and ordinary copies, and rub out or change parts of the designs conveniently. Objects within a diagram may act as though they were made of plasticine, demonstrating the ease with which they can be reshaped, moved and rotated. When these sets of commands are created and stored, their recall can give the effect of movement or *animation*. This can be an excellent technique to use in presentation graphics as well as being useful to simulate the effect of changes in wind patterns on bridge or building designs.

Although standard printers are adequate for many business graphics applications, CAD applications usually require a sophisticated plotter. This will give a much higher degree of accuracy. The use of a mouse, joystick, light pen or an equivalent device is also essential. A keyboard is designed for the input of text and numbers. The use of commands such as 'up', 'down', and 'right' or 'left' or the use of the arrow keys on the keyboard are very tedious. Some systems provide a **tablet**, which is a flat surface whose boundaries represent the boundaries of the screen. A mouse can run on the tablet allowing the user to 'draw' a picture or design which will be reproduced on the screen.

ACCOUNTING AND RELATED DATA PROCESSING APPLICATIONS

Microcomputers, like minicomputers and mainframes, are frequently used for accounting and related data processing applications. The applications discussed in this chapter are for general business accounts requirements. Packages for professional accounting companies are not covered, as these are more specialised. Even so, many of the general accounting packages that are available do require the knowledge of a company accountant and may not be suitable for the smaller firm whose manager may only wish to produce the basic business accounts to satisfy the law.

The basic accounting routines include sales, purchase and nominal ledgers, which are discussed in sections 6.3, 6.4 and 6.5. Related applications include sales order processing and invoicing (section 6.6), stock recording (section 6.7), costing (section 6.8) and payroll (section 6.9). Not all of these modules will be included in all accounting packages and some may include other modules, such as a register of company assets.

There are many packages available for accounting applications and some are integrated so that the accounting routines can be processed in a similar manner and the basic accounts modules can 'talk' to each other. The data required for one of the modules will be required by others, indeed this may be automated in the package. There will not be any necessity for duplicating data collection and storage. Integrated packages are discussed in section 6.10.

As with most applications, a lot of effort is required in planning the implementation of the new system. With accounting systems, however, this is particularly critical because accounts systems tend to run in a yearly cycle and therefore the best time for the new system to be operational is at the beginning of a new accounting period. This can be crucial, and planning for implementation should allow for possible unexpected delays.

We first look at a number of features which apply to accounting systems in general. This first section is followed by a discussion of a particularly important requirement of all accounting systems – that of good control.

6.1 FEATURES OF ACCOUNTING SYSTEMS

In this section we look at a number of features which, although by no means relevant only to accounting systems, can take on particular importance in the context of these applications. We first look at **cost justification**, which is sometimes easier to prove in accounting systems. Even so, the **choice of hardware** will probably not rest on cost factors, but on the numbers of records and transactions to be processed. Although accounting systems are required by all firms, procedures do differ, and we look at the requirement of packages to be **flexible**. We then describe some aspects of **design**. There may be a need for **multi-user systems**, and we discuss the problems that this may cause. Although we look at the various applications separately (apart from section 6.10), the accounting applications do link together and the last part of this section examines the **integrated nature of accounting routines**.

(a) Cost justification
Accounting packages are sometimes the easiest to cost-justify in a feasibility study amongst the applications discussed in this text.

- (*i*) Faster invoicing to customers will lead to faster payment from them.
- (*ii*) Quicker (and better) decision-making, say on sanctioning credit, will generate more business which produces profit.
- (*iii*) Better credit control will encourage debtors to pay up.
- (*iv*) Better payment control will enable the business to take advantage of cash discounts.
- (*v*) Better stock control will minimise stock-outs and reduce over stocking.
- (*vi*) Good reporting, such as regular profit and loss reports and actual against budgeted accounts, will enable management to keep track of the business.

It is therefore not surprising that the various accounting routines together account for about half of the commercial application packages available on microcomputers.

(b) Choice of hardware and software

The difference between what is a powerful microcomputer and what is a minicomputer or mainframe has become blurred and the decision about which hardware to use is of secondary importance to choosing the software which must satisfy the following requirements:

- (*i*) the number of records to be maintained;
- (*ii*) the number of transactions processed each period;
- (*iii*) the number of types of item:
- (*iv*) the number of users on a multi-user system; and
- (*v*) the number of companies and departments into which the business is divided, and so on.

In many small and medium-sized businesses, microcomputers may well be adequate for running the company accounts.

(c) Flexibility

Although accounting routines are required by all businesses and must conform to standards such as compliance with VAT rules, the packages should have some flexibility. To give some examples, it should be possible for accounting packages to handle different:

- (*i*) accounting periods (for example, four weeks or one calendar month);
- (*ii*) ways to draw up coding structures;
- (*iii*) payment terms;
- (*iv*) currencies (and exchange rates);
- (*v*) languages; and
- (*vi*) credit periods.

There should also be flexibility in report design. Although most packages offer 'standard' reports, it is important that they also allow the user to redesign these standard reports and to create new ones. Management information requirements for decision-support systems can be extensive, and therefore the reporting system should be comprehensive as well as flexible. It should be possible to review summary information, in order to look at the overall financial health of the company, as well as to look in detail at a single transaction or account.

The user may state the processing requirements by choosing from a menu of options listed by the package or through the specification of parameters. Systems wholly menu-driven can be difficult to customise to the user's exact requirements, although they tend to be easier to learn and have the advantage of consistency.

In a parameter-driven system, the user specifies options that are required on a parameter record. These requirements will include:

(*i*) period dates:
(*ii*) file locations;
(*iii*) VAT rates,

and so on. The contents of these parameters may vary according to the particular customers and suppliers being processed.

Frequently, but not always, complexity is a corollary of flexibility. However, if the package has been well designed, few problems will be encountered in the company's accountancy department, as the various options offered by accounting packages ought to be well understood and easily specified.

As with all application packages, accounting systems are only flexible for customisation up to a point, and it may be necessary for the business to develop a total accounting system in-house. No two businesses run their accounts in exactly the same way, so that a package needs to be as flexible as possible to avoid businesses bending their systems to the package. Alternatively, some suppliers will sell the source code which users with the necessary programming expertise could adapt to suit individual requirements, although the user must be careful to ensure that the source code (that written by the originator of the package) can be readily modified when required.

There may be problems with these 'own programming' solutions, particularly in that the package might be difficult to maintain. Accounting routines must keep pace with legislation, and whereas a standard package should be updated by the suppliers automatically as part of the maintenance contract, this will be more difficult to apply with regard to a package that has been changed by the user.

(d) Design
As with all applications, the new user will need to spend some time on design. For example, a comprehensive coding system needs to be devised for the ledger systems to cover categories of:

(*i*) expenses;
(*ii*) assets;
(*iii*) income;
(*iv*) debtors; and
(*v*) sales.

Cost centres are also normally devised. As with any multi-user facility, there needs to be some overall administrator to assign access privileges and, in general, control usage. These are allocated to departments or items of equipment. By incorporating these cost centres into the accounts, it will be possible for managers to see the profitability of each part of the business.

(e) Multi-user systems
Some accounting packages also offer a multi-user capability. There must be record-locking facilities so that one user is not updating a record whilst another user is attempting to update the same record. Two users should have the ability to update different records, however, so that, for example, operators can enter details of orders from different customers. This multi-user facility may be supported by a multi-user computer or by being part of a computer network.

(f) Integrated nature of accounting routines
In this chapter (apart from the last section) we will look at each application area separately. However, the reader should bear in mind that these modules are related and may be integrated.

This applies to sales order processing, invoicing and stock recording, as well as the basic accounting routines. Thus, as sales orders are received, the system will check that the goods are in stock, make the necessary adjustments to stock as the goods are sold, and print out the invoices. The package may also produce reports detailing the levels of stock available of each product, provide an analysis of sales, and print out letters re-ordering goods whose stocks are depleted.

Managers may also want the flexibility to integrate accounting information with other files and microcomputer packages.

6.2 CONTROL

Another feature of the packages will be the emphasis on control procedures. Problems with these programs such as:

(a) employees not being paid on time;
(b) invoices for the wrong amounts;
(c) customer details lost; or
(d) updates due to the Budget or other legislation not being correctly implemented,

could prove very costly to the firm. Only well-tried and tested software should be considered, and suppliers should be able to provide immediate help on problems. There should also be good training facilities available.

In choosing accounting software, the purchaser should ensure that the package conforms to established practice. Packages that allow the user to cut corners may eventually lead to problems with external auditors. Indeed, it is usual to seek approval (or at least acquiescence) from the external auditors before a package is purchased. We will return to auditing later in this section.

The control procedures that are internal to the system should be rigorous and comprehensive. Good validation procedures should be a feature of all computer systems, but accounting systems should also include procedures to detect fraud and promote efficiency. Validation procedures will include, for example, checks to ensure that:

(a) data is numeric or alphabetic as expected;
(b) particular customers exist;
(c) particular items are feasible (for example, credit limits fall in a particular range);
(d) date fields are plausible (the date exists and it conforms to the period being processed);
(e) all fields are completed,

and so on.

There should also be administrative controls over staff to ensure that responsibilities are known to them and that these procedures are followed. These controls will help to ensure that the system is working efficiently and effectively.

Program disks and data disks must be clearly labelled and stored, so that there is no confusion as to which disk is the latest.

There must also be *security measures* to prevent unauthorised access. Much of the data in these systems, such as that held in payroll records, is 'sensitive'. Security measures should at least include passwords with a limit on the number of attempts to enter the system with an illegal password. This password security should be available separately for each module in an integrated package.

There must also be good backup procedures so that files can be restored if disks are corrupted. Many systems do not permit the deletion of records in one operation, rather they mark records for deletion. Only at period end procedures, frequently referred to as *housekeeping procedures*, are the records actually deleted. This caution applied to data that is about to be deleted provides added security.

Accounting systems will also be open to *internal and external auditing*. Auditors have to satisfy themselves that the business figures are accurate and thereby assure shareholders, tax authorities and management that the firm is being run properly, and that fraud or mismanagement would be detected if it existed. Where it is possible to predict auditors' requirements, these should be built into the system and package evaluation should take these requirements into account. Packages should at least be capable of giving a printed record of all data handled by the system. This **audit trail** should include listings of amendments and an end of run set of control accounts.

6.3 SALES LEDGER

The purpose of a sales ledger system is to record sales and remittances, provide statements of any balances owing, produce anlayses of debtors' balances and possibly generate letters to overdue debtors. The sales ledger system will access and maintain a file of customers with details about them including any balances owing. There are three types of system.

(a) Balance-only
In this type of system a record of the debtor's balance is maintained.

(b) Balance-forward
In this type of system a balance is maintained for the previous accounting period, plus the details of all transactions relating to the debtor for the current period. These details will not appear on future statements, whether the transactions have been settled or not.

(c) Open-item
This is the most detailed. Details of all transactions are recorded and retained until the net amount due is zero. Thus if a company is delivered goods in one month, but pays in three stages, the transaction will only be closed when the last cheque has been cleared. A further complication that the system should deal with is the allocation of sums received from a customer to a number of different transactions.

Most companies require an open-item sales ledger system and many computer packages facilitate this. Some give the user an option of choosing between the ledger types. The computer system will maintain the records and produce the sales ledger report, name-and-address lists and labels, and also provide statistics of sales, and reports on debtors. Some systems also facilitate on-line access supporting user enquiries.

In order to provide this information, files must include:

(*i*) customers' names and addresses (an administration address as well as delivery address);
(*ii*) credit limits;
(*iii*) tax details of the customers;
(*iv*) settlement terms;
(*v*) discount details,

and so on, as well as details of the transactions and therefore the balance data. The transaction types will include:

(*i*) opening balances;
(*ii*) invoices;
(*iii*) credit notes;
(*iv*) journal entries; and
(*v*) cash receipts.

The transaction type ought to be dated, so that reports can be produced according to the age of the transactions. Typically, users require an **aged report** into overdue amounts of 30 days, 60 days, 90 days and so on.

A number of reports can be generated by sales ledger systems. A sales account is given as Figure 6.1. Some systems give the flexibility to produce reports of debtors by:

- transaction date;
- due date; or
- invoice date.

fig 6.1 *sales ledger report*

OUR COMPANY   3 APRIL 1986

SALES LEDGER ENQUIRY

ACCOUNT NO: 76513   BIG CUSTOMER PLC

		DATE	DESCRIPTION	DEBIT	CREDIT
RECEIPT	R746	10 3 86	Sales Receipt		£90.00
	R748	21 3 86	Sales Receipt		£64.00
INVOICE	I764	17 2 86	Car Parts	£85.76	
	I799	28 2 86	Car Parts	£81.00	

AMOUNT OUTSTANDING	£1,563.75
AMOUNT PAID TO DATE	£1,400.00

There may also be a facility to surcharge overdue accounts as well as calculating cash settlement dates. There will normally be a facility to write off bad debts, so that transactions which will not be paid are not kept on file indefinitely.

The customer reports might include a listing of sales of customers according to:

- area;
- sales representative, or
- customer group.

The control account report shows what should be posted to the nominal ledger at the end of the accounting period.

6.4 PURCHASE LEDGER

Purchase ledger systems are similar to sales ledger systems, except that they record information about the firm's purchases rather than its sales. They need to store details about:

(a) suppliers (rather than customers);
(b) purchase invoices (rather than sales invoices); and
(c) creditors (rather than debtors).

Figure 6.2 shows a purchase ledger record. The highlighted aspects are:

(1) the company name and address;
(2) the supplier name and address; and
(3) a list of all transactions.

The transaction types are as follows: invoice (**IN**), credit note (**CR**), cash (**CA**), transfer (**TR**), and outstanding balance (**O/BAL**).

The purpose of a purchase ledger system is to:

(a) record purchases and remittances to suppliers (allowing for adjustments for returns);
(b) provide statements of any balances owing to creditors; and
(c) produce analyses of creditors' balances.

As with sales ledger systems, there are three types; balance-only, balance-forward and open-item. Again, most companies require the latter, as it is more detailed.

fig 6.2 *purchase ledger record*
   Source: Apricot (UK) Ltd

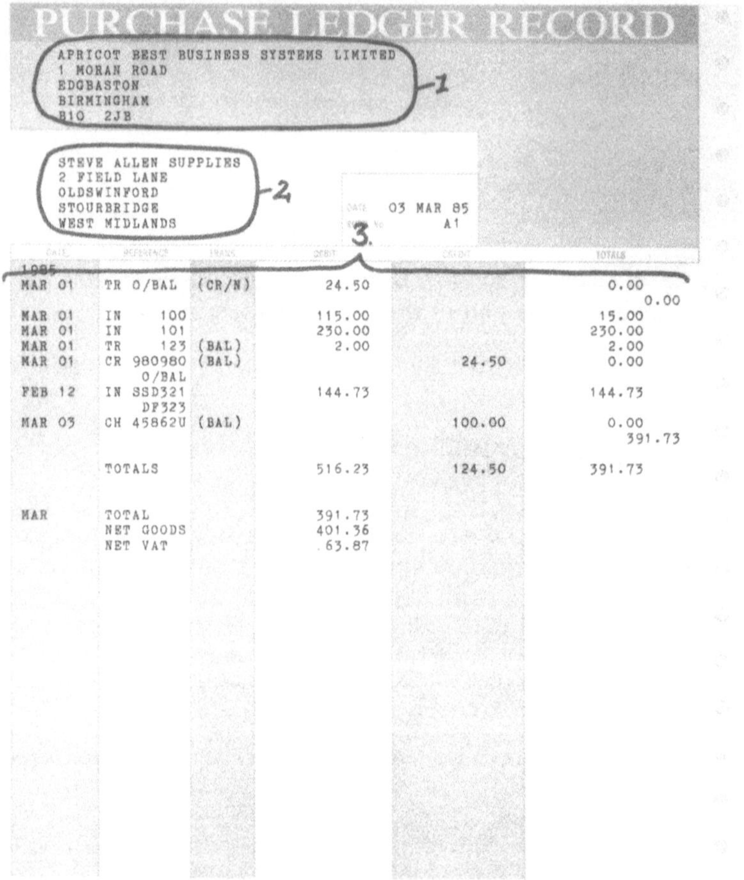

PURCHASE LEDGER RECORD

```
APRICOT BEST BUSINESS SYSTEMS LIMITED
1 MORAN ROAD
EDGBASTON                                    —1
BIRMINGHAM
B10  2JB


    STEVE ALLEN SUPPLIES
    2 FIELD LANE
    OLDSWINFORD                    —2
    STOURBRIDGE              DATE  03 MAR 85
    WEST MIDLANDS                  A1
                                 3.
```

DATE	REFERENCE		DEBIT	CREDIT	TOTALS
1985					
MAR 01	TR O/BAL	(CR/N)	24.50		0.00
					0.00
MAR 01	IN 100		115.00		15.00
MAR 01	IN 101		230.00		230.00
MAR 01	TR 123	(BAL)	2.00		2.00
MAR 01	CR 980980	(BAL)		24.50	0.00
	O/BAL				
FEB 12	IN SSD321		144.73		144.73
	DF323				
MAR 03	CH 45862U	(BAL)		100.00	0.00
					391.73
	TOTALS		516.23	124.50	391.73
MAR	TOTAL		391.73		
	NET GOODS		401.36		
	NET VAT		.63.87		

Most computer packages prepare lists of:

(a) payments due;
(b) name-and-address lists;
(c) audit reports;
(d) ledgers; and
(e) creditor lists.

A payments due list is shown in Figure 6.3. The highlighted
sections show:

187

fig 6.3 *payments due list*
Source: Apricot (UK) Ltd

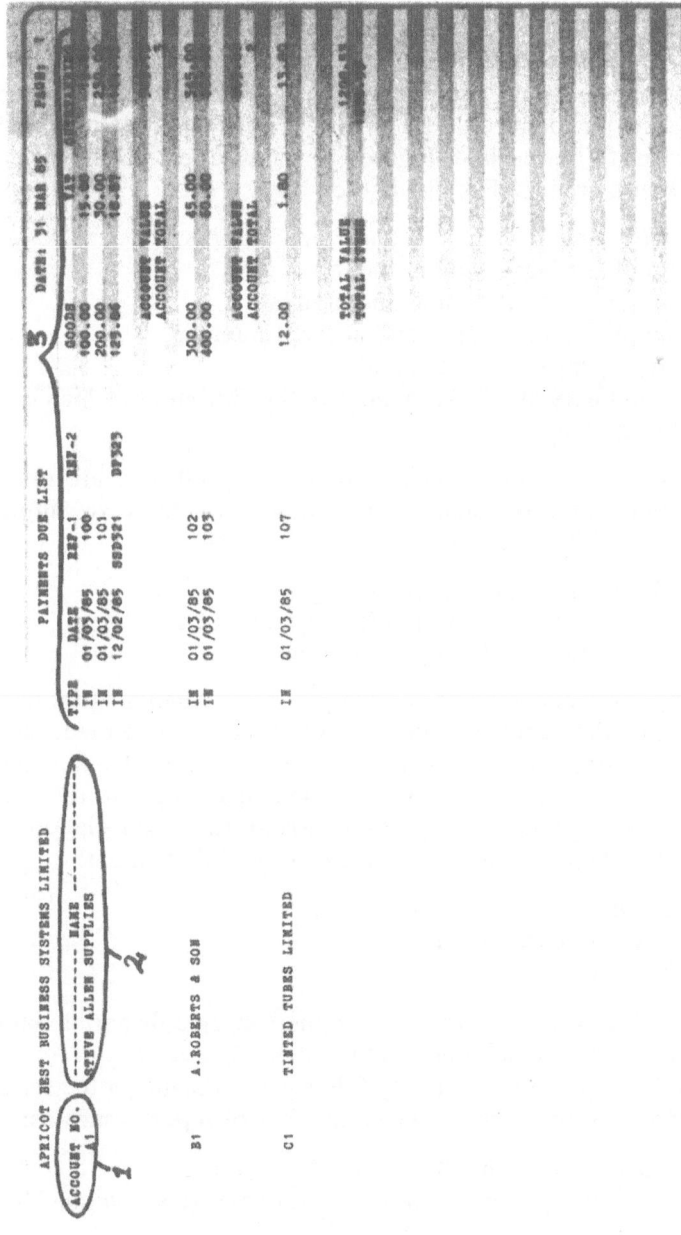

(1) the account number;
(2) the supplier name; and
(3) details of all transactions which are due for payment.

There may also be routines to produce cheques for payments and to generate bank giro credits. The system may be designed to generate payments only when the payment-due date or a credit limit is about to be reached. Figure 6.4 shows direct payment details via bank giro credits. The highlighted parts are:

(1) your company's bank's name and address:
(2) supplier's bank code;
(3) supplier's bank's name and address;
(4) supplier's name and bank account number;
(5) your company's name; and
(6) a summary of all transactions in the current run which is used for internal use.

Security measures, such as password protocols, are essential to prevent fraud or unauthorised access to sensitive information. Obviously there must be other checks, such as:

(a) did the delivery take place?
(b) were the goods returned for any reason? and
(c) is the price on the invoice correct?

Some systems provide a cheque reconciliation routine, which matches the cheques issued against cheques presented. Banks can provide firms with a bank account statement tape detailing the latter. This tape can be copied on to a floppy disk, input to the microcomputer system and then used as a basis for the reconciliation routines. The purchase ledger system needs to hold data about:

(a) suppliers' names and addresses;
(b) buying contracts; and
(c) credit limits.

It may be possible to refer to suppliers using only partial name keys, as well as full name or account number. By using any of these keys, it should be possible to display full account details on the screen.

Most systems will produce a number of reports, such as:

(a) balances according to age by due date;
(b) a list of suppliers' names and addresses (and mailing labels);
(c) audit trail reports;
(d) VAT analysis; and
(e) payment details.

fig 6.4 *bank giro credit to suppliers*
Source: Apricot (UK) Ltd

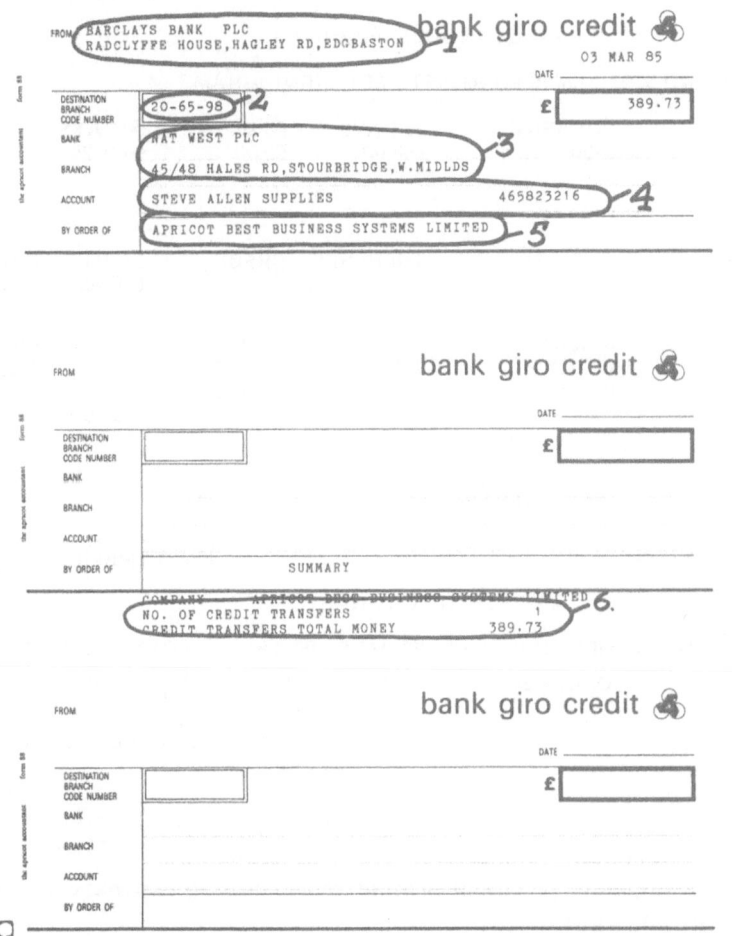

Figures 6.5 and 6.6 show a purchase ledger enquiry and an aged creditor analysis respectively.

6.5 NOMINAL LEDGER

The nominal ledger, sometimes called the general ledger, summarises sales ledger and purchase ledger details, providing the information required to produce the following items.

fig 6.5 *purchase ledger report*

OUR COMPANY   8 NOVEMBER 1986

PURCHASE LEDGER ENQUIRY

ACCOUNT NO 5366 JAMES LONG, ASTON ST, BIRMINGHAM

BALANCE	CURRENT	30 DAYS	60 DAYS	90 DAYS
£259.25	£-300	£58.00	£0.00	£501.25

DATE	OUR REF	THEIR REF	CREDIT	DEBIT B/Fwd	BALANCE £0.00
04 5 86	B713INV	176	£184.75		£184.75
19 8 86	B771INV	981	£201.25		£386.00
17 10 86	B775INV	1387	£358.00		£559.25
1 11 86	C74CSH	1711		£300.00	

fig 6.6 *aged creditor analysis*

OUR COMPANY   8 NOVEMBER 1986

AGED CREDITOR ANALYSIS

ACCOUNT	NAME	CURRENT	30 DAYS	60 DAYS	90 DAYS	OLDER
5366	J. LONG	−300	58.00	0.00	501.25	0

BALANCE 259.25

(a) Profit and loss account
This is a summary report of income and operating expenses for the company and each department.

(b) Balance sheet
This is based on the assets and liabilities of the company.

(c) Trial balance
This lists the balance of each account at the end of the financial period.

These reports are usually produced monthly, and there will be a set of accounts produced annually.

The nominal ledger can therefore be seen as the central part of the business accounts: a record of the incomings and outgoings, which also gives a general picture of the company's trading position. It also records information about the assets and liabilities of the business and keeps these up to date by recording details about relevant transactions.

Using the data held in the nominal ledger files, the balance sheet and profit and loss accounts are constructed and printed, usually along with a report of the previous period for comparative purposes. There will be a number of accounts kept to provide information to management on the assets and liabilities of the business and perhaps details of sales and purchases under various categories.

For the trial balance, each aspect of the ledger such as:

- (*i*) stocks;
- (*ii*) cash in hand;
- (*iii*) wages; and
- (*iv*) sales,

are listed as a debit or a credit. It is also possible in most systems to produce detailed analyses of sales and costs by department, product or capital item.

The profit and loss account represents the company's trading position showing items relating to revenue and expenditure. Typically, profit and loss items will include:

- (*i*) sales;
- (*ii*) cost of sales;
- (*iii*) staff costs;
- (*iv*) accommodation;
- (*v*) advertising;
- (*vi*) motor and travel;
- (*vii*) financial charges;
- (*viii*) depreciation charges; and
- (*ix*) professional charges.

These are usually assigned codes, and monies are allocated to the relevant cost centre.

Figure 6.7 gives an overview income statement showing revenues, costs and expenses, and uses that data to produce gross income and net income (after tax).

Where the nominal ledger package is integrated with a sales ledger and purchase ledger package, the entries for these will be posted directly to the nominal ledger files, so that the latter can summarise

fig 6.7 *income account (created using Wing Z)*

	1988	1987	1986
Revenues			
Sales and other operating revenues	$20 186	$18 273	$28 923
Consumer excise taxes	1 833	1 754	1 614
Other income	340	199	339
Total revenues	22 359	20 226	30 876
Costs and expenses			
Purchased crude oil, products and merchandise	8 940	7 591	12 569
Operating expenses	3 318	3 316	3 740
Petroleum exploration expenses, including exploratory dry holes	645	926	1 428
Selling and administrative expenses	1 428	1 379	1 392
Taxes other than income taxes	2 849	2 591	3 441
Depreciation, depletion, amortization, and retirements	2 296	2 418	2 059
Interest expense	398	447	435
Total costs and expenses	19 874	18 668	25 064
Income before income taxes	2 507	1 588	3 812
Income taxes	1 149	851	1 854
Net income	$1 369	$754	$1 952

the month's incomings and outgoings. This is much more convenient than batching and keying-in these entries again. However, in order to avoid security and handling problems regarding swopping floppy disks, it is much more convenient for such systems to use a hard disk.

Although much of the data is posted to the nominal ledger via the sales and purchase ledgers, some are **journal transactions** such as those relating to:

(a) rates;
(b) rent;
(c) electricity; and
(d) gas.

These journal entries are repeated each financial period and do not relate to the general purchases or sales. Journal transactions have to be entered directly into the nominal ledger system, and are not posted by the sales ledger and purchase ledger systems.

For each of these accounts there may be budget ledgers as well as actual ledgers. Thus the figures that were budgeted at the beginning of a period can be compared to the actual figures.

6.6 SALES ORDER PROCESSING AND INVOICING

When a customer orders from the company, the transaction can be validated and recorded in a sales order processing system. Stock files need to be accessed to ensure that the stock is available. This stock ought to be *allocated* so that it is not assigned elsewhere. This means that the stock file should also be updated in the sales order processing system so that a stock level of, say, 30, should be reduced to 4, if 26 of the product have already been allocated. Otherwise a new order of 20 will be 'accepted' even though this amount of stock will no longer exist in the warehouse. In a multi-user system, it is important that other users cannot gain access to the stock records being updated.

It is reassuring to the customer to send a confirmation of the order. The customer will want to receive the goods as soon as possible. The despatch note can give:

(a) **picking information**, which gives the warehouse instructions on the most efficient way to pick the goods from the shelves;
(b) **packing instructions**, which will give instructions on the box type to be used and other packing material to ensure safe delivery at the least cost; and

(c) **delivery instructions**, giving information to the driver on how best to get to the customer,

which will all speed up delivery. The quicker the goods are delivered, then the quicker the bills go out. If all bills go out one day sooner, then payments are also likely to come back one day sooner. This can make a marked improvement to a firm's profitability and cost-justify the use of the computer system in itself. In some businesses it will be possible to give the invoice with the goods.

An invoicing system will prepare the invoices, taking account of discounts relating to the:

(a) customer;
(b) product;
(c) early settlement; or
(d) size of order

and print out the invoices. Many packages provide a default invoice format which the user can customise. The user may specify the exact requirements through a question-and-answer session or through a parameter record.

Useful management reports may include an analysis of sales by type, department, salesman, and so on.

Figure 6.8 shows a typical invoice. The highlighted aspects are:

(1) The company address, which would normally be pre-printed on stationery,
(2) User-defined information for head of invoice,
(3) The customer's name and address,
(4) User-defined messages,
(5) The invoice columns,
(6) VAT analysis, and
(7) The facility to key in the delivery address, if different from the invoice address.

In the same way that the purchase ledger system is similar to the sales ledger system, purchase order processing, that is, the processing of orders to suppliers (rather than orders from customers), is similar to sales order processing.

fig 6.8 *invoice*

Source: Apricot (UK) Ltd

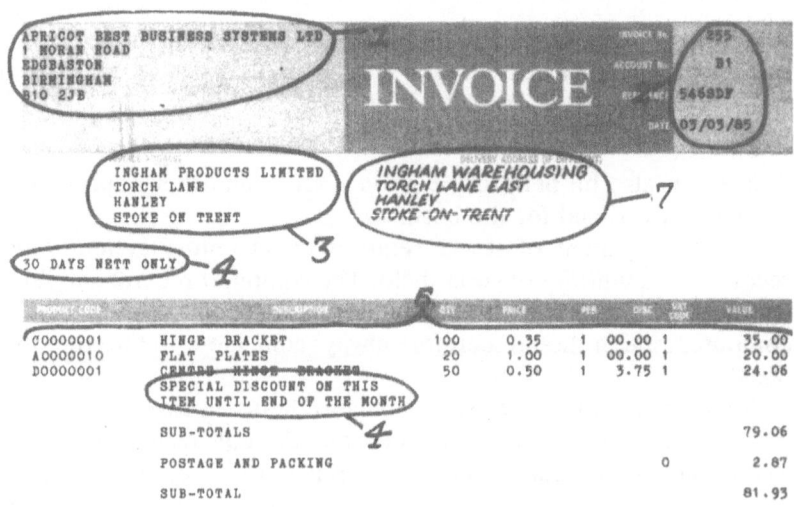

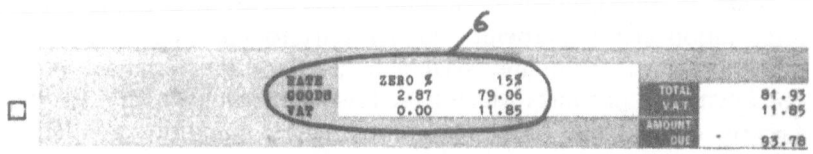

6.7 STOCK RECORDING

(a) Stock can include:

- (*i*) finished goods;
- (*ii*) work in progress; and
- (*iii*) raw materials.

(b) The transaction types will include:

- (*i*) goods received notes;
- (*ii*) customer returns;

(*iii*) production receipts; and

(*iv*) production issues.

(c) Stocks can be held for three main purposes:

(*i*) to meet the normal transactions of the business;

(*ii*) to serve as a safety stock in case of unexpected increase in demand or late delivery times; and

(*iii*) to speculate for an expected increase in price.

Stocks can also be held for *no good reason*, and then represent an expensive overhead for the business.

The management of stocks requires an inventory system which records the quantities of goods held. The computer records should be updated continuously, as stocks are depleted or added to. The computer system should therefore always coincide with the true stock position.

Stock levels should represent a balance between two dangers: that of not being able to supply customers and thereby losing custom, and that of having too much money 'tied up in stock'. This is itself costly, as the monies could be better spent elsewhere, and there may be consequent losses through deterioriation and/or obsolescence.

Stocks may be replaced when the amount of a product in stock falls below a pre-determined **re-order level**. There is some scope here for the computer system to continually review re-order levels and indicate to the user those products that need re-ordering. This information can be provided in a report to the user. It may be possible for the computer system to produce the purchase order documents for products which have low stock levels directly. In this case the computer files must hold the re-order quantities and details of suppliers.

An alternative system is for a **periodic review** of stocks. On the basis of stock levels at that time, the re-order quantities (if any) are determined and the orders placed. This approach is preferable where demand fluctuates considerably. The order quantity is calculated on the basis of an amount to bring the stock level equal to a maximum quantity. This value will also be held in computer files.

Most computer packages available follow the former (re-order level) strategy for replenishing stock.

As well as maintaining records of stocks, including periodic adjustments to take account of goods returned from customers and pilfering, and triggering re-ordering, a package is also likely to provide reports giving information on, for example:

(a) slow-moving stock;

(b) stock-outs; and
(c) slow deliveries.

Some packages 'recognise' that stocks may be held at different warehouses and keep tags on stock levels at each warehouse. This makes possible one warehouse 'feeding' another, and avoids unnecessary re-ordering from suppliers.

Some packages contain a **forecasting** element. Such aspects as the re-order level and the re-order quantity could be established by analysing the previous demand levels. They may therefore incorporate features such as exponential smoothing that are normally associated with a full statistics package (see section 7.3).

As well as keeping stock records, the system is also likely to keep records of suppliers, including their names and addresses and details of a 'contact person' who can be contacted for urgent requirements. Data might also be kept on the delivery times and reliability of suppliers.

Another aspect of stock is its *evaluation*. This is not as simple as it seems, and yet the basis on which stocks are evaluated will be critical to income measurement. Stock evaluation could be based on the selling price or cost price of the product. The cost price could be based on present prices or the price when it was produced or bought. Conventionally, the evaluation of stocks is based on some form of weighted average of these cost prices.

The reporting facilities of a stock control package are important. There should be exception reports giving details of slow moving stock or items frequently out of stock. These can also be displayed as warning messages on the screen. The package should also provide general reports, such as:

(a)   the location of items of stock in the warehouse;
(b)   outstanding allocation of stock (goods which have been allocated but for which the official customer order has not been received or the stock has not been replenished);
(c)   total movements of stock in a year; and
(d)   checklists for stocktaking.

Figure 6.9 shows a typical checklist for stocktaking. The highlighted values are:

(1)   product number;
(2)   description;
(3)   location;
(4)   status;
(5)   selling unit;

Source: **Apricot (UK) Ltd**

APRICOT BEST BUSINESS SYSTEMS LIMITED
STOCK LIST

STOCK CONTROL

02/05/85

DESCRIPTION		QUANTITY	VALUE	CODE	ORDER POSITION	HISTORY	
A0000001 ANGLE PLATE	1 EACH	900	90.00	0.10	0		0.10
ROW1		3250	1324.00	0.12	0		0.12
S		5010	501.85	0	2660		0.14
		2660	121.85	0	2660		00.00
					2660		00.00
A0000002 SUPPORT BRACKET	1 EACH	250	62.50	0.25	0		0.25
ROW2		1000	250.00	0.15	1250		0.55
S		2000	500.00	0	1250		0.75
		0	-125.00	0	1250		00.00
		1250	187.50	0	0		00.00
A0000010 FLAT PLATES	1 EACH	38	38.00	1.00	0		1.00
ROW1		15	8.25	0.55	23		2.00
S		0	-17.10	0	23		3.00
		23	12.65	0	23		00.00
							00.00
B0000001 DOOR PLATE	1 EACH	90	90.00	1.00	0		1.00
ROW2		1370	1370.00	0.65	-1280		1.50
S		0	448.00	0	-1280		2.00
		-1280	-832.00	0	-1280		00.00
B0000002 SEAT BRACKET	1 EACH	50	25.00	0.50	5		0.50
ROW2		95	48.75	0.25	950		0.75
S		1000	500.00	0	950		1.00
		955	238.75	0	0		00.00
B0000012 RAIL FITTING	1 EACH	12	120.00	10.00	0		10.00
ROW1		52	520.00	7.00	-40		12.50
T		0	0.00	0	-40		15.00
		-40	-280.00	0	-40		00.00
C0000001 HINGE BRACKET	1 EACH	1000	350.00	0.35	166		0.35
ROW1		-156	-78.10	0.15	1000		0.38
T		0	-253.20	0	1000		0.40
		1166	174.90	0	0		00.00
C0000002 LADDER CLIPS	1 EACH	200	100.00	0.50	0		0.50
ROW1		0	0.00	0.21	200		0.00
T		0	-58.00	0	200		00.00
		200	42.00	0	0		00.00
C0000020 WALL FIXING	1 EACH	20	30.00	1.50	10		1.50
ROW1		5	7.30	0.65	25		1.60
T		20	30.00	0	25		1.70
		55	22.75	0	0		00.00

(6) selling prices;
(7) discount levels;
(8) re-order details;
(9) an additional report column; and
(10) cost price.

Stock control packages are frequently integrated with the other accounting routines.

(a) Integration with sales order processing can ensure that data is used to update the stock files and therefore save the raw data being keyed in again for the stock system.

(b) Integration with the purchase order system can ensure that re-orders are made automatically when stocks become depleted.

(c) Integration with sales ledger and purchase ledger systems can ensure that these details are recorded on the ledgers.

(d) Integration with the invoicing system will enable the triggering of the invoices when the goods have been taken.

Obviously it is important to have a standard and unique identifying code for each item of stock in each system, although it is usual to provide a visual check to the operator of the product name when entering data.

6.8 COSTING

The costing of jobs is important in estimating the price to be charged to the customer for a product or service, and is therefore a standard accounting application. However, surveys of available software show that this application is less frequently available than most other accounting routines discussed in this chapter. The main reason for this is that costing procedures tend to be industry-specific, and there are some costing packages available which relate to a particular industry, such as those for the construction industry. '

Associated with the costing module are a set of expense codes relating to each type of expense. Attributing these to a particular job will enable the user to cost that job. The costing package will keep a record of the costs in each category for a job over time.

One of these costs is that for labour, and therefore some form of integration with the payroll system will reduce the amount of data that has to be keyed in. Labour costing can be complex, particularly where some form of piece rate and overtime scheme is used for the payment of employees. Added to the basic labour charge will be a charge for the overheads of employing each worker.

Another cost is related to raw materials used in a job. Job costing packages may have access to the stock control system where details of stocks can be found. The costing package may update the stock records as stocks are drawn off for particular jobs. Associated with this module (or the stock control module) may be 'bill of materials', that is a list of materials required for any product or job, and the quantities of these materials.

An important facility for management is the comparison of estimated (budgeted) with actual costs. Even if estimates were incorrect this time, the accountant – helped by the costing system – will be able to learn from this experience and future estimating should be more accurate. The more accurate costing is, then the more likely it is that the firm will make a 'reasonable profit' for work and at the same time win orders from customers.

6.9 PAYROLL

Every organisation has employees, and so every company will have a payroll system of some kind. There are a number of computer systems available, and it is essential that any system that is implemented is reliable, for mistakes in pay details or the failure to run the payroll on time will cause many problems.

For every employee, the payroll system will calculate:

(a) gross pay for the particular payroll period; and
(b) deductions, such as tax, social security, and superannuation.

Payroll systems for salaried staff can be less complex than for employees receiving a weekly wage. Salaried staff will have a fixed annual salary, whereas the gross pay for wage earners will be calculated using normal time rates and overtime rates and multiplying these rates of pay by the appropriate hours worked.

Most systems offer a number of ways of payment.

(a) Cash
Should payment be paid by cash, the system is likely to offer a **coin analysis** whereby the wage of each employee is analysed and a total

requirement for the various notes and coins made. There may be an optional rounding of net wages to avoid 'coin nuisance'.

(b) Cheque
If payment is made by cheque, the cheques sometimes are printed by the system. Alternatively they can be written manually to the amounts advised by a system printout.

(c) Bank transfer
This is a method of payment where payment is sent directly to the bank of the employee from the company's bank.

Payroll packages may offer all these alternatives and the user specifies the exact requirements before running the system.

Figure 6.10 shows two payslips. The highlighted aspects show:

(1) titles, defined by the user;
(2) the hourly rate;
(3) pre-printed titles;
(4) cash analysis;
(5) number of payments this period; and
(6) cumulative deduction fields.

Payroll packages need to be particularly accurate and timely. Late payment of salaries causes much distress to employees and is frequently used to cite a company about to go bankrupt. Further, these packages need to be very secure, both to prevent fraud and to prevent unauthorised access to sensitive data.

The package also needs to take account of legislation in relation to salaries, social security and pension arrangements, and be maintained so that it is always in step with these legal and social requirements. The various forms required for tax purposes need to be printed out using pre-printed stationery. Ideally, the system will be easy to adapt to such changes as statutory sick pay requirements, national insurance and tax rates.

Considerations such as a good maintenance and software support contract and a reliable supplier are particularly important in the context of payroll systems. Updates of the package to take account of changes in legislation need to be implemented at the right time and be correct. Because government requirements and rates do change frequently, it is important (as it is with most packages) to take out a maintenance contract with the supplier so that updates are given automatically. It is also important to choose a supplier which is likely to stay in business for some time.

fig 6.10 *payslip*
    Source: Apricot (UK) Ltd

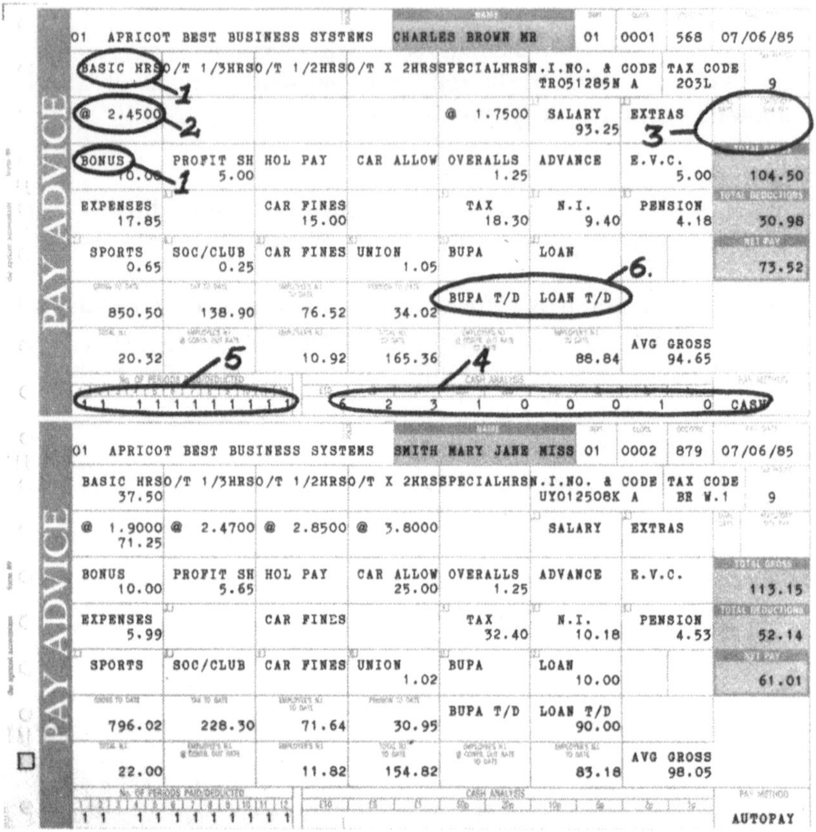

Reports provided by the system are likely to include:

(a) a listing of employee details;
(b) wage costs by department;
(c) total tax and national insurance contributions; and
(d) total funds transfer to each bank.

6.10 INTEGRATED ACCOUNTS

There are many application packages available for accounting applications and some are *integrated* so that all the accounting routines can

be processed in a similar manner. Data collected and validated for one module can be used by others (see Figure 6.11). In this way, duplicating data collection and storage is avoided. This transference of data from one part of the system to another is called **posting**. Integrated packages may also provide management information which derives from data coming from a combination of the individual source modules.

Integrated accounts packages can be complex to use and necessitate swopping floppy disks in and out. It is therefore advisable to have a larger microcomputer (with at least 512k) and hard disks. These will be able to hold several years' comparative data for statistical analyses and decision support, as well as accounts data for the present year to date.

fig 6.11 *integrated accounts – collecting data once for all accounts systems*

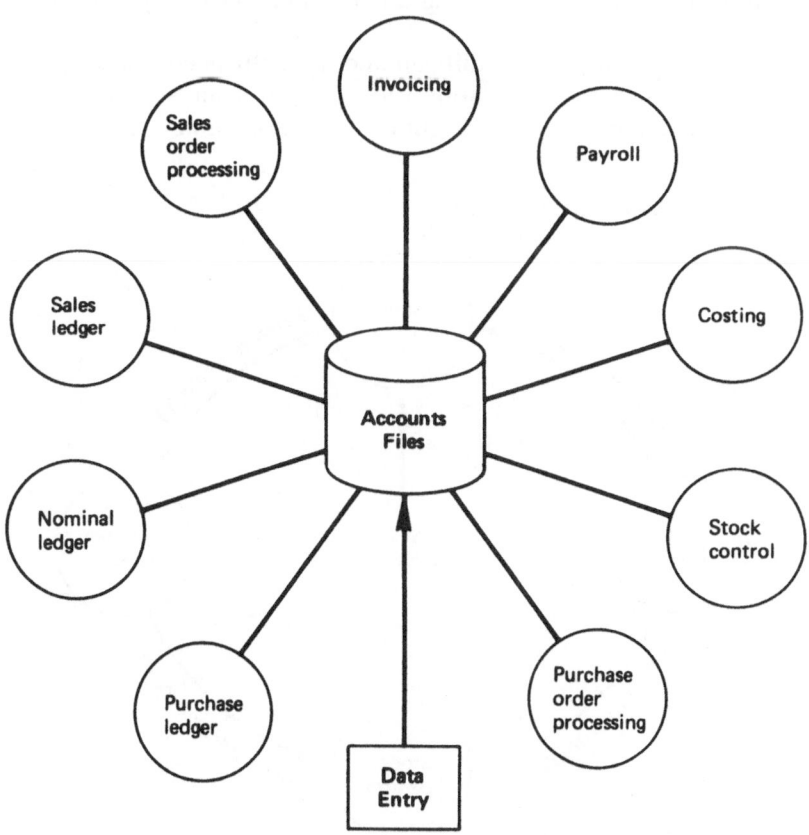

Fully integrated packages represent only one end of the spectrum and some packages are more limited, being designed to maintain, say, only customer, personnel and VAT records. This may be all that is necessary for the particular business. Sometimes many of the features of an integrated system will not be used, and therefore much of the investment will be wasted should a fully integrated system be purchased.

One solution will be to purchase individual modules of the integrated package. For example, the basic modules such as sales, purchase, and nominal ledgers and stock control may be bought separately, even though they are designed to integrate to form a complete ledger package (see Figure 6.12). This does mean that some of the advantages such as single data entry and validation will be lost.

Integrated systems will use a common style for presentation, and the commands will be similar for each part of the system, so that although the whole system is large and perhaps difficult to learn, it is likely to be easier than learning about a number of separate packages.

Installation can be more difficult and normally needs the help of a dealer, although the installation procedure of some systems is well documented and proves straightforward. Sometimes, the user is

fig 6.12 *integrated accounts (part)*

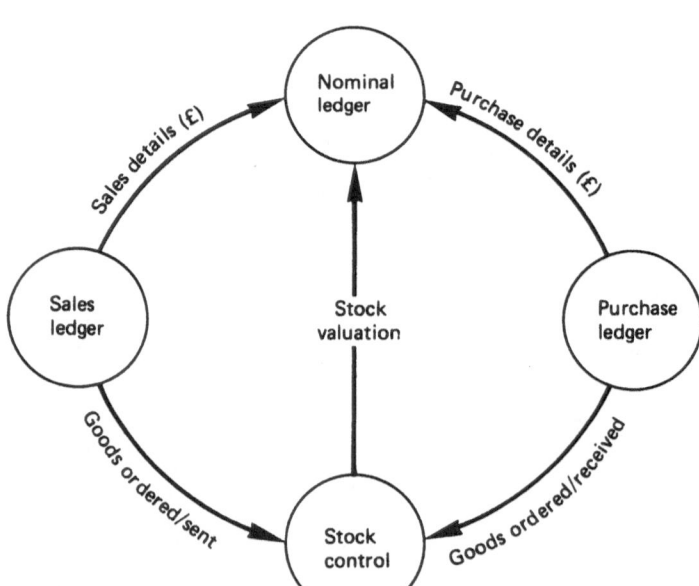

faced with so many options that it is difficult to know, without having had experience of the package, what the right answers are for any particular installation.

One of the important advantages of an integrated accounts system is that of verifying the integrity of the subsystems which make up the accounting package. For example, it will be possible to check that the total amount owing to the business in the sales ledger files equals the total amount owed by debtors in the nominal ledger. Further, there should be a common and safe policy recommended for the backup of files so that recovery from any inconsistencies discovered or from a 'crash' of the system is possible.

An audit trail, which checks the processing of transactions, keeping track of what has happened, can be followed through *all* the accounts. This may be particularly useful in an external audit, such as the one carried out by tax inspectors. They will not be satisfied with cumulative totals only, they need to know how these totals have been derived, and with an integrated package it is easier to follow the transactions through the system.

INTEGRATED SYSTEMS

AND

OTHER APPLICATIONS

We have already discussed the fundamentals of word processing, file management, spreadsheet and graphics packages, and although many users do buy separate systems for each of these, the alternative does exist of buying a single integrated package which contains all these elements (and sometimes others as well). Integrated packages are discussed in section 7.1.

Many integrated packages have communications modules. These provide the ability for the microcomputer system to link with other microcomputers or to act as a terminal to a minicomputer or mainframe system. The opportunity is also taken in this section to discuss communications facilities in the context of integrated systems.

Project control packages are discussed in section 7.2. These help managers schedule projects and allocate people and other resources to them. Although many spreadsheet and file management packages do have statistical routines included amongst their operators, sometimes the facilities of purpose-built statistical packages are required. These are discussed in section 7.3.

We have assumed in this text that readers will not be prepared to write their own computer programs, or at least that they would prefer to avoid this if possible. However it may be necessary for users to write additional procedures to an application package and to generate applications in some circumstances. Aids to help users generate their own programs are discussed in sections 7.4 and 7.5.

The last section in the chapter discusses one of the newer applications of microcomputers, that of expert systems, which represent attempts to develop computer programs which simulate the role of the expert.

7.1 INTEGRATED PACKAGES

Many packages can claim to be integrated to some extent. A spreadsheet package is likely to have good graphics facilities so as to present the basic data in the most attractive way. Similarly, data base systems are likely to have graphics facilities. In integrated systems the packages are designed for efficient integrated use rather than to have one main use which is extended to have features of others (see Figure 7.1).

The main advantage of an integrated system is that data for each module can conveniently be used by the others. This may be very useful. For example, a manager may be producing a report on a word processor. It would be advantageous if it is possible to include in that text a table of values set up in the file management system or display these values as a pie chart or bar chart set up in the graphics module.

There may be disadvantages too:

(a) Some functions rarely required
The user's application may be a single system application, such as one requiring only a spreadsheet. This means that the other functions are required only rarely. Yet these have been paid for in terms of money, memory requirement and complexity.

(b) Absent facilities
Some of the facilities in a good specialist package may be absent in the attempt to keep the integrated package as small and as simple as possible. For example, an integrated word processor may not handle foreign language characters or may not have a spelling checker or the choice of charts in the business graphics part may be too limiting.

(c) Time and money already invested in a single function package
There may be a reluctance to pay for the new package and to devote the time and effort necessary to convert the data from one system to the integrated system.

(d) One application featured very strongly
Many of these systems feature one of the applications very strongly, typically the spreadsheet, and other parts of the integrated package are less sophisticated and sometimes rather weak.

fig 7.1 *integrated packages*

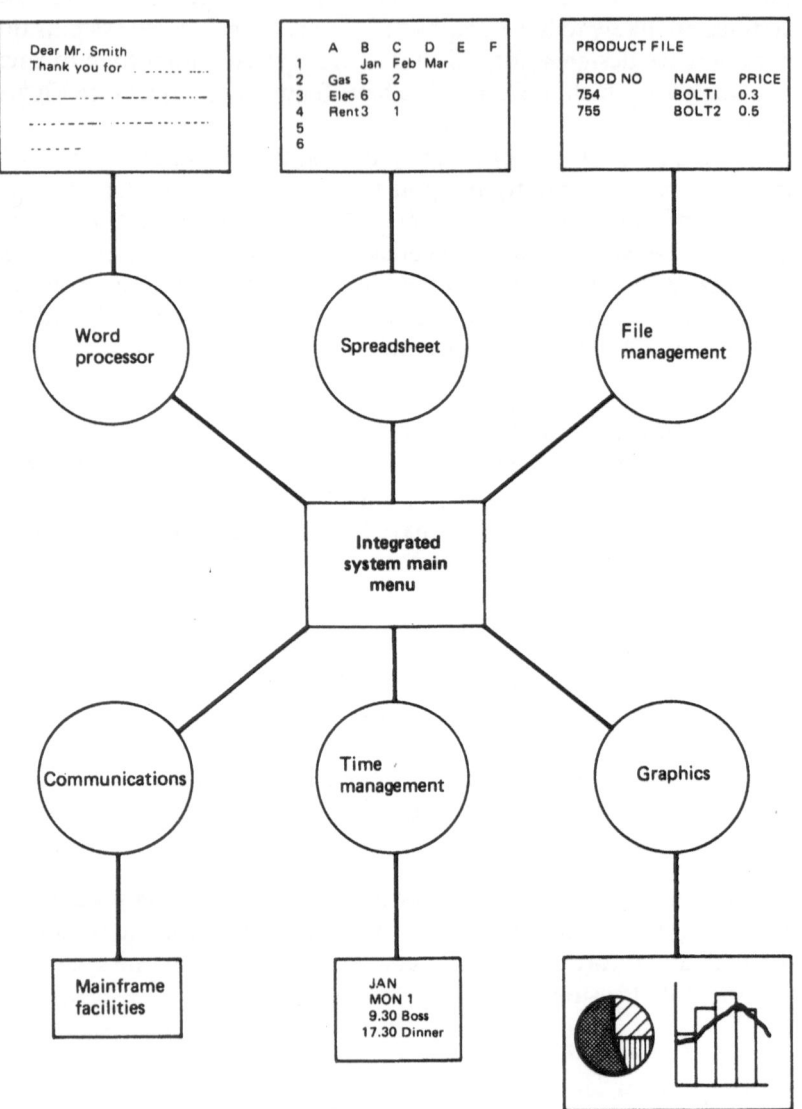

(e) Only two or three types of application featured
Some of these systems feature only two or three types of application, such as spreadsheet with graphics or word processing with a data base.

There is an alternative to integrated packages. Where there is a strong case for choosing a particular word processor, particular business graphics system, and so on, the users may be able to 'mix-and-match'. There are programs available which are designed to enable your 'separates' to communicate with each other using a common language. In this case, the files of each system need to be readable and writeable in a single format, usually one of the following standards:

(a) ASCII (American Standard Code for Information Interchange);
(b) DIF (Data Interchange Format), which is the standard used initially by the early spreadsheet package *Visicalc*; or
(c) 123 format, used by the package *Lotus 1-2-3*.

However, the degree of genuine integration (for example, common styles of messages and use of function keys) will be limited by following this solution, and the rest of this section will be devoted to purpose-built integrated software. This software may be supplied as a set of one or two disks which hold the basic application programs. The user will normally load these as the first task of the day. Alternatively the package may be supplied as a set of floppy disks, a basic disk and then one disk for each application. The former approach avoids the necessity of having to change disks on each change of application and, in general, simplifies procedures. In the attempt to keep the whole system simple, however, their facilities may be more limited.

An integrated package *can* be large and expensive and installing and learning about the system may be quite time consuming. However, these systems are usually menu-driven so that the user can specify those aspects of the system that are required. In this way, learning about the system may not be too difficult a process. Sometimes the learning process is divided into basic, advanced and professional levels, the user specifying the 'confidence level'. Most integrated packages will come with a tutorial program which will go through each aspect of the system step-by-step.

There are other factors which will help ease of learning. Many packages will make full use of the function keys of the particular computer so that each command may be simple to execute. Further, similar types of commands, such as deleting, reading, printing, and moving to a new VDU page, can use the same procedure in each program, so that the total familiarisation process should be easier than learning about the equivalent number of separates. *Consistency betwen modules* is a goal of most integrated packages, although sometimes commands good for one application are not necessarily suitable for the other applications. Another aspect of consistency in integrated packages is that the general appearance of the screens is likely to be similar, whichever module is being executed.

Most integrated packages are fairly complicated to set up in the first place, and it is advisable to ensure that this is performed by the supplier as part of the contract. Of course this advice holds true for any package, but an integrated system is likely to double or treble the problem, because of its scope.

One important aspect of integrated systems is the amount of memory needed, for although it may be possible to run them on a basic or 512k machine, most will be very sluggish unless user documents are very small. For this reason integrated packages normally need at least one megabyte to run, and preferably more.

In order to avoid the problem of constantly changing disks, a hard disk system is preferable. Even so, some systems require a 'systems disk' to be in the floppy disk drive to enable the system to operate. The reason for this is to prevent non-registered users using the system illegally. This may be sensible from the supplier's point of view, but is a nuisance for the user.

Many integrated systems follow a principle known as virtual memory. When the module is loaded in, there may be, say, 200k bytes left for the spreadsheet. If a user wants a spreadsheet bigger than this, then he is unfortunate unless the data can be swopped in and out of disk. The user is then given a memory as large as the disk space, rather than the memory left in the machine. There may be a penalty in speed, because writing data on disk is slower than writing on main memory.

Another useful facility provided by most integrated systems is the ability to write a series of procedures as a macro and execute this whenever the same procedures are required. The macro can include calls to a number of the modules. Usually the user writes the set of procedures which can then be tested, corrected, and stored, and run as required.

Alternatively, the process may involve the following steps. First the system is switched to 'remember' mode, then the set of processes is 'acted out', and if it works, this set of procedures is stored and can be executed again when required. This process of writing macros is sometimes referred to as 'programming by doing'.

Most integrated packages are *not* **multi-tasking** in the true sense. This would imply that the user could set a spreadsheet in calculating mode, and whilst the system is busy with that, go into another module and work with that. However, most *are* **multi-task-active**, that is, they will allow the user to work on one module (the others being held in a 'frozen state'), then pass over to another module, then go back to the first, and so on, without it being necessary to write files out on disk at each stage. This saves a lot of user time.

Sometimes it is possible for both tasks to be displayed on the screen as separate windows. Part of the spreadsheet can be in one window, whilst the text for word processing can be in another. The joy of integrated packages comes when the user is at the point in the text when a table from the spreadsheet can be incorporated in the text, in other words, the two windows can be merged. Data is said to be **piped** between the applications. In this way a change in the data base, for example, can effect an equivalent change in the final report, without the data having to be transferred again. Most systems allow a number of modules to be active or 'live' at one time. The limits will be determined by the main memory available and the ability of users to keep track of what is going on.

There is a similar but alternative system to windows, known as the **frame** which has been adopted by some integrated package writers. A frame is a development of the window concept in that frames can contain parts of the constituent modules (part of a spreadsheet and file for example) but can be arranged in a hierarchy so that one frame can contain elements of others which can themselves contain further frames. Thus one frame can hold the main headings of a document, the next the subheadings within any of these main headings, and the next the text which is within any subheading.

Most integrated packages have word processing, file management, graphics and spreadsheet as elements, but some systems have time management and communications modules as well. On entering the package, the user is normally given a list of these options as a menu, from which the choice of option is made.

The time management module enables the user to create a diary, telephone and address book, and can be used for meeting arrangement, as it will be possible to find a time slot when all participants are free. Tasks may be displayed by time and priority. With the diary system, daily, weekly and monthly schedules can be printed or displayed. It may even be possible to list jobs by priority. Some of these applications were discussed in Chapter 2.

The **communications** module is particularly useful and the rest of this section will be devoted to this topic. The communications module enables files to be transferred between users on different machines. Once the parameters for a particular communication have been set (see below), the second computer is dialled and the user follows the protocols of that computer. These protocols will include correct user number and password. Assuming that these protocols are correct, the user has access to the programs and data on the remote microcomputer.

The parameters are:

(a) speed – defined as a **baud** rate (baud = bits per second);
(b) size of character transmitted (the number of **data bits**);
(c) size of boundary between characters, the number of **stop bits**; and
(d) the checking mechanism (the **parity** bits).

These settings for the two systems need to be known, otherwise successful communication will not be established.

The communications package may also be used for remote access to a central computer data base such as library data, government statistics, or an up-to-date listing of stocks and share prices. These data bases can be pulled into the system as a spreadsheet or file. The user can then use the facilities of the integrated package to analyse, manipulate or print the data. Thus the data can be expressed as a graph, a facility which may not be available on the host data base.

There may also be a facility to use the various electronic mail services such as Telecom Gold and Easylink. With this facility it will be possible to send and receive messages to and from subscribers of the electronic mail service using your electronic **mailbox**.

The communications facility normally requires additional hardware, that of the **modem**, which facilitates the transfer of data between the computers. The word is short for modulator-demodulator and it allows computers to 'talk' to each other using telephone lines. Its function is to translate digital signals (the kind used by computers) to signals acceptable in the telephone network. It will also translate these signals back again so that the computer at the other end can pick them up digitally. There will therefore be a modem at both ends of the communications link. The telephone number of the receiving computer is dialled (or keyed in, depending on the system) and there is a link established between the two machines. Many modems have automatic dial and answer facilities, which reduces the amount of work.

Although most systems do require additional equipment, some computers now come with a 'communications module' which includes a telephone, modem and communications software. At least in this purchase, the user should avoid possible problems such as non-compatibility and the lack of the correct interface or cable.

The acoustic modem (or **coupler**) is an alternative to the standard modem. The user dials the telephone number of the receiving computer system and, once communication has been established, the headset of the telephone is placed in the two cups of the acoustic coupler. Such links are easy to set up, but acoustic couplers are prone to picking up spurious noises and a permanent hook to the telephone system is better in the long term.

Another facility of some communications modules is that of **terminal emulation**. This is the ability to change the role of the microcomputer to that of 'dumb terminal' to another computer. The user can then take advantage of the computing power of that computer. Messages are transferred from the microcomputer keyboard and replies are displayed on the VDU attached to it.

Some packages enable the user to emulate particular terminal standards (such as ANSI or VT100) and the host computer cannot distinguish between this terminal and any others that conform to its standards.

Using the microcomputer as an intelligent terminal, rather than simply keyboard and VDU access to the host computer, allows the user to store data on that machine and to format data which will be sent to the host machine. This will not be possible if the microcomputer is simply a dumb terminal.

7.2 PROJECT CONTROL

One of the most important tasks of a manager is project planning and control. Projects which take longer than scheduled cause a loss of money as well as embarrassment, particularly if the delays were unexpected or cannot be explained easily. The use of a project planning package can ensure that projects are scheduled at the earliest possible date, with the least drain on resources, and that there is a good chance that this date will be met. If there are delays, then at least the managers have information about them. Projects may include the launching of a new product, developing a piece of software, producing a set of documents, or building a house.

Project control techniques start with an attempt to break down the large and complex project into tasks, normally called **activities**. Once the activities have been identified, a time and resource requirement is assigned to each of them, and the interrelationships between them established. In other words, those tasks which are dependent on the completion of other tasks are identified. These activities, and information about them, can be entered into a project control package (see Figure 7.2). The more powerful packages now available can handle thousands of activities and many packages are geared towards multi-project management and departmental planning so that the whole department is run as efficiently as possible. Many systems will handle multi-project management on the basis of priorities assigned to each project, as well as other factors such as resource management.

Using this information the computer package can draw up a **network**. In a network, the activities are represented by the arrows which join the nodes. These represent events, that is, the completion of activities.

As for all the applications discussed in this text, project control, even with the help of a good computer package, requires careful and detailed work:

(a) to identify tasks;
(b) to establish the interrelationships between tasks; and
(c) to allocate their resource needs.

This is an analytical process which is time-consuming.

Figure 7.3 shows a network. The arrows represent the activities, though the length of the arrow does *not* indicate the time taken for each task. Arrows drawn in parallel indicate tasks that can be carried out simultaneously. Arrows following others indicate tasks that are dependent on the completion of those other tasks.

The manual development of networks is lengthy and project control packages can make the task much easier. They can draw the network and highlight **critical** activities on which any slippage of time will cause the whole project time scale to suffer. The path of the critical activities joined together forms the **critical path** and it is useful for the package to highlight these activities. In Figure 7.3, the activities A-B-C-E are on the critical path. If it is possible to reduce the time of these activities, possibly by moving to them resources allocated to other activities, then the overall project time should decrease. Activity D is not on the critical path, and there is a slack of 7 days on this activity. In other words, there can be a delay of up to 7 days on D without delaying the overall project.

Figure 7.4 shows a network drawn on a plotter. The conventions are slightly different in this system, with the nodes representing events containing most of the information about the particular network.

fig 7.2 *activities with resource requirements*
      Source: Abtex Software Ltd

Acme Construction Ltd   NEW HOUSING ESTATE, MOSELEY

REPORT TYPE: ACTIVITY LISTING   Printing Sequence :: Node, Activity Number Sequence
PLAN ID HOUSE   Version 1   Selection Criteria :: All
                                       Time Now Date   :: 11 Jul 89

DUR	PREC NODE	SUCC NODE	DUR	DESCRIPTION	RESOURCES	
	START=> 10			UNSCHEDULED		
	>> 10 <<	MILESTONE START				
START	=> 10	=> 12	4	Clear Site	5 labourers / 1 excavator	2 dumper trucks / 100 cost in £
		=> 32	14	Deliver Windows		
		=> 35	12	Deliver Roofing		
	>> 12 <<	MILESTONE START CONSTRUCTION				
4	10	=> 12	=> 14	4 Excavate for drains	3 labourers / 1 excavator	1 dumper truck / 80 cost in £
			=> 16	3 Prepare foundations	3 reinforcers / 3 carpenters / 1.75 tons cement	4 labourers / 120 cost in £
			=> 20	4 Drain connections	2 labourers	70 cost in £
4	12	=> 14	=> 20	2 Construct drains	3 labourers	150 cost in £
3	12	=> 16	=>18	2 Prepare and cast concrete foundations	3 concreters / 200 cost in £	3 labourers
2	16	=> 18	=> 20	10 Underground walls	4 bricklayers / 75 cost in £	2 labourers
4	12	=> 20	=> 24	3 Prepare and cast concrete floor slab	3 concreters / 1 carpenter	3 labourers / 170 cost in £

215

fig 7.3 *project control – the network and critical path*

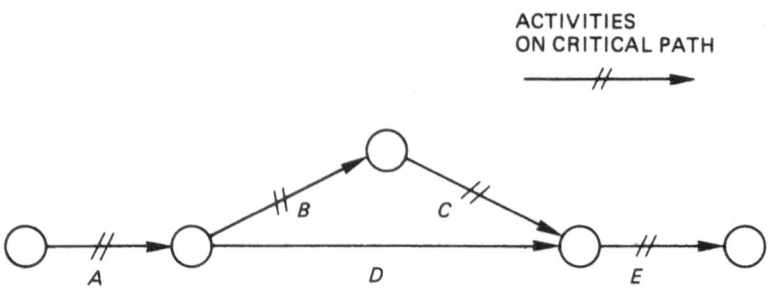

ACTIVITIES
ON CRITICAL PATH

Activity	Dependence	Duration (days)	Start	Finish	Slack
A	–	5	0	5	0
B	A	3	6	8	0
C	B	8	9	16	0
D	A	4	6	9	7
E	C,D	3	17	19	0

fig 7.4 *network drawn on plotter*
Source: Abtex Software Ltd

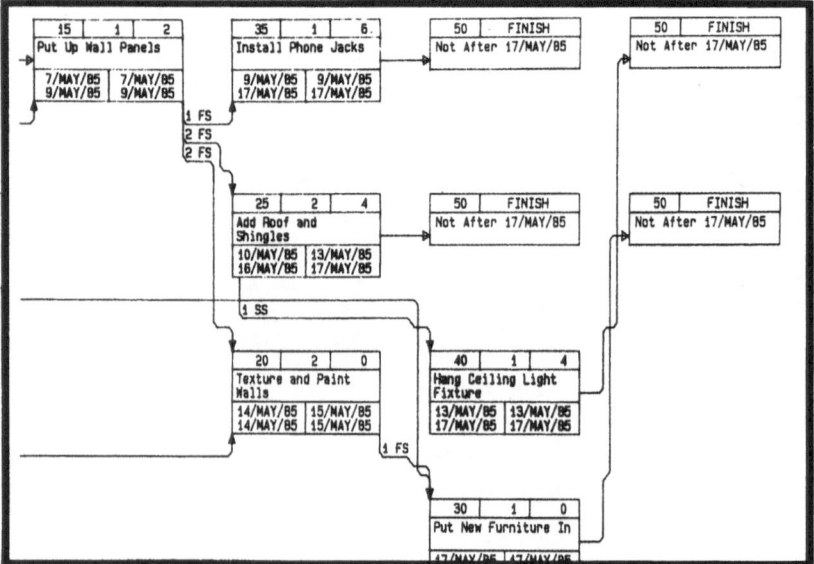

Computer packages may handle a large number of resources; for example, they may schedule, say, 200 resources over a period of eight years, aggregate the various resources, such as the number of people working on the activity, and level off the use of these resources throughout the project. It is usually better to use resources as smoothly as possible in the lifetime of the project. Once this has been done, a bar chart showing the resource allocation over time can be displayed and printed (see Figure 7.5).

Many packages will report on inconsistencies within the network, such as the same resource being used in two places at the same time. The package will normally convert days into calendar dates and allow for weekends, bank holidays, and other holidays.

Normally there is a trade-off between time and cost, in other words the more resources allocated (and the more costly the project), the quicker it can be finished. The user may like to input:

(a) the minimum;
(b) the most likely; and
(c) the maximum

resource availability so as to get three different results for time/cost comparisons. Such an exercise would be very laborious if drawn by hand.

As with a spreadsheet, project planning packages may permit the user to ask 'what if?' questions so as to see the consequence of certain actions, for example of:

(a) a strike;
(b) an overtime ban;
(c) a machine breakdown,

and so on.

Useful reports from the package include a list of activities presented in order of:

(a) latest starting date;
(b) earliest starting date;
(c) department;
(d) resource; or
(e) by responsibility.

Information relevant only to a particular department or sales area can be created so that people are not given unnecessary information.

fig 7.5 *resource scheduling*
Source: Abtex Software Ltd

Acme Construction Ltd   NEW HOUSING ESTATE, MOSELEY

REPORT TYPE: HISTOGRAM   Report Basis   : Activities at last start
                                 Resource examined : Labourers
PLAN ID HOUSE   Version 1   Time Now Date   : 11 Jul 88

8 12 16 20 24 28 32 36 40 44 48 52 56 60 64 68 72 76 80 84 88
15 Jan 89 31 Jan 89 18 Feb 89 6 Mar 89 22 Mar 89 9 Apr 89 25 Apr 89

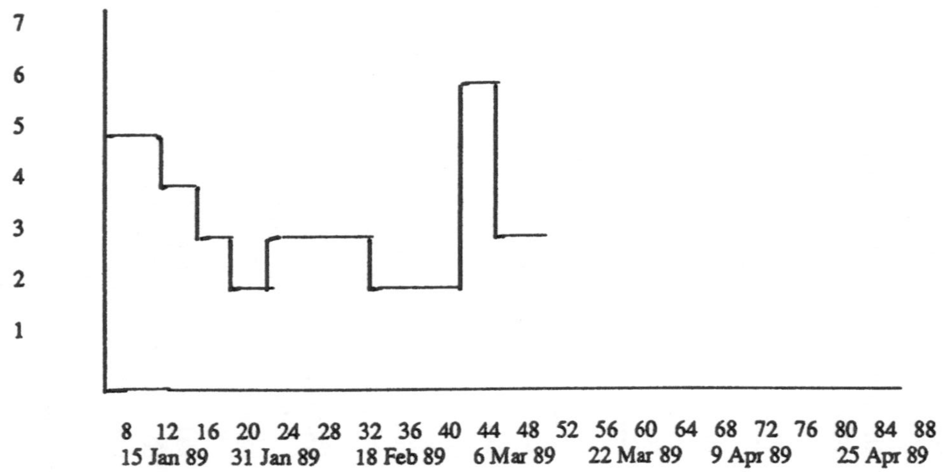

Furthermore, it may simulate the effects of:

(a) prolonging an activity;
(b) reducing resources applied to it; or
(c) adding new activities

to the total project time.

Once the project is underway there will be progress reporting. This can be used to:

(a) compare the schedule with progress made;
(b) detect problem areas; and
(c) provide a historical record which can be used for future project planning.

The system may also give information about how to act so as to put right any deviance from the schedule. This may be achieved by, for example, increasing the resources on some activities and rescheduling others. This goal seeking type of analysis, almost impossible manually, is achieved by a number of computer packages.

Many packages support colour and advanced graphics and have the degree of sophistication previously restricted to large mainframe systems. For example, probability analysis can be used to estimate the likelihood of a project being completed on time. This will be based on various statistical analysis routines being applied to the individual activities and costs.

7.3 STATISTICS

Statistics packages are designed to give statistical analyses of data sets. Some statistical analysis functions may be available in a spreadsheet package and integrated package, but the facilities of a purpose-built statistical package are likely to be more wide-ranging.

The data has first to be presented to the package. It may be created directly for the statistical package. This is commonly achieved in the manner of creating a file in a file management package or spreadsheet. Alternatively the file may be transferred from another system to the statistics package for statistical analysis. The latter therefore should be capable of 'understanding' files presented to it in standard ASCII and possibly also as DIF files or 123 files.

The basic mathematical functions, present in some general-purpose packages, include calculating for a set of numbers the:

(a) average;
(b) sum;
(c) total number of occurrences;

to which may be added

(d) absolute value;
(e) exponential;
(f) factorial;
(g) OwenT;

and many others.

It may also be possible to draw a scattergraph, and, on categorising the data, to plot a frequency histogram. These latter two functions require at least rudimentary graphics facilities, and many statistics packages are really statistics/graphics packages. A graphical means of presenting statistical data can be very useful. It may therefore be necessary to purchase an extra 'card' (printed circuit board) for graphics and a plotter or graphics printer. Frequently, a statistician requires a three-dimensional plot, for example 3-D scattergraphs and histograms (see section 5.2).

More advanced features of a statistics package, less common in general packages, include:

(a) weighted averaging (the user may wish to stress certain values as being more important than others);
(b) percentiles (calcluating the value below which a certain percentage of values fall);
(c) simple and multiple regression (relating a dependent variable to one or more independent variables);
(d) analysis of variance between expected and observed values;
(e) a plot with logarithmic scaling (to give a different view of the data); and
(f) various tests of the data against various standards such as:

   (i) Poisson comparisons;
   (ii) Beta tests;
   (iii) Student's T;
   (iv) Chi-squared distributions;
   (v) Binomial;
   (vi) F;
   (vii) non-central distributions;
   (viii) standard deviation, and so on.

A further feature of statistical packages, providing management information for decision-support, is the forecasting of future values based on an analysis of previous values. There are in fact a large number of smoothing and trend fitting techniques which can be used for this purpose, such as:

(a) exponential smoothing;
(b) trend analysis; and
(c) seasonal smoothing.

Typically, a statistical package may have 300–500 routines which can be used for analysis.

Figure 7.6 shows a cross tabulation of two variables which have been classified. Figure 7.7 shows the various statistical values of this cross tabulation which can be produced using the cross tabulation produced in Figure 7.6.

fig 7.6 *cross tabulation*
   Source: Mercia Software Limited

		CLASS 1 78	CLASS 2 79	CLASS 3 80	CLASS 4 81	CLASS 5 82	Row Total
CLASS 1		22	23	7	13	20	85
	1	61.1	79.3	24.1	43.3	64.5	54.8
CLASS 2		6	4	9	5	2	26
	2	16.7	13.8	31.0	16.7	6.5	16.8
CLASS 3		8	2	13	12	9	44
	3	22.2	6.9	44.8	40.0	29.0	28.4
COLUMN TOTAL		36 23.2	29 18.7	29 18.7	30 19.4	31 20.0	155 100.0

fig 7.7 *statistical analysis based on the cross tabulation figures in fig 7.6*
   Source: Mercia Software Limited

```
Chi-square = 24.6933 with 8 D.F.    Sig. Level = 1.75183E-3
Contingency Coefficient = 0.370701
Lambda (Asymmetric) = 0.0857143 with Rows Dep.
                      0.0756303 with Columns Dep.
Lambda (Symmetric) = 0.0793651
Cramer's V = 0.282234
Uncertainty Coeff. (Asym.) = 0.08866 with Rows Dep.
                             0.0544539 with Columns Dep.
Uncertainty Coeff. (Symmetric) = 0.0674691
Kendall's Tau B = 0.0984313 with Sig. Level =  .1528
Kendall's Tau C = 0.101394
Conditional Gamma = 0.139952
Somer's D (Asymmetric) = 0.0846451 with Rows Dep.
                         0.114463 with Columns Dep.
Somer's D (Symmetric) = 0.0973213
Eta (Asymmetric) = 0.356115 with Rows Dep.
                   0.145805 with Columns Dep.
Pearson R = 0.120258
```

Another application of statistical packages lies in the field of **quality control**. Again, there are a series of techniques which can be used to ensure that the quality of finished products or raw materials is good enough. As it is not practicable to test all examples, a sample is taken of the items which are then inspected. A statistical analysis of the proportion of defective items of those tested (using, for example, comparisons with the Poisson distribution and Pareto charts to isolate frequent sources of defects by category) can lead to predictions on the proportion of those goods produced or received which are defective.

With this information, decisions can then be made about whether this proportion is acceptable or not. These tests will also highlight an increase or decrease in the levels of acceptability. It is important that the sample taken is adequate, in particular that it is large enough to be a basis for any conclusions drawn. Again, a statistical package can be used to check that the sample is in fact large enough.

7.4 WRITING YOUR OWN PROCEDURES

The reader of this text has been assumed to be either someone who has an application for which a microcomputer system may be appropriate or someone who wishes to know what applications can be implemented using a microcomputer system. Either way, you are unlikely to be a computer expert and unwilling to spend the many hours necessary in designing, writing and testing programs in a computer programming language. However, most programming language compilers can be obtained for microcomputers and there are other texts in this series designed to help you in this task (see, for example, *Mastering Computer Programming, Mastering Cobol Programming*, and *Mastering Pascal Programming*).

Nevertheless, as we discussed in the first chapter, a particular package may perform something like 80% or 90% of the requirements in a particular application, leaving 10% or 20% of the work undone. It may be that these tasks can be done manually or that a consultant can be afforded to write the software necessary to execute these tasks. Some packages provide another alternative: the ability to write user procedures. This gives additional flexibility and it is frequently not beyond an *interested user* to write the procedures necessary to fulfil all the required tasks.

Packages adopt one of two approaches. In the first, the user writes procedures in the programming language used by the writers of the application package. In this case, the microcomputer needs to have the compiler of that particular programming language. Otherwise the code cannot be executed. If this approach is adopted, then the host language needs to be a particularly easy one for the user to learn, or at least the proposed subset of the language that is recommended needs to be fairly easy to learn.

The second approach is to propose a 'very high level language' which is easy to use and which the package can execute. A specially designed set of procedures is usually much easier to learn and to use than a conventional programming language. These commands should give the user the flexibility necessary to allow the production of routines required to 'individualise' the package so that it can meet all the user's requirements. Even so, it is probably necessary for the user to have attended a training course in the use of the package, usually lasting a few days, to gain a fair command of the system's capabilities.

7.5 APPLICATIONS GENERATORS

Some applications are unique to a company or at least are so different that it is impossible to find a suitable application package available. If there is no in-house software specialist who can write the computer programs in Cobol, Pascal or another high level programming language, there is still an alternative: that of using an applications generator.

An applications generator (or **user workbench**) is a package designed to help the user build a system without using a conventional programming language. An applications generator may consist of a number of tools, frequently called **fourth generation tools**. The facilities that they provide are likely to include:

(a) prototyping;
(b) design aid;
(c) screen formatting;
(d) data base handling;
(e) test data generation;
(f) report generation;
(g) data dictionary handling; and
(h) document generation.

Many of the systems advertised under these banners are designed for applications programmers – aids to speeding up their work – particularly the more mundane work such as screen and report design.

However, there is a way that even specialist tools can be helpful, for users and programming people can sit together at a work station and try out a **prototype**. This is a trial system which can be developed by the computer person with the applications knowledge of the user. The prototype can be modified a number of times, until a system is developed which is satisfactory to the user. This process of developing application systems has two main advantages: first, it is quick, and secondly, because the user is involved, it is likely to produce a system that meets the user's requirements.

This section will concentrate on the attributes of those systems designed especially for the user. There are packages with facilities similar to those described above but usable by the untrained person. These systems will therefore be:

(a) easily learned;
(b) require few statements to do a particular task;
(c) adopt default settings should the user not specify certain details; and
(d) provide productivity and cost gains over programs written by programmers in conventional programming languages.

These facilities form a user workbench – as against the programmer workbench and analyst workbench, which are subsets of the fourth generation environment designed for the more technical people. Many systems have only a few of the facilities discussed below, but it is likely that newer systems will contain most of these facilities designed for the user in a complete 'fourth generation environment'.

Some packages which help users generate their own applications provide aids to help users analyse, design and document the application, as well as generate the programs. The main feature of these tools is graphic support to create and amend diagrams used in analysis and design. Some of these diagrams may be standard, as they follow methods used by professional systems analysts. Indeed, some design aids, usually called computer-aided software engineering (or CASE), support methodologies for systems and software designers. Nevertheless, many are easily learnt and there are likely to be standard symbols for data flows, processes, decisions, transitions, and so on. The design aid may have validity checks, so that detectable flaws in design are not permitted. By going through the diagrams, users may also detect conditions which have not been considered or errors in logic.

A **screen painter** (or formatter) enables the user to set up a screen layout for such requirements as menus and screen reports. The system itself generates the programming language statements necessary to produce the particular screen layout required. A series of similar screens can be set up easily. This will be useful for the entry of data which is similar but not the same. The system should also enable screens to be changed easily. This means that the tool is far more flexible than conventional application systems.

One feature that most of these fourth generation systems will have is **data base handling**. The user may not have to collect the data for the application, it may be already in the data base. However, it is necessary to specify what data is required. The system may do this by asking the user a set of questions – a series of prompts – and, according to the user's answers, generating the code necessary to derive the information required.

Alternatively, the user's requirements might be specified by 'filling in a form' displayed by the system on a VDU. It may even be possible to use an 'English-like' code and, should the system not understand this fully, it clears up ambiguity by asking the user a further set of questions. A further facility provided by the data base will be the raw material to **generate test data** from the data base, so that the users can satisfy themselves that the applications that have been developed do work.

From the user requests, the system will generate a programming code. This code may well be in a high level language but there is no guarantee that the code generated is efficient. Indeed, it is not likely to be very efficient and such systems often require a microcomputer with a large memory. The code generated by experienced programmers is normally more efficient, but their time is more expensive.

The simplest request is usually one of **report generation**. This may also be specified by *completing a form* giving details of:

(a) the data required;
(b) headings;
(c) titles;
(d) totals;
(e) page breaks; and
(f) sort and print criteria.

As well as having a data base, these systems normally have a **data dictionary**, which gives details of the data stored. This enables the user to specify the correct name of the data required and to see how the data has been validated, when it was set up, and so on.

Forms may also be created by the user for data entry into the data base, and the user should also be able to specify data validation procedures, so that data entering the data base is valid. Another important tool is the ability to create menus for future users as well as reports and forms. The menu may consist of a series of options expressed in English phrases or icons. The person creating the application may also wish to set up help screens for users of the system being developed. In designing screens and forms, such requirements as:

(a) top and bottom headings;
(b) colours;
(c) column placements; and
(d) when to produce a new page

should be specified very simply using such a tool. All these facilities give the user a powerful soft copy and printed **document generating** tool.

Another principle of many of these systems is that of development by example. The user 'ticks' those items on the screen that are required. A report screen could also be presented to the user who specifies areas where more detail is required (a 'zoom in') and other areas where a summarised format would be more appropriate.

Although such systems may be used to develop applications, they may also document the systems produced, or at least ease its production. For example, initial 'skeletons' of document types can be provided. These will not only help and speed up the production of documentation, but also ensure that standard layouts are followed and documentation is complete. Indexes can also be built up to cross reference elements of the documentation and the system itself. This also means that documents can be retrieved conveniently and altered if necessary.

Another way of developing applications is through hypertext. This could be considered as a data base system, because it is a way of storing and retrieving information, but the data is associated through its content (meaning) rather than form (structure). Further, it has links with graphics systems, as it displays data using graphical techniques. It is frequently used by end users as an environment for building applications which are under their control. It can be inefficient for larger applications, but it enables simple applications to be built simply and easily.

In the Macintosh environment, the hypertext system is called Hypercard and the associated programming language is called Hypertalk. Each object of data may have associated Hypertalk scripts attached to it. This might be as complex as a set of routines which are executed when the object is encountered or it might be a mechanism to link objects together. In Hypercard, this linking mechanism can be achieved using the mouse, by pointing to a button and clicking. The button may lead to another object, or be used to exit from Hypercard. Objects are organised in stacks of cards, equivalent to a file of records, but stacks contain data and scripts. The cards will hold more than data, having buttons and 'ornamentation', which can make cards equal the best produced by many graphics packages.

Figure 7.8 shows one card from a stack of cards of names and addresses. The left and right arrows are buttons which allow the user to go to the previous or next card. The column of buttons on the left include that to go to the home card (the starting place to choose the stack required), a calendar stack, a diary stack and a stack of reminders. The next to last button activates a procedure which displays all cards in the stack quickly and the last button activates a procedure to sort the stack.

Figure 7.9 is a card from one of the many stacks which are provided with the Hypercard system (others can be obtained from third party suppliers). This stack contains a number of art ideas, parts of which can be copied to users' own stacks or to non-Hypercard applications.

Different user levels are catered for, from the 'browser' who can read the information, to levels which enable users to change the information on the stacks, through to designing and building the stacks themselves. At the browser level, many of the menu items are hidden, and therefore users find it easy to grasp the basics of the system.

7.6 EXPERT SYSTEMS

An expert system is a system which will simulate the role of the expert. It is distinguished from other applications because its usefulness is derived from the knowledge and reasoning ability of the expert system package and not from number crunching (carrying out large and complex calculations) or the repetitive processing of data, which distinguish most commercial microcomputer applications.

An expert system stores the knowledge of the expert in a **knowledge base** and uses this knowledge to deal with problems by making inferences from it. The part of an expert system which does this is the **inference engine**.

Most expert systems that are available provide a **shell**. This combines the inference engine with a user interface which allows the knowledge of the expert to be input into the knowledge base. Thus they are not usable in themselves as expert systems but are tools to build expert systems. The knowledge base is usually formed using a question-and-answer session. In truth, the expert will probably spend

fig 7.8 *Hypercard, part of a stack of names and addresses (created using Macintosh Hypercard)*

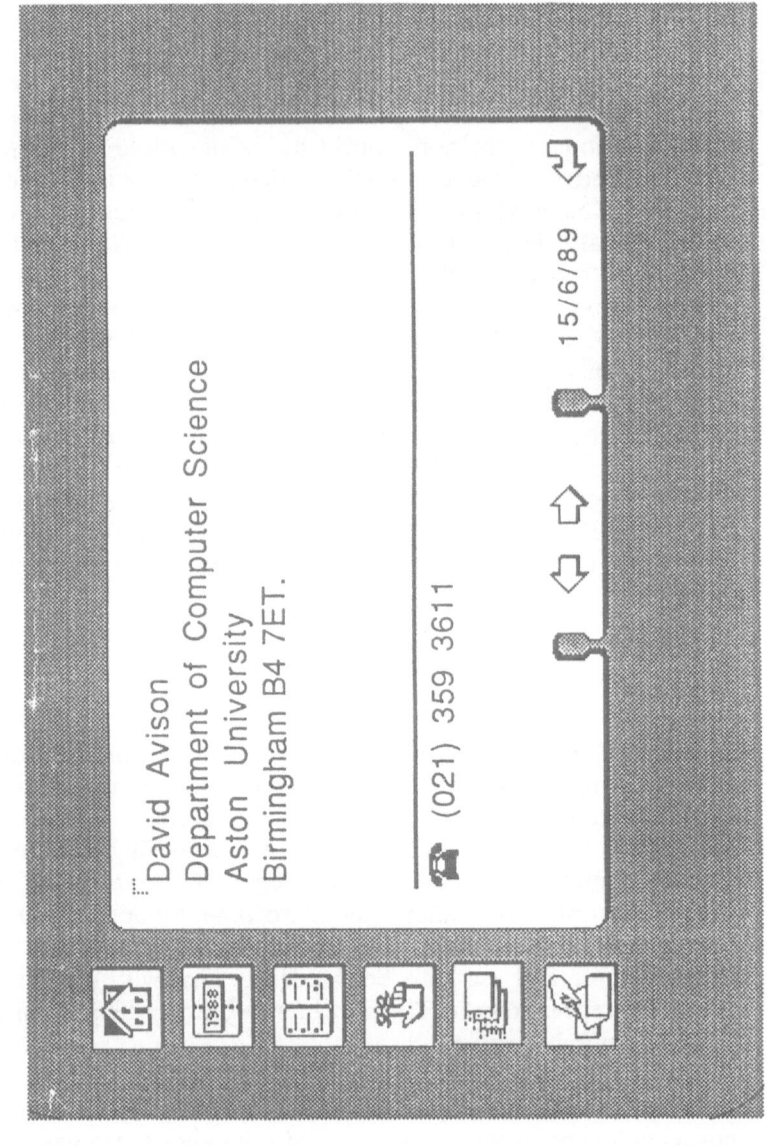

fig 7.9 *Hypercard, part of a graphics stack (created using Macintosh Hypercard)*

Books, Articles, Newspapers

some time getting this knowledge into the system. This knowledge may be in the form of facts, rules and regulations or as **knowing precedents**. Some systems may be able to incorporate probabilities, giving a rule of the type:

> If A is true and B is true
> There is a 75% probability that C is true.

Such a rule could be:

> IF the car does not start
> AND the starter motor does not turn the engine
> THEN there is a 70% probability that the battery is flat.

The expert system itself does not think. It is given these rules by humans and makes deductions from these rules. The rules have to be verified by humans or the deductions made could be nonsense. Knowledge may be coded in a number of ways. For example, some information may be classified into 'good' and 'bad' categories which can be useful in quality control applications.

In certain application areas, there may be a **customised expert system** available. In other words, the package comes complete with a knowledge base. These may be more suitable to the commercial user because the shell-only type expert systems will be very difficult for users to set up to form the true expert system. The use of a customised system may prevent problems that might be caused because the particular shell is not appropriate for the application.

A customised system may be available for car fault diagnosis or minimising tax payments. These applications require different types of reasoning. The first is **forwards reasoning**; that is, diagnosing a particular fault from a list of problem areas or symptons. The latter is **backwards reasoning**, where there is a set goal and the reasoning is backwards to assess how the goal might be achieved.

One of the requirements of a 'textbook' expert system, not always provided in microcomputer shells, is the ability not only to 'reason' and come to a conclusion, but also to *explain* its reasoning. The system should backtrack through the 'chain of reason' which led to the conclusion reached. With this knowledge, the user may modify the rules stored in the knowledge base so as to improve the reasoning of the system. It should be possible to add to the knowledge base and therefore improve the success of the expert system.

Some systems may be designed not to come to any specific conclusion but, for any particular problem, to list alternative courses of action and give the advantages and disadvantages of each. This type of system is known as a **decision-support system**. The system may typically be used to evaluate different investment proposals, screen job applicants, or, in our context, select from a range of software. packages.

Expert systems are available on large computers as well as micro-computers. The limitations of microcomputer systems are related usually to their capacities, for example the maximum number of rules allowed. Microcomputers are not presently appropriate for very complex application areas. In any case, the development costs of developing an expert system relative to an off-the-shelf package may be high. Time spent by valuable experts from the company, perhaps with the additional help of a 'knowledge engineer' in giving the expert shell information about the application, can be a major commitment and disruption to the company.

GLOSSARY

access   The retrieval of data, hence access time is the time taken to search for and retrieve data.

address   This locates a record on disk or in the computer's memory, just as the address of a house locates the house in a street.

alphanumeric   A character set containing alphabetic, numeric and special characters, such as +, -, *, ! and?.

applications generator   A package which eases the process of building application systems.

application package   The programs to carry out business and other functions which can be bought 'off the shelf' from a supplier.

area (or block)   The dividing of the text or other file into a section or sections to move, copy or delete portions of a file or between files.

ASCII   The American standard code for information interchange is a widely accepted format for data on computer so that it can be exchanged between computer systems.

backing storage   Connected to the computer, usually a disk storage system which will be used to hold computer programs and data.

backup   A copy of a file which will be used if the primary copy is lost or destroyed.

baud   Measure of transmission speed (actually a number of bits per second).

bespoke program   A program written for a particular user rather than 'generalised' for many users.

binary   A number system which has two states, 0 or 1.

bit   The basic unit of storage, a binary digit.

buffer   An intermediary storage area, for example, used before printing out.

byte The smallest addressable unit of a computer, consisting of 8 bits, capable of holding one character or number.

cell A particular row-and-column coincidence in a spreadsheet.

central processing unit (CPU) The hardware hub of the computer controlling the operations of the computer.

centring The position of text or numbers in the middle of a spreadsheet cell, screen, etc.

check digit A number added to a code to make the code self checking and improve data validation.

chip A small piece of silicon on which the processing circuitry or memory can be held.

commands Instructions to run software.

communication The hardware and software allowing data transfer between computer systems.

compiling Translation of computer programs into machine code.

consolidation Merging files or spreadsheets.

control Measures to ensure that a system is working as expected.

cursor A marker on the VDU screen which appears where the next instruction (correction, insertion or deletion) will be made.

data Facts.

data base An organised and integrated collection of data (facts).

data dictionary A directory of information about the data base.

decision-support system An application providing managers with information, usually derived from a data base.

dedicated system A computer system designed and used for one application only.

default A value which is assumed by the application package unless altered by the user.

desk top publishing (DTP) An extension to word processing to include complex page set-up features required for brochures, reports and so on.

disk A medium for storing data.

documentation A set of explanations and instructions to help users use hardware or an application package.

dot matrix printer A type of printer that forms a character by a matrix of dots.

dots per inch (DPI) A standard for printers, where (all other things being equal) the more DPI, the better quality of print.

editor The system which facilitates the amendment of data or text.

electronic mail The process by which users convey messages to each other using computers and terminals, rather than conventional post or telephone services.

electronic office   A development of the new technology to automate more and more aspects of office work.

ergonomics   Aspects relating to the working environment, such as temperature, comfort, and lighting.

error message   A message provided by an application package to inform the user that an error has occurred and the reasons for that error.

expert system   A computer system which simulates the role of the expert.

facsimile (fax)   The transfer of pictures and text along telephone lines, using computer systems.

feasibility study   An investigation of the problems of the present system, setting up a requirements definition for the new system, looking at alternative solutions, detailing their costs and benefits, and recommending a solution.

field   One data element in a record. For a product file, the fields could include a product number, description, and selling price.

file   A collection of related data in a specific application area. Firms are likely to have a customer file, product file, payroll file, and stock file.

file management system   An application package to organise and enable access of data.

floppy disk   A medium for storing data and programs.

form-driven system   A way of presenting options to the user who completes the form displayed on the visual display unit.

fourth generation system   A series of tools designed to help all types of users develop applications quickly.

function keys   Keys on the computer keyboard which perform specific functions such as 'help' which provides the user with information on how to use the system.

goal seeking   A requirement of spreadsheet and financial modelling systems where a target is specified, and the system informs the user which are the required values that associated variables must achieve to satisfy that target.

graphics   The representation of statistics in pictorial form on screen or paper.

hacking   Breaking into confidential systems, for 'fun' or gain, proving that a security system can be broken.

hard copy   A printed copy of a report or a diagram.

hard disk   A storage medium for data and programs.

hardware   The microcomputer and associated equipment.

housekeeping   A set of procedures for tidying up files, for example deleting unwanted data, on a routine basis.

human-computer interface The way in which computers and users communicate, particularly the design of messages presented to users.

icon A pictorial representation of information.

implementation The stage when a new computer application system is made operational.

information centre The service through which users have ready access to tools and guidance from data processing staff.

input Data and instructions entered into the computer.

integrated circuit A group of hardware instructions mounted on a chip.

integrated system A package of separate applications, such as file management and word processing, linked together.

interface Communication, e.g. between computer devices or devices and people (human interface).

inverse (or reverse) video The inverse of normal display on a visual display unit, for example white on black, instead of black on white. Used for highlighting.

joystick A handle, similar to that in an aeroplane, which is moved left and right and up and down thereby moving the cursor in the required direction.

justification The process of moving text or numbers left or right so that they occur at a predefined position on the screen and are aligned.

key field This is used to identify a particular record occurrence on the file, for example, a customer number might identify a customer record on the customer file. The key field 'labels' each record in the file.

keyboard This is based on the conventional typewriter keyboard, although there are additional keys, for example function keys which are used to perform special functions.

light pen An instrument which locates an item on the visual display unit for processing.

local area network (LAN) A communication system used to connect computers and other elements of hardware.

machine code Series of bit patterns forming instructions to be executed by computer.

macro The way of defining user's own procedures, usually a set of commands, which can be executed as and when required.

mainframe computer A large and powerful computer requiring a specially conditioned environment.

maintenance Regular cleaning and checking and the repair of equipment, and the correction and updating of software.

marking Placing a mark at the beginning and end of part of a file, spreadsheet or text for deleting, moving or copying a block of data.

mask The structure of a record of data on a file.

mega Approximately 1 million (e.g. megabyte).

memory The storage area of the computer usually quoted as a multiple of one 'k' byte where one 'k' is 2^{10} or 1024 bytes. The minimum business computer memory requirement is now 512k.

menu A list of options from which the user chooses.

microdisk A small floppy disk (normally 3 ½") which is protected by a stronger plastic casing than a conventional floppy disk.

microprocessor An integrated circuit containing much of the logic of a microcomputer on a chip.

minicomputer A computer about half way in its size, cost and facilities between a microcomputer and mainframe computer.

modem Equipment to transfer computer (digital) code through the conventional telephone network.

monitor Visual display unit.

mouse This is a small box which is connected to the computer by a wire and can be used to move the cursor to an option which is then activated by pressing a button on the mouse. There is a ball at the bottom of a mouse and it is the movements of this ball which moves the cursor.

multi-user system Computers which allow more than one user on the computer at one time using separate keyboards.

near letter quality (NLQ) The ability of some dot matrix printers to produce output which is similar to, but not as good as, daisy wheel printers.

network A communication system to join many computers and other hardware devices so that they can pass data between them.

open systems architecture (OSA) The aim of permitting any type of device and different devices of each type in any location on a network.

operating system This organises the running of user programs and the transfer of data between the various devices. It monitors and controls the use of the hardware. This can be described as the software which carries out the computer's housekeeping, as against the applications package which carries out the users' requirements.

option area Part of the VDU screen on which an application package displays the various options open to a user.

output Data, text or graphics produced by the computer system.

painting Marking parts of the screen, by colour or patterns, to highlight areas of, for example, a spreadsheet or graph.

parameters The specification by users of a set of options as a list to the application package.

participation   The process of involving the people who are going to operate and make use of the new technology in decisions about them.

password   A code which prevents unauthorised access to data or software.

piping   The transfer of data from one part of an integrated system to another.

pixels   The basic picture elements on a VDU screen.

plotter   A printer designed for displaying graphics output.

portable   This refers to the ability of software running on one computer system to run on another system without amendment.

presentation graphics   The production of slides, photographs, video images, pictures and graphs, for presentation at lectures, seminars, and so on.

printed circuit board   A series of chips and circuitry mounted on a plastic board held in the computer.

printer   Whereas messages on the VDU ('soft copy') are not permanent, 'hard copy' can be obtained by attaching a printer to the microcomputer (a daisy wheel printer, producing letter-quality but slowly; dot matrix, fast but near letter quality (NLQ) at best; laser, high quality but expensive, and so on).

program   A set of instructions to perform a particular task.

project management   An application helping management to control jobs by giving estimates of resource requirements.

prototypes   Trial versions of an application system.

query language   A series of commands by which users can retrieve information from a file or data base.

random access memory (RAM)   This is memory available to the user for programs and data. RAM is for the temporary storage of data and programs, and on finishing the session the user must transfer the data on to backing storage if it is worth keeping.

read   Obtain data from a storage device (e.g. disk) or keyboard.

read only memory (ROM)   This is memory used for the operating software of the computer and, unlike RAM, its contents will not be lost if the machine is turned off.

record   A file is made up of a collection of records containing the same type of information. For example, there will be one record for each product on the product file.

replication   The duplication of a procedure on a spreadsheet by referencing cell locations relative to those on the original procedure.

report generator   A system helping the user to set up printed reports.

scrolling   Moving up, down, left or right in a file, text or spreadsheet continuously when the document is larger than the display size.

security   The arrangements restricting the access and protecting the contents of files from accidental or malicious damage.

soft copy   The display of data on the visual display unit.

software   The programs that make the hardware perform particular tasks or functions. Software drives the computer system in such a way that a particular function or set of functions is carried out.

sorting   Programs which re-order a file or part of a file in a particular sequence required by the user.

spooling   The simultaneous printing of a text or data file whilst the user is engaged in some other activity, such as editing another text.

spreadsheet   A matrix of data (in rows and columns) on which calculations can be performed.

status line   A line of information displayed on the visual display unit for the user, for example, showing the current time and date.

streamer tape   Magnetic tape system which is used to backup data held on a hard disk quickly.

teletex   A publicly available electronic mail service more powerful than the conventional telex service.

teletext   A publicly available service for the transfer of data by televised signals which are received on television sets.

terminal   An input and output device, usually the combination of a visual display unit and keyboard.

turnkey system   A hardware/software combination which has been designed for easy and immediate use. Once it is delivered and set up it should be utilisable 'at the turn of a key'.

users   The people in an organisation who may use computers.

viewdata   A publicly available service for the transfer of data in the telephone system displayed on adapted television sets.

virus   A program which attempts to damage other programs and data covertly.

visual display unit (VDU)   The computer can send messages to the user on the VDU, a kind of monitor. The user can return messages by typing on a keyboard attached to it.

wildcard   The selection of text or data using any characters following or preceding the known characters specified.

WIMP   The design of a human-computer interface using windows, icons, mouse and pull down menus (sometimes windows, icons, menus and pointers).

window   A rectangular subdivision of the visual display unit screen.

word processing   The preparation of text using computer technology.

workstation A combination of input device, output device and, usually, very powerful computer, frequently connected to other computers and devices on a local area network.

wysiwyg (what you see is what you get) Where a display produced on a screen will be reproduced exactly when printed out.

INDEX